M

...ston public library

DAMAGE NOTED

Item was damaged prior to
checkout. Do not remove this
slip, or you may be held
responsible for damages.

SPECIFY DAMAGE:

Cover damaged

STAFF INITIALS: DS

DATE: 10/21/2019

E

JUN 0 6 2007

DEMCO, INC. 38-2931

DISHWASHER

One Man's Quest to Wash Dishes in All Fifty States

Pete Jordan

HARPER ● PERENNIAL

NEW YORK ● LONDON ● TORONTO ● SYDNEY

HARPER **PERENNIAL**

Some material in this book previously appeared in slightly different form in the zine *Dishwasher* and on the radio program *This American Life*.

The names of some characters have been changed.

P.S.™ is a trademark of HarperCollins Publishers.

HarperCollins books may be purchased for educational, business, or sales promotional use. For information please write: Special Markets Department, HarperCollins Publishers, 10 East 53rd Street, New York, NY 10022.

FIRST EDITION

Designed by Jaime Putorti

Library of Congress Cataloging-in-Publication Data is available upon request.

ISBN: 978-0-06-089642-3
ISBN-10: 0-06-089642-6

07 08 09 10 11 ❖/RRD 10 9 8 7 6 5 4 3 2 1

For Amy Joy,
and in memory of my dad

"[Dishwashers] are quintessential dirty workers, necessary for operating the establishment, but functionally non-persons."

—Gary Alan Fine,
Kitchens: The Culture of Restaurant Work

"And yet the *plongeurs,* low as they are, also have a kind of pride."

—George Orwell,
Down and Out in Paris and London

Part I

Initiation

1

Wine O'Clock

Abead of sweat rolled from my forehead, down my nose and into the greasy orange sink water. I wiped my face with my apron, lifted my baseball cap to cool my head and sighed. As I picked at the food dregs that had coagulated from the sink water onto my arm hairs, I surveyed my domain—the dishpit. It was a mess. The counters were covered with the remains of what, not long before, had been meals. But the dishmachine stood empty. No dirty dishes were in sight. No one yelled: "More plates!" or "Silver! We need silverware!" For the first time in hours, a calm settled over my dishroom. Having successfully beaten back the bulk of the dinner rush, I was caught up and it felt good.

Time for another go-round. On my way to the waitress station, I grabbed an empty bus tub and twirled it on my middle finger—a trick I'd perfected while working at a bagel shop in New Mexico. I lowered the spinning tub from my finger to my cap—a new trick I'd yet to perfect. The tub sputtered from my head and plummeted into the full bus tub that awaited me. A couple plates smashed to the floor.

The crash rang throughout the restaurant and was followed by a shocked hush from employees and customers alike. I, too, observed the moment of silence for the departed plates. But I wasn't sad to see them go. If dishes had to break—and they *did* have to—then it was best to break the dirty ones rather than the plates I'd already worked to clean.

In some Illinois cemetery, Josephine Cochrane was spinning in her grave. She was the 1880s socialite who'd grown fed up by her servants breaking her precious china as they washed it by hand. Cochrane presumed that by reducing the handling, there'd be far less breakage. So she invented the motorized dishwashing machine. Her contraption became an instant hit with large restaurants and hotels in Chicago. Even the machine I was using at this place—a Hobart—was a direct descendent of Cochrane's. But now, more than a century since the introduction of her innovation, human dishwashers—particularly this one—were just as cavalier about dish breakage as they'd been back in Cochrane's day.

As I looked down at the wreckage at my feet, the boss-guy charged around the corner wide-eyed with his hand clutched to his chest as if he'd been shot.

"Plates fell," I said.

"*Again?*" he sighed. "Try to be more careful, Dave."

Six weeks earlier, when a fellow dish dog had tipped me off about this gig—an Austrian-themed inn at a ski area in Vermont's Green Mountains that came complete with room and board—I was immediately intrigued. I'd pictured myself isolated in the mountains and hibernating through the winter at this job while getting caught up with my reading, saving up some money and crossing yet another American state off my list. When I called about the job from Wisconsin, the boss-guy assumed that if I wanted to come all that way to dish in a ski area, then I must've been a ski nut.

"No," I told him. "Actually I don't ski."

That made him suspicious. He then asked, "Do you have long hair?"

"Not anymore," I said.

"Okay," he said. "If you can get here by next week, the job's yours."

I rode the bus most of the way and hitchhiked the rest and when I arrived, the boss was no longer suspicious. I was willing to dish and that was enough for him. In fact, he gave so little thought to me that by the second day, he started calling me by the wrong name.

"And Dave, clean it up," he said, looking at the broken plates on the floor.

I'd never bothered to correct him.

"All right," I said.

When he turned and walked back to the dining room, I kicked the debris under the counter and headed back to the dishpit with the full bus tub.

While unloading the dirty dishes, I mined for treasure in the Bus Tub Buffet. The first find was fool's gold—a half-eaten schnitzel. I couldn't blame the diner who'd left the second half uneaten. It was the place's specialty, but it wasn't very special. I snobbishly passed on it as well and continued excavating.

I unearthed more dishes and then struck pay dirt: some garlic bread and remnants of crème brulée. I smeared the crème brulée on the garlic bread and scarfed it down. Scrumptious, said my taste buds. Queasy, countered my stomach. The gut had a point. Bus Tub Buffet? More like Bus Tub Roulette: you win some, you lose some. So far I was losing.

As I was guzzling water from the tap, the call went up in the adjacent kitchen: "Wine o'clock! Wine o'clock!"

I looked at the clock. Indeed, it was already wine o'clock.

Dick, one of the cooks, entered the dishpit with a grin on his face and a jar in each hand. He handed me a jar and held up the other in a toast.

"Wine o'clock," he said.

"Wine o'clock," I repeated.

We clinked jars and then downed their cooking sherry contents. Wine o'clock was eight o'clock—an hour before closing time and an occasion observed by the cooks with rounds of sherry. Closing time—nine o'clock—was celebrated in a similar fashion except with shouts of "Five o'clock! Five o'clock!" and the consumption of Five O'Clock brand vodka.

A couple of weeks earlier, the inevitable cook/waitress tension had come to a head here over the question of how the waitresses should place their orders. The waitresses wanted to just give the ticket—the food order—to the salad cook, who in turn would relay it to the line cooks and then to the dessert cook. The cooks argued it'd be better if the waitresses wrote their tickets in triplicate and distributed copies to each of the three cooking stations. The waitresses were less than thrilled.

From the dishpit doorway, while consuming Bus Tub Buffet strudel and wine o'clock sherry, I watched the two groups bicker. The cooks had their clique and the waitresses theirs. But as the dishman, I kept to myself and labored alone—the way I liked it.

But then a cook suddenly shouted, "Let's ask the dishwasher then!"

Looks from all twenty or so eyes darted my way. I quickly averted them all. I looked down at my hands, down at the strudel, down at . . . the cooking sherry. Wine o'clock. I'd been accepting the wine o'clock sherry from the cooks. The waitresses never gave me any sherry.

I cleared my throat and then announced, "Triplicates sounds better."

The scales tipped. From then on, the order placing was done the cooks' way.

But that'd been a couple weeks earlier. Now wine o'clock had struck once again. I emptied my jar and dove back into the sinks. As my stomach settled, I sweated out several more rounds of clean dishes. Then someone behind me said, "Hon?"

In the doorway stood the waitress who'd never before uttered a word to me. Now that I was "Hon," she probably wanted me to do some part of her job like empty the waitress station trash can.

I hesitated before answering, "Yeah?"

"Is it true what Linda just told me?" she said. "That you go all over washing dishes?"

Of course it was true. It was my life's mission, after all. But that didn't mean I wanted my cover to be blown.

I hesitated again. "Um . . ."

I now regretted having cracked under the intense questioning from that nosy Linda. My anonymity had been compromised.

"Uh, yeah," I finally stammered as I nervously picked at my arm hair boogers. "I guess it's true."

"Wow!" she said. "So, you like, go all over?"

She was hooked. I'd seen it so many times before: a waitress who barely notices a quiet dopey dishman suddenly gets interested once she finds out that he's a *traveling* quiet dopey dishman.

"Yeah, sure," I answered.

"That's so cool!" she said, entering the dishpit. "I wish *I* could do that."

I shrugged and asked, "Why don't you?"

"I don't know," she said. "Seems hard."

"*Hard?*" I asked. "No, staying in one place is hard."

"You think?"

For the first time, I realized how cute she was. Tall, bobbed dark hair, glasses, requisite black skirt and white blouse. If only she'd flirted with me like this weeks earlier, I would've sided with the waitresses in the order-placing debate. That would've scored me some points. Who knows, maybe she'd have started dropping by my basement room behind the inn after work. If so, I wondered, could I stay indefinitely at this job? Could I hack coming to it every day? Could I handle living in the mountains of Vermont for good—or would she lose interest if her quiet dopey dishman shed the mystique of being a traveler?

She had other ideas in mind.

"Maybe I can tag along with you," she said.

Could she be serious?

"Yeah, sure, tag along," I said. "You can wait the tables and I'll wash the dishes."

"Ha! That'd be a blast!" she said, squeezing my arm.

Looking down at her delicate hand on my grungy arm hair, I took a deep breath and then asked, "So, what are you doing after work?"

She let go of my arm.

"After work? My boyfriend's picking me up."

"Boyfriend, huh?"

What had I been thinking? Of course she had a boyfriend! Of course I couldn't stay at this job—or in these mountains—forever.

"Hey, you should come out with us!" she said. "He'd really get a kick out of meeting the guy who washes dishes all over."

"Nah," I said, pulling some plates from the bus tub. "No thanks."

I never could anticipate what it would be—that one thing that'd made me crack. But once that notion of quitting entered my head, there was no use fighting it. The whim could strike at any time: on an ordinary morning, waking up to see it snowing outside, just like it had in Pittsburgh. Or the idea could hit mid-shift when someone tried to boss me around, like what happened in Reno. The feeling could even overcome me when I learned a friend was leaving town and that I could catch a ride with her, as it had in Seattle. Whatever the case, once the notion hit, I was powerless. And now, just hearing mention of this flirty waitress's boyfriend, I knew it was time to go.

Six weeks earlier, upon my arrival, I sincerely thought I'd last the whole winter. Then again, I sincerely believed all my grandiose plans would pan out despite a lengthy track record that proved otherwise.

My chat with the waitress was interrupted by Dick.

"Five o'clock," he said, handing me a jar of vodka.

"Five o'clock," I repeated.

Vermont was the twenty-third state I'd conquered. By the time I was due at work the following day, I was already seeking out my next dish job in another state.

2

Maps

*I*f, indeed, I was born to wash dishes, no one had ever bothered to tell me that it was my calling. I didn't grow up dreaming about becoming a dishwasher. I never yearned for the prestige of being an unskilled laborer. I never craved the glory of scrubbing the crap off America's pots and pans. If I had, though, having such fantasies could've saved me a lot of time trying to figure out what I was going to do with my life.

I thought I had figured it out early on. In fifth grade, for a "What I Want to Be When I Grow Up" essay, my classmates followed the nun's prodding by writing that they'd grow up to be lawyers and doctors and presidents. When called upon, I read aloud my essay about a dream life as a house painter.

"Peter Jordan," the teacher, Sister Peter John, interrupted, "you can be *anything* you want."

"What?" I said. "I wanna paint houses."

"A *house painter*?" she scoffed.

She pointed at the future lawmakers and doctors and presidents around the room as proof that my goal should be loftier.

I didn't buy it. We were all immigrants or children of immigrants or African Americans. And I couldn't see any of us rising out of that decaying school (that'd be shut down within a few years) and attaining any lofty goals. Sure I wanted encouragement—I didn't exactly want the nuns to tell us we were losers and would always be losers. But I wanted *realistic* encouragement.

Growing up in a family of seven in what was built as a one-bedroom apartment in the pre-yuppified Haight-Ashbury district of San Francisco in the 1970s, I figured I was destined for a life of drudgery. My father had grown up in an impoverished family of eight living in a two-room tenement apartment in Glasgow, Scotland. He was still living in those two rooms when, at nearly forty, he married and emigrated to San Francisco in pursuit of a more prosperous life. For decades, he held a steady job at a customs office. He always arrived on time, worked without complaining and was the model employee. But those who got ahead, it seemed, were the bullshitters and the backstabbers. Being the good employee counted for little. He was passed over for promotions and raises . . . and he remained poor.

As the youngest of five kids, I came along at a time when my dad seemed bitter about his lot in the world, as if he'd realized that the American Dream was a sham. Watching him trudge up the street after work and then collapse on the couch in frustration, I learned very early on how one could start out poor, work hard all his life—and still end up poor.

Since I was going to start out poor and most likely end up poor, I decided not to waste time in between. Climb the career ladder? Hope to be patted on the head by bosses while trying to get rich in the American Dream scam? I decided, instead, to start out on the bottom rung—and stay there.

Months before writing the fifth grade essay, I'd no aspirations for an adult occupation. I only knew that, whatever it'd be, I didn't want to work hard doing it. Then, when a house painter spent weeks working on a building across the street from our apartment, I took notice. Every day he sat on the scaffolding planks with his lunch pail on one side of him and his transistor radio on the other. As he hummed along to the music, one hand dragged a paintbrush up and down against the building while the other hand stuffed sandwiches into his mouth.

Awed, I thought, *I* could do that!

But Sister Peter John thought otherwise.

"Look at Felicitas," she said. "She's going to be a nun! I think she'll make a wonderful nun."

"Yeah," I muttered. "Then she can yell at kids for wanting to be house painters."

That's the quip that got me sent to the principal's office.

It's not that I was merely a lazy kid who didn't want to work hard later in life. If anything, I wanted to work *less* when I grew up. Throughout my childhood, I held lots of jobs: passed out flyers for several restaurants, folded pizza boxes at a pizza joint, sold stationery sets and seed packets door to door. Every week I used to clean the dog shit out of one neighbor's backyard and take out the garbage for the old lady next door. And every day, from when I was eight until I was fifteen, I delivered newspapers.

On many mornings, my routine was to rise at five a.m., deliver one paper route (if not more), go home and eat breakfast, go to Saint Agnes's Church on Masonic Avenue to serve mass as an altar boy, go to Saint Agnes's School on Ashbury Street to work in the cafeteria in exchange for eating whatever I wanted (which really meant drinking cartons of chocolate milk throughout the schoolday), and then finally, go to class to try—often unsuccessfully—to stay awake.

I worked the paperboy gig till the summer that I signed up with a municipal program designed to get poor teens off the streets and into jobs. Two of my friends had already been hired through the program to hang out in city parks and paint park benches green. Upon signing up, I expressed my desire for the bench-painting dream job. Apparently, my passion for bench painting was overshadowed by the program's need for lifeguards. I was assigned to the swimming pool at the neighborhood boys club—even though I didn't know how to swim.

At the beginning of each shift, I stood poolside in my street clothes and announced to the kids in the water that if any of them planned to drown, they'd be better off waiting till my shift ended. If need be, I could throw in a Styrofoam lifesaver but I wouldn't be getting in the water no matter what the emergency.

It took a few weeks of me refusing to get in the pool before I was transferred upstairs to the crafts room. The crafts room coordinator wasn't happy to have a deadbeat from the pool foisted on her; she already had more "employees" from the jobs program than she knew what to do with. Since there wasn't much for me to do, I favored sitting around. But she always dreamt up some pointless task for me that involved lifting and moving things. One day, after she had me haul all the supplies out of a closet, I became frustrated when she then told me to simply put it all back. I went and sat down and said, "Do it your fuckin' self!"

Fired from the boys club and dropped from the jobs program, I turned to the "Help Wanted" section of the newspaper's classified ads to find a new job. The hundreds of listings all seemed to say something about needing experience. Without experience, or even a desire to have experience for any job that required it, I remained jobless the rest of that summer.

My time, instead, was spent riding buses. One thing I'd inherited from my dad was his passion for maps. When I was eight years old, I used to study his atlas of the fifty states and have him quiz me on the capitals. Later, as a teen, I'd buy road maps from the Rand McNally shop on Market Street and pore over them as I envisioned traveling the nation. I wanted to see the rivers, mountains and towns in person. I wanted to walk the endless number of streets I saw in the street maps of America's big cities, and know people in all those places, have friends from coast to coast—and maybe even have a girlfriend somewhere.

In the meantime, though, I carried around a map of San Francisco and traveled as much as I could within its borders by attempting to walk the city's every street and ride the entire length of every bus line. It was thrilling to travel through neighborhoods that were—in my small world—far-flung. Less thrilling, though, was being singled out in those areas for no other reason than for being a kid from another neighborhood. Whether it was white kids at the end of the L-Taravel line in the Sunset District or black kids in Visitation Valley while waiting for the 15-Third, the local teens didn't discriminate when it came to singling me out and kicking my ass.

When I wasn't busy worrying about being assaulted, I was worrying about getting arrested. My being on the streets was reason enough for cops to stop and search me and my friends. Of the score of times I was picked up, it was usually for legitimately dumb stuff like trespassing or stealing booze from liquor stores or crowbarring open laundromat coin boxes. But there were also plenty of cockamamie arrests— for malicious mischief (I was waiting for a streetcar) or male prostitution (I was standing on a corner waiting for a friend).

Still, in my circle of friends, I was the angel. As petty criminals, my cohorts were in and out of detention centers and group home facilities. Bragging rights went to those who could boast of their latest crimes or stints of imprisonment. And to those with the bragging rights flocked the girls in my neighborhood. The girls also went for guys with capacities for heavy drug usage—another realm in which I was a lightweight.

When three of my friends took to shooting up—first speed, then heavier stuff—not only did I pass each time the syringe was passed around, I was even square enough to try to get them to kick their habits. It wasn't out of a concern for their health or well-being, though. They'd just become so boring. There was nothing more tedious than loafing around a basement with them as they zoned out or worried about their next fix.

One afternoon, in their dealer's apartment, I implored them to give it up. Apparently, such sentiments were bad for business. First, the dealer threw a beer bottle that just missed me. Then he pulled out a gun and threatened to pull the trigger if I didn't shut up about the lameness of shooting up. So I got up and left. He followed me out. When I reached the sidewalk, he stood on the building's front steps and waved his gun around menacingly. Two guys I knew, Kevin and Baldwin—both recently released from juvenile facilities—walked up. When they saw what was happening, they started yelling at the drug dealer, "*You* wanna play with guns? Okay, then we'll go get *our* guns!"

As the three of them crowed about who would shoot who, I stood to the side—my hands in my pockets—unimpressed. My three junkie friends inside all had girlfriends. Kevin and Baldwin both had girlfriends. And the lunatic waving around the gun? Even he had a girl. And then there was me: not an addict, not a criminal—seemingly a nice guy. That was just the problem, though. As my friends often told me, to the girls in my neighborhood, I was *too* nice.

After the standoff ended with no one shooting anyone and no one quitting shooting up, I went and jumped on the streetcar alone and rode it to the end of the line.

When I was sixteen and my friend Jimmy told his dad that he was dropping out of high school, his father appealed to me.

"C'mon, Pete, *you* go to school," he pleaded. "Tell Jimmy not to drop out."

But dropping out of school was hardly unusual. In fact, I named twenty-one of our friends who'd already dumped school. Of those who still bothered to attend, I could only come up with three names—mine included.

My dad had also dropped out of high school—but that was because he had to work to help support his mom and siblings. To me, he always pushed going to college, as if it were an elixir against a life of drudgery. And I did see college as an elixir, though not because I had any grand career aspirations. Rather, I figured it could help me to achieve my goal of simply getting out of San Francisco. Away from my prison-bound, drug-addled friends. Away from the pesky neighborhood cops.

So I went to high school and did as well as one could who'd never participated in a single activity or even brought a book home. Just before graduation, I applied to a Catholic liberal-arts college that was twenty-five miles east of San Francisco. I didn't know much about the school other than it was far enough away from my neighborhood that I'd have to move out of the city, but near enough that I could easily scramble back if need be. I was accepted and, fortunately, was poor enough that much of the tuition and expenses was covered by grants from the college and the state. A $2,500 loan paid for more.

I was on my way.

3

A Date with the Dishes

Within minutes of my arrival, my new dorm room-mate, Tom, complained about his Chevy Camaro. It'd been brand-new when his parents gave it to him for his sixteenth birthday. Now the car was getting too old for his liking.

"What do you drive?" he asked me.

Not only did I not possess a car or even a driver's license, I'd never before met a teen who owned a car. Sure, a few times I'd gone joyriding as a passenger in vehicles friends had stolen. But a teenager owning a car—a *new* car at that? This was my first clue that I'd landed in a foreign world.

As Tom unpacked, he lined our sink and medicine cabinet with all kinds of shampoos, conditioners, gels and sprays for his hair. He apologized for taking up so much shelf space. It wasn't a problem, though. I didn't have much to contribute—

not even a bottle of shampoo. My lone hair-care product—given to me a few years before by my sister after she'd complained about all the knots while cutting my hair—was a plastic brush.

Tom found this strange, as he did my clothing. I was wearing the going-off-to-college shirt my mom had bought me the week before. It had a little turtle on it. Tom's shirts had little alligators.

"You can't possibly wear that," he said.

He claimed my shirt was a cheap imitation of his and that it'd be foolish to be seen in it. I didn't get it. A shirt was a shirt. Why would anyone care what tiny creature inhabited its breast? But, as stupid as his comment sounded, Tom was right. That first week, several other students also took the effort to point out that my shirt was a shoddy excuse for whatever was cool.

Located in a wealthy suburb, the school was populated with suburban students from well-off families. I found myself in the land of mid-1980s preppies—without even knowing such creatures existed. Unlike my overly groomed male classmates, who were decked out in Top-Sider boat shoes and pastel Izod shirts, I had long, greasy hair, a scruffy face and wore whatever clothes fit me from the all-you-can-fit-in-a-bag-for-five-dollars thrift store. And while the girls in my neighborhood had thought I was too nice to garner their attention, now the pendulum swung far in the opposite direction. The rich, blond, ponytailed coeds in their convertible VW Rabbits gave me a wide berth.

Judging by how often I was asked what the hell was I doing at this college, it became obvious that I looked and acted out of place. At first, I took offense at being singled out. The implication was that everyone else belonged there and I didn't. But then again, everyone else was there to get a career-inducing education. I, on the other hand, was only there because it was somewhere other than my old neighborhood.

During those first weeks of school, whenever I was walking down the street with any of my new classmates, I'd look around nervously for approaching cop cars.

"Cops coming!" I once said to Tom. Then I turned my back to the street and pretended to look in a shop window.

"Yeah?" Tom said. "So what?"

"In case you've got warrants or are on probation or you're carrying something."

"Why would the cops bother with us?" he asked. "We're just going to the store."

"That's plenty enough reason," I said.

But, it wasn't. Here, remarkably, cops drove right past me without even slowing down. And even when I'd mosey along sidewalk-less, six-lane suburban boulevards, carloads of teens might yell, "Loser!" But they never bothered to beat me up. Though I found this rich-kid environment bizarre, at the same time, I kind of liked it. I was able to stop worrying about being assaulted or arrested for merely being in public. I relaxed. College felt like vacation.

While my goal to escape the city had been achieved, I was now stuck trying to figure out what to make of my education. I didn't know what to study. Unlike my classmates, I had no major, let alone a career path.

Tom was going to be a lawyer. Other classmates talked about becoming lawyers. Still others aspired to being accountants and dentists. When asked of my own plans, I always said the future didn't include a professional career. What I wanted was to be free of a job; to travel the country and have friends nationwide whom I'd visit. So my standard answer was, "I'm just gonna come crash on your floor when you're a successful lawyer/accountant/dentist."

It was a claim many took as a joke. Years later, they'd discover firsthand that I wasn't kidding.

Though my financial aid grants and loan paid for most of my schooling, to cover the rest, I had to work. Through the school's job placement center, I got hired to unload boxes at the campus bookstore. The work went well the first six weeks. Then, one quiet afternoon while I was unpacking, a customer—who happened to be in one of my classes—asked for help finding a particular book. As I searched the shelves with him, the assistant manager yelled across the store, "Pete, get back to work!"

Work? I *was* working.

"I'm helping this customer!" I shouted back.

"You're just talking to your friend," came the reply. *"Now get back to work!"*

As I returned to the box I'd been unpacking, I began to fume. What *was* I expected to do if a customer asked for my help? Then, conscious not to cuss, I screamed my answer across the store.

"The next time a customer asks for my help, I'll tell them to *go to hell!*"

When I arrived the following day, the store manager called me into her office and told me she had to let me go.

"But I didn't even *swear!*" I protested.

That didn't matter.

But I'd no time to dwell on the injustice. My college plan depended on me working. So I marched straight from the bookstore back to the job placement center.

"I need a job," I told the lady behind the counter.

"What kind of work are you interested in?" she asked.

"Doesn't matter," I said. "Just as long as they'll hire me."

"Then you should go to Jack in the Box," she said. "They're always asking us for applicants."

I caught the bus to Jack in the Box, filled out the application and was told to start the next day.

Less than 24 hours after I got the axe from the bookstore, I stood wearing a paper hat and a polyester knit shirt sizing up the vats of hot grease. As fry cook, I was responsible for deep-frying French fries, fruit pies and tacos—scutwork that any simpleton could do. Except for this one. The tacos just weren't my forte. I'd stuff the taco shells with so much lettuce and cheese that they'd crack. Customers would complain. So to prevent the shells from busting, I'd then put almost no lettuce or cheese inside. Again complaints. So then I'd cram the damn stuff in again until the shell broke.

My ineptness quickly earned me a new assignment. As cashier, I faced the even trickier responsibility of handling customers. Again, a seemingly straightforward task. Again, I was the exception. Some customers were actually polite and patient. To them, I was courteous in kind by sliding them large orders of fries in place of the small ones they'd paid for or by giving them two cheeseburgers for the price of one. That was easy.

Much more challenging was trying to remain courteous to the many jerk-off customers. If I'd been on the other side of the counter and out of uniform, these same people would've been courteous enough to hold a door open for me. But because I stood *behind* the counter, I was nothing more than a shooting-gallery target to them. The five bucks they spent on crappy eats was the price of admission for them to take shots at the sitting duck in the paper hat.

But this duck shot back.

Once, while I was making a milkshake, a customer called in my direction, "Shawanda! Shawanda!"

I looked at him and wondered why he was yelling at me.

"Sha-wan-da!!"

Oh yeah, I remembered. Customers actually read the requisite nametags. I'd promptly thrown away each *Pete* nametag issued to me. But I still complied with Jack in the Box's rules by digging through the collection of old nametags and choosing one with a name least like my own: *Tawasha, Shondrella, Shawanda*.

"Shawanda! Can you move any fuckin' slower?"

"Yep," I said, then shuffled in half-inch steps toward him with his milkshake. "See, I can move *a lot* slower."

"Just gimme my food, asshole!"

"Wait, you haven't seen how slow I can move."

I stopped dead in my tracks.

"Gimme my food!"

The manager rushed over, grabbed the milkshake and handed it to the customer. Then he turned to me and scowled, *"You* just earned yourself a date with the dishes!"

Since the place employed no dishwasher, the manager would try to recruit a cook or a cashier to hit the sinks. My coworkers—who considered the task filthy and degrading—all balked at those requests. Foolishly, without any firsthand experience, I'd done the same.

And if no volunteer came forward, then the chore was meted out as punishment.

"Aw, you're fucked," one cashier said to me as I trudged toward the back with my head down.

Crap, I thought, I don't want to do this.

In the rear—out of sight of both customers and my co-workers—I found a sink full of dirty spatulas, trays, food storage containers, French fry racks and the like. I wanted to slip out the back door and split. But then what? Slink back to the job placement office to ask them, now that I'd blown a second job, could I please have a third?

As I stood at the sinks, a cook sidled up to me. He looked over his shoulder, then slipped me a burger.

"That's a raw deal you got," he said.

I thanked him for the free grub.

After filling the sinks with soapy, warm water, I sunk my teeth into the bacon cheeseburger and made a stab at the dishes. Without much conviction, I dragged a scrub brush back and forth across a French fry rack.

Meanwhile, the bustle of the operation echoed around me: the frying food sizzling, the employees barking out orders, the customers whining. . . . It was a relief to be out of the food ordering/preparation/serving loop and away from the constant pressure that accompanied those jobs.

I took another bite of the burger.

A little radio sat above the sink. I flipped it on.

Another bite, another swabbing.

Then I looked around. No one could see what I was up to. So I set the scrub brush down, finished the burger and fiddled with the radio dial.

Why the others despised this chore was beyond me.

Filthy? Manning the vats of hot grease was far filthier. Degrading? Kowtowing to the customers was far more degrading.

This ain't so bad, I thought. Not bad at all!

When the manager approached, I grabbed the scrub brush again.

"You learning your lesson?" he asked. "See what happens when you're a smart-ass?"

I most surely did!

After that, I never missed an opportunity to clash with a customer. If a woman paid by throwing her money on the counter, then I threw back her change. If a guy bawled at me about having given him the wrong size soda, then I gave him the correct size—of the wrong soda. The result—spending a couple hours *away* from the bastards—hardly felt punitive. In the back, out of the limelight, I could lollygag to my heart's content. Freed from the shackles of responsibility, I'd listen to the oldies station and drink chocolate milkshakes while dragging out the chore for hours on end. The boss—relieved that the chore was being done at all—never complained.

Eventually, I chose to forgo the customer confrontations and just volunteered outright for dish duty. But I had to do so grudgingly. I feared that if the manager discovered my affection for the loathed chore, then he might punish my slack work with the dishes by forcing me instead to cook food or, ugh, ring up customers.

But if dishwashing was my calling, I wasn't listening. I soon quit Jack in the Box to take a job as a church janitor—a plum position that involved plenty of pew-napping.

Since accepting that initial $2,500 loan, I'd resisted borrowing any more money for school. The idea behind the loans was that a student could rack up a bunch of debt and then pay it off when he had a degree-required high-paying job. But in my case, I had no desire for a job like that. So taking on any more debt was a scary thought. That twenty-five hundred bucks was already giving me enough worries.

But the janitorial gig didn't pay nearly enough to cover my school costs. So when the tuition for the approaching semester was due in the middle of my third year, I was at a loss about what to do. Then, a couple days before the semester began, I drunkenly destroyed the furniture in my campus apartment for little more reason than because it was fun to do so. The dean of students—who'd once chastised me for having "a complete lack of respect for authority"—booted me out.

So, sprung from school sooner than expected, I kept my word to my classmates: I slept on their dorm room floors. In the meantime, dreams of finally seeing the rest of the country filled my head. To save up money, I fulfilled my fifth grade fantasy by picking up work on some house-painting crews.

My childhood fantasy of idly painting while listening to the radio and munching on sandwiches wasn't one shared by my employers. My first paint-job boss often complained of me being the straggler on the crew. The boss of the second crew echoed that sentiment. The boss-guy of the third outfit was even worse. He was so ambitious about working at a breakneck pace that he had us painting three different houses simultaneously—even though the whole crew totaled only him, me and my friend Tony.

When this boss first complained about my tempo, he said, "*This* is what you need."

He held out to me the secret of his own speediness: a palmful of amphetamines.

Pick-me-ups still put me off. I passed on the pills.

Then, one day, I spent hours sitting on a roof with my transistor radio and my sandwiches while painting some eaves. That afternoon, Tony came over from the house he'd been painting. He said he was sick of trying to keep up with the job's manic pace and was going to quit as soon as the speed freak arrived with our pay. If Tony was leaving, then there was no way I was going to be left behind to paint three houses with that fiend.

When the fiend in question arrived, Tony quit and was paid in full. When the boss then noticed that I hadn't come close to finishing the eaves, he said to me, "You're the *worst* employee I've ever had."

"Yeah?" I replied. "Well, I quit too."

"You can't quit," he said, "'cause you're fired."

How pathetic, I thought.

"I already quit," I said. "You can't fire me."

"Yeah I can."

"No you can't."

"Yeah I can."

He then proceeded to count out exactly half the cash he owed me for the week.

"Where's the rest?" I asked.

"That's all your slow ass deserves," he said with a wild glint in his drugged eyes.

Though I was pissed, he had me.

I left with my half-pay.

4

Fragile

School had already gotten me a few miles out of San Francisco. So I used the experience as a springboard to get me even farther away to see other parts of the country. After scouring a college guidebook for a school that was both cheap and in an enticing locale, I found one—in Kentucky. A state university there was so desperate to attract students that it had a wide-open enrollment. Out-of-state students were charged the same low tuition as Kentucky residents.

Weeks after being canned from the paint crew, I was in Kentucky and in need of a job again. I meandered around town one Friday morning until I saw the marquee sign of one of the Perkins chain restaurants: "Dishwasher Wanted." The sign didn't necessarily call out to me. But, remembering Jack in the Box and how I'd enjoyed the dishes, it didn't sound half bad.

I went in and filled out an application. When the manager asked if I could start the next day, I told her no. My buddy Phil—only one of two friends I still had from my teen years in San Francisco—would be passing through town that weekend.

"I can start Monday, though."

"Come in Monday at eight a.m.," she said.

That weekend, Phil and I went on a bender. Monday morning, hung over, I dragged my sore body and aching head over to Perkins, managing to arrive only twenty minutes late. When I entered through the back door, the lone person in sight was a guy washing the dishes. He explained that, with my arrival, he was now the *old* dishwasher. Timmy handed me an apron and described the operation step by step. When the training ended five minutes later, Timmy embarked on his new prep cook job and I embarked on my new dishwasher job.

From the pile of dirty dishes, I grabbed a couple of plates. Now what? In my muddled state, I hadn't followed Timmy's instructions. I called him back over. Again he explained what to wash and where to put things once they were clean. This time, I concentrated.

Waitresses—whose faces I couldn't see, only their hands—would shove the dirty dishes through a waist-high hole in one wall. I was to wash the dishes and then shove them through a waist-high hole in another wall to the cooks—whose faces I also couldn't see, just their hands. The only person ever in view was Timmy, who—content in his new position—whistled cheerfully as he chopped vegetables.

Each time I cleaned all the awaiting dishes, my queasiness subsided. But then the waitresses would shove through another load and I'd feel ill all over again. As the minutes passed with agonizing slowness, a longing for a well-earned meal break kept me going. In the meantime, I scrounged through the meager food scraps and snacked on toast crusts and fatty bacon remains.

After an hour, it was an accomplishment that I hadn't passed out. But then the faceless waitresses suddenly started yelling, "More silverware! We need more silverware out here!"

As instructed by Timmy, I'd been dumping the dirty silverware into a large metal container to let it all soak. The cutlery lay at the bottom of the container, under about eighteen inches of hot water. The water was too scorching for my bare hands so I donned some gloves. But the gloves were too short to reach all the way down; tongs weren't long enough either. I tried to pour the water out, but the container was somehow affixed to the wall. Then I tried to bail the water out, but the container was too narrow for a soup ladle.

After ten minutes of futile attempts at problem solving, I called Timmy over.

"How d'ya get the silverware out?" I asked.

"You pull it out," he said and then plunged his arm into the hot water. His face lit up, his mouth popped opened and his arm shot back out. He shook it around wildly to numb the pain and when he finally stopped, I was horrified to see his beet-red arm. It looked like it was starting to welt.

When he caught his breath, Timmy calmly said, "Somebody musta put hot water in there."

Then he returned to his vegetables.

"Where's the silverware?!" cried the faceless waitresses, their hands waving frantically through the little waist-high hole. *"We need more silverware!"*

I was at a complete loss.

During the time I'd spent trying to recover the silverware,

I'd washed nothing else. So then the faceless cooks poked their hands through the other hole.

"Plates! We need plates *now*!"

It felt like all the menacing waitresses and cooks were going to crawl through their holes to get me. When the room began to spin, I knew there was no way I could survive until a meal break.

My calling? *This?*

I pulled off my apron and laid it like a shroud over the stack of dishes.

"I gotta go," I told Timmy.

"Shit," he sighed. "Guess I'm back to dishing."

"Sorry," I said.

As I stumbled home, I vomited up the bacon and toast scraps into some bushes.

A couple of days later, I was hired to work in a warehouse that stored the university's old desks, chairs, typewriters and other supplies. My lack of qualifications perfectly prepared me for the job; almost all I ever did was sit at a counter and read. Once a week, a truck would drop off some old desks and I'd find space for them in the warehouse. Then I'd resume my reading. If anything, *this* seemed like a calling.

Though I was able to use the four months at the warehouse job to read twenty-six Mark Twain books in a row, I made no friends and got lonely. Before long, I was back in San Francisco, living in my friend Karl's basement apartment—less than a hundred feet from the apartment I grew up in.

So much for traveling and seeing the nation. I made the most of my circumstances by pulling out my old marked-up map of San Francisco and reviving my attempt to cover every street in the city by foot.

Karl got me hired at the UPS warehouse on Potrero Hill, where he was working loading trucks in the middle of the night. My new job was simple, yet bewildering. As the packages wound their way through the building on a series of chutes and conveyor belts, they'd pass the rear of the parked trucks. Loaders would pull off the packages to place them in the proper trucks. If the packages on one particular conveyor belt had found their way onto the wrong belt or had been missed by a preoccupied loader, then they'd reach the end of the conveyor belt and plunge six feet to the floor.

My sole task was to pluck these forlorn packages from the floor, wheel them on a cart to the head of the conveyor belt and place them back on for another go-round. By the time I'd return to the far end of the conveyor belt, a new pyramid of fallen parcels would be awaiting me on the floor. If a fallen box was damaged, I was expected to try to smooth out its dented sides. Though I wasn't asked to shake each package to listen for broken contents, I took it upon myself to do so anyway. The packages that rattled most were usually those that looked to have been most carefully wrapped with FRAGILE written innocently on the outside.

So why couldn't a table at the end of the conveyor belt catch the packages? Or better yet, why not a little slide installed to glide the packages down to the cart? Or, best yet, a *circular* conveyor belt that sent the parcels around and around like an airport baggage carousel?!

Well, UPS didn't pay me to think. It paid me to plod back and forth with the dented packages—grunt work any numbskull could handle. Or so I thought.

One night, at three a.m., I arrived to start my shift. On my way to the conveyor belt, I was called into the supervisor's office.

"We need to talk about your work performance," he said.

"Oh?"

"Yeah, you're not cut out for working here," he said. "You have a lack of enthusiasm for your work."

Enthusiasm? I picked up smooshed boxes off the floor. What was there to be excited about?

Well, I never found out because as an ex-employee, I didn't stick around to meet my more enthusiastic replacement.

A couple of weeks later Karl asked for my half of the rent. I was flat broke and unemployed. He was pretty pissed to hear that I couldn't pay up.

"Take it easy," I told him. "I'm gonna find a job *right now*."

I left the apartment intending to wander around the neighborhood long enough for Karl to cool off.

I had no clue how an unskilled, unkempt and unmotivated man was to find work. By looking through the newspaper classifieds? If I wasn't even qualified to pick up packages off a floor, then I definitely wasn't qualified for any of those jobs that demanded "experience." By sending out a resume? What employer wouldn't love to read a resume from someone kicked out of college, fired from several shit jobs and with a peculiar talent for sitting and reading for hours on end without complaint?

After I had strolled three blocks from Karl's apartment, a sign in a café window caught my attention: "Dishwasher Wanted."

I stepped inside and inquired about the position. The boss-guy asked if I could start in the morning. I could.

That was it. I was hired.

"There's just two things," he said. "First, you can eat or drink whatever you want—except the beer and wine."

"Okay."

"And second, don't just up and quit on me."

"All right," I said.

Back at the apartment, no matter how much he wanted to, Karl refused to believe that I'd found work in only ten minutes.

Early the next morning, I showed up at the café—a brunchy place that was open from 7 a.m. until 3 p.m. The boss-guy showed me how to clock in, where to put the clean dishes and then his brief tour ended at the dishwashing station: a sink with a spray hose and an under-the-counter dish-machine.

While rinsing the first few dishes, I bumped my head on the low, slanted ceiling that sliced diagonally across the dish station. And then I bumped into a customer who was on her way to the bathroom. Wedged in under the stairs and in the pathway to the toilet, the dishwashing area was obviously an afterthought to whoever had laid out the café.

After I rinsed a few more dishes, one of the cooks reached over and handed me a plate of French toast.

"You want 'em?" he asked. "I screwed up an order."

Ten minutes into the shift and I was already being fed. This was a good sign.

Throughout the morning, the cooks sent other food my way. Poached eggs, bacon, oatmeal. They got a charge out of offering me more and more grub since I refused nothing. Buttermilk pancakes, bagels with lox, burgers. I'd taken the job for the cash. The chow was an unexpected bonus.

Come three o'clock, the cooks and waitresses raced through their closing chores and then split. The boss-guy guided me through my own closing chores. After I finally finished the dishes, I was then to sweep and mop the whole place, hose off the kitchen mats out back and drag all the garbage cans out to the sidewalk. When I was done, I was to lock up and then push the key back through the mail slot.

"One last thing," he said. He showed me the reach-in fridge. "The waitresses fully restocked the beer so I'll know tomorrow morning if there's any missing."

As he was leaving, the boss-guy said it should take me an hour to close up.

An hour later, I'd only managed to finish the dishes. Then, while searching for the broom in the upstairs storage area, I noticed the cases of unrefrigerated beer.

Hmmm.

I grabbed a bottle of warm Anchor Steam, took it downstairs and swapped it for a cold one.

The next morning, I arrived at work with an empty stomach and big plans for what I could eat that day.

"You came back!" a waitress remarked upon seeing me.

"Yeah," I said. "Why wouldn't I?"

"Lotta dishwashers never come back after that first day."

When the boss-guy walked by, he said nothing about the missing beer or the fact I'd clocked out an hour later than he'd predicted.

When I was left alone to finish up that second afternoon, again I sat and rewarded myself with a beer upon finishing the dishes. Another reward came after the sweeping was done. It was even later when I clocked out that day.

Every afternoon after that, I spent increasingly more time sitting and drinking congratulatory beers. Eventually, the damn closing chores started to get in the way of my sitting around. So if I pulled a dish from the bus tub that didn't look too dirty, then I just reshelved it with the clean ones. I stopped hosing off the kitchen mats. The sweeping went half-assed.

Mopping? Why bother? Before long, Karl was even stopping by to partake in the sitting-around and beer-drinking.

Eating so much while at work and taking home enough leftovers from the kitchen to see me through my off days fell right in line with my ongoing plan to simplify my life: now I didn't have to grocery shop or even pay for food. By then I'd been paring down my belongings—not that I ever had many to begin with: mostly just books, LPs and maps. But after giving away more stuff, I wondered why I needed to live in an apartment. I didn't need it for storage or for cooking. In fact, since most nights I was crashing on floors and couches around town anyway, I decided to once and for all pare my belongings to the point where I could fit everything in a large plastic garbage bag. I could cycle to work with all my stuff and then over to a friend's apartment for a night on the floor in my sleeping bag.

One day, when I showed up at my parents' place on my bike with my garbage bag and sleeping bag in tow, I told my dad about my new living arrangement. He was baffled.

"What? You're living like a turtle?" he asked.

The remark was meant to be dismissive yet, actually, it was perfectly apt.

"Yeah, exactly," I said. *"Like a turtle!"*

Then one afternoon, while the café's other employees rushed to heap all the closing-time dishes on me, I was staring at the stacks. The boss walked up with my time card in hand. Rather rudely, he said, "What the *hell* are you doing that takes you so long to close up?"

His grievance was legitimate; by then I was routinely

clocking out much later than he'd said I should be. But he picked the worst time to gripe. After having slaved all day and dreading the dishes that awaited me, I snapped.

"Look at all these dishes I've still got!" I said. "Then I gotta sweep and mop and hose the mats off and take out the trash. I'm doing everything you told me to do, *so fuckin' lay off!*"

As soon as the words left my mouth, I knew what to expect. Mouthing off at bosses had gotten me fired from the boys club and from the campus bookstore. Working at a snail's pace had gotten me fired from house painting and from UPS.

Now, another job would be added to those lists.

But he didn't can my ass on the spot. Actually, he kind of cowered.

"Uh, okay," he said. "I'm sorry."

A couple minutes later, after he'd left, I sat down with a beer and suspected there might be something to this dish-washing business. But I wasn't completely sure. After all, why *would* he fire me when there were still stacks of dishes to be washed? If I was to be sacked, he'd be smart to wait until I'd finished out the day. Supposing that was the case, I sat around even longer after closing time and hardly swept or mopped.

That night, I wrote a couple letters to pals who, coincidentally, had also fallen into dishwashing. Tony—my buddy from the paint crew—was dishing with his friends on a five-man crew at a large college cafeteria up in Davis, California. He'd written me a letter about his stubborn refusal to wear the requisite plastic apron because of his aversion to plastic clothing. My pal Dave was working two different dish jobs in Olympia, Washington. He wrote me about his struggles with the alcoholic owners at one of the restaurants.

Reading and writing these letters about dish work gave me an idea: collect these tales and print them up in some sort of pamphlet. The other guys liked the idea, too. But the problem with starting a publication devoted to the work of laggards was that Tony and Dave were too damn lazy to send me their promised contributions. Then again, when it came to lethargy, I had them both beat.

The morning after cussing out the boss, I wasn't terribly motivated to go to the café. Not only did I presume I'd be canned upon my arrival, I was also hung over. But since I was hungry, maybe the cooks would slip me something to eat even if I was no longer an employee. So I peeled myself off the floor, rolled up the sleeping bag and biked down to the café.

When I walked in more than an hour late, the place was already packed with customers. A waitress saw me and said, *"Thank God you're here!"*

When the boss-guy approached, I expected him to cuss me out and tell me to beat it. Instead, he looked relieved.

Here I'd yelled at the boss, done a lousy job closing up, taken too long to clock out, helped myself to the forbidden beers, arrived late (unshaven, unbathed, unkempt and hung over). . . . And what was the response? Relief that I'd shown up at all!

As easy as this job had been to get, it appeared even harder to lose.

That's when I heard it, loud and clear. There was *definitely* something to this dishwashing business—something I liked. Quite possibly, this *was* my calling!

●

There was one last appeal of the profession that didn't reveal itself to me until the following week. Upon awakening on a morning that I was due at work, I rolled over on the couch and went back to sleep. That was that.

I'd already routinely broken the boss-guy's rule about drinking, so I couldn't pass up breaking his other rule.

Without notice, I'd just up and quit on him.

5
A Three-Day Soaker

I took my stuff up to Davis, crashed on Tony's floor and then applied for a job in the university cafeteria dishroom where he and his friends worked. Despite my getting hired, I was told there wouldn't be an opening for me in the dishroom for another week. In the meantime, I was expected to work on the cafeteria floor as the "beverage person."

Early one morning, I was handed a kelly-green polyester knit shirt and matching baseball cap. It was my uniform to wear while keeping the soda, milk and juice dispensers stocked and cleaned. Then, at 7 a.m., the cafeteria doors opened and students began to stream in.

Standing at attention at the drinks station, I saw my reflection in the window. There I was, looking like a damn clown in my kelly-green outfit.

Then some girl whined to me, "The nonfat milk is warm."

This was no way to land a dish job—a job where I could wear my own grubby clothes and avoid the gabby customers. At 7:05 a.m., I grabbed my shirt and escaped with a vow to never again wear company garb.

A couple days later, I studied dozens of three-by-five-inch index cards on the campus ride board. One read: "Two guys driving up to Alaska looking for a third person to help share the cost of gas." I called them and was told they were heading up to find work in the oil spill cleanup. It was April 1989. A few weeks before, the oil tanker *Exxon Valdez* had struck a reef and dumped at least ten million gallons of crude oil into the Prince William Sound. It sounded intriguing, so I bought a fifteen-dollar tent and left with Jack and Ali a couple days later.

It was dusk when we arrived in Valdez—namesake for the doomed oil tanker and epicenter for the cleanup effort. The place was a madhouse. The town of four thousand residents was overrun with upward of ten thousand job seekers. Everywhere we looked, people were camped out in tents, cars and makeshift shacks. It was so crowded, we had to drive a mile out of the boomtown before we found a vacant patch for ourselves among the hordes.

As I pitched my tent, a party atmosphere raged around me. Campfires and drinking were in full effect. The three middle-aged guys sitting around the nearest campfire invited me over to join them. One of them handed me a can of beer.

They were down from Fairbanks, filled with enthusiasm and chatty. All they talked about, though, was the available work (cleaning the oil off coastlines) and the pay ($16.67 an hour).

"They should have one of these spills *every year!*" one of them said. The others raised their cans in agreement.

When I finished my beer, I got up and moseyed around. The conversations overheard at the other campfires echoed the sentiments of the Fairbanks trio. Witnessing all the boozy, charged anticipation was surreal. It seemed more fitting for a parking lot the night before a rock concert than for the site of an immense environmental disaster.

The more I heard about the work, though, the less interested I became in doing it. Sure the wage was stratospheric. And using a high-pressure hose to wash oil off rocky shorelines could be fun. But what got me was the workplace location: isolated coastlines accessible only by boat. Inevitably, I'd grow sick of the job. And once that happened, how could I flee a job site on some remote island? I'd be left stuck, unable to leave—and absolutely miserable. No wage, no matter how astronomical, was worth tempting a fate like that.

In the morning, I packed up my tent. Turned off by the town's get-rich-quick vibe, I said so long to Jack and Ali and hit the road. On my way out of Valdez, a driver in a pickup picked me up. He was heading all the way to Anchorage—120 miles away. Now, so was I.

"You just finished safety training, too?" he asked.

"No," I said. "What's that?"

"It's like boot camp for cleanup workers," he said.

The day before, he'd completed that final step in the hiring process and was now on his way home to Anchorage to await a call-up for duty. When he learned I had no interest in the work, he responded the same way the Fairbanks guys and Jack and Ali had: he was flabbergasted.

"It'll be *cool*," he said. "You'll see!"

He wanted to turn around and take me back to Valdez. I told him not to.

Then, he tried to pressure me: "Man, you're really gonna regret this one day!"

Finally, he got mad: "I can't believe you'd shit on this golden opportunity!"

It didn't matter what tactic he used, my mind couldn't be changed. Eventually he fell silent and I was left in peace to watch the passing parade of pine forests and snowcapped mountains.

While I was traipsing around Anchorage, my garbage bag luggage fell apart. My crap had to be cradled in my arms for a couple hours until I came upon an army-navy surplus store. There, I broke down and blew seven of my thirty-two bucks on a secondhand duffel bag that was big enough to accommodate my sleeping bag, tent, T-shirts and books.

My new duffel bag and I then headed south sixty miles to the town of Kenai, where I picked up work at a fish cannery and pitched my tent outside the plant. My job was to "slime" salmon by gutting them and slicing off their fins. That is, when there were fish to be processed. Despite our being far from where the tanker had struck the reef, the oil slick covered such a large area that "tar balls" were turning up in the local fishing grounds. Each time a tar ball washed up, the fishing ceased and the cannery shut down for a few days. After several weeks of working sporadically, I quit and hitchhiked another sixty miles down to the where the road dead-ended in Homer.

Again, I got hired at a cannery. Again, the work was intermittent due to the oily waters. And again, I quit after a few weeks.

While I was in Homer, a coworker told me that volunteers were needed at the place that treated spill-affected sea otters. When oil got into their fur, the animals would try to lick themselves clean. Swallowing the indigestible oil could be fatal. So they were captured and brought to a rescue center where their fur was cleaned by volunteers.

I was fascinated. But not because I was any big animal nut. Rather, I was smitten with how otter fur was cleaned: washed by hand—using household *dishwashing detergent*!

So I thumbed it the eighty miles to Seward and arrived in the evening. In the morning, I offered my services at the rescue center but was rejected—there was already a glut of otter washers. In the afternoon, on the edge of town, I caught a ride. The driver had just spent more than a month on a boat plucking the oiled otters from the sea. Now he was on his way home for a week of R & R. When he heard about my attempt at volunteering, he offered to get me a job on the boat he worked on.

Me work on a boat? I explained to him how that wasn't likely.

"Let me get this straight," he said. "You'll wash otters for *free*. But you won't go out on a boat and catch 'em for *eighteen bucks* an hour?"

"Yeah," I said.

"And you'll wash dishes for a measly *four bucks* an hour but you won't wash rocks for *sixteen-sixty-seven* an hour?"

"That's right," I said.

He looked at me cockeyed and said, "Something don't add up."

"No," I assured him. "It all adds up to me."

I caught rides around for another week and ended up back in Valdez. The town was now completely transformed. Gone were the encampments of job seekers. All those folks I'd seen weeks earlier were now scattered around the coastlines and islands of the Prince William Sound scrubbing those rocks and getting rich quick.

From Valdez, I caught the overnight ferry (a five-and-a-half-hour trip) to the town of Cordova. There, I got hired to work on yet another slime line. But, like at the other canneries, there wasn't much work for me to do due to oily local fishing grounds. Though I was hardly earning money, I *was* being housed and fed in exchange for barely working. One couldn't complain—but *I* did. After four weeks of "working," I quit and caught the ferry back to Valdez. Then I hitchhiked around for a couple weeks and made it to the town of Haines with my money budgeted perfectly: exactly enough dough to buy a loaf of bread, a jar of peanut butter, a jar of raspberry jam and a $205 ferry ticket to Seattle.

As a growing aficionado of ferries, I was excited to embark on America's ultimate ferry service—a three-day, thousand-mile sail through the Inside Passage. As the ship weaved along mountainsides of rain forests that plunged down to the seas of southeast Alaska and British Columbia, I slept at night on the deck in a deck chair. By day, I spotted killer whales and humpback whales and porpoises and bald eagles. The scenery from the ship was absolutely amazing.

The scenery *on* the ship was even more amazing; a Native-Alaskan passenger with long, wavy hair caught my eye three different times. On each occasion, I considered approaching her. But then I figured, if women had scant interest in me even when I had access to bathing and clothes-washing facilities, then why would one so gorgeous take interest now? I hadn't shaved in months, bathed in weeks and was wearing the cleaner of my three filthy T-shirts (meaning whichever one I hadn't worn the previous two days). So each time I saw her, I chickened out.

Then, on the final night of the voyage, *she* cornered *me*.

"Can I buy you a beer?" she asked, then proceeded to buy me a pitcher in the bar.

In turn, to impress her, I pulled out my sandwich fixings and made her a PB&J so overstuffed, the fillings oozed out its sides.

I didn't know if it was the cuisine or my stench, but for the first time, a woman was interested in me. Actually, as we spoke, it seemed what attracted her most to me was simply that I was a traveling man.

When we docked in Seattle, I was still as penniless as when I'd boarded the ship and didn't know what to do next. Melanie, who'd just finished working the summer as a fisher-woman, was heading down to college in Arcata, California. When she offered me a ride, I didn't hesitate to accept it. By the time we reached her destination a couple days later, we were like turtledoves. And when Melanie then invited me to stay with her, who was I to say no?

Exxon sent me a check for $1,500 for the time I was em-ployed at idled canneries. Those funds held me over for four months. When they ran out, I hoofed it all over town only to find every dishwashing position already filled. The newspa-per's want ads had no dish positions either. Looking through the ads that were listed made me ill, precisely as it had when I was a teenager. I still wasn't qualified for any of the other jobs. But given my concern over losing Melanie if I couldn't bring in some income, this time my lack of experience didn't deter me from applying for any kind of work.

I tried for not one, but two different seamstress jobs, fig-uring, how hard could it be to sew?

Apparently, harder than I'd assumed. I was rejected at both places.

I even applied for a job as a meter maid. When the chief of police interviewed me, he asked, "Have you ever been arrested?"

"Yeah," I said, "but who hasn't?"

"Wrong answer," he said.

As my cash decreased, my stress increased. Without the allure of traveling, I feared Melanie would see me as worthless and dump me. She still had money from her summer of fishing. With it, she treated herself to frivolous things like eating out. I passed on each of her invitations to join her because I was clutching tight to my dwindling funds. Besides, I hated eating out. Restaurants cost money. Money meant working. And to offset the working part of the equation, I was perfectly content to subsist on a PB&J diet.

For my twenty-third birthday, though, Melanie dragged me to a snazzy restaurant that had white starched tablecloths. Sitting there at the table while trying to act proper was enough to make me anxious. But my nervousness grew when Melanie pulled her napkin off the table and put it somewhere. The act seemed to be some mysterious custom. Eventually, I broke down and asked her, "What do I do with my napkin?"

Melanie looked at me for a second, then said, "You put it across your lap."

In his book *Ham on Rye*, Charles Bukowski—her favorite author—had scoffed, "What woman chooses to live with a dishwasher?"

At that moment, she was probably asking herself the same thing.

●

Then one day, Melanie invited me to go to lunch. As usual, I declined. She went off to eat alone and I felt like a louse, wondering how much longer it'd be before she told me to hit the road.

But then an hour later, she ran in excitedly.

"They need a dishwasher at the place I just ate at!"

"How do you know?" I asked.

"I watched them put up a sign in the window," she said.

I ran the eight blocks to the restaurant and saw the hand-written sign: "Dishwasher Wanted—Ask for Charlie."

I went in and asked for Charlie. A minute later, a white-clad old man stepped out of the kitchen and said, "I'm Charlie."

"I want the job," I told him.

"You washed dishes before?"

I started to tell him about the café in San Francisco but he cut me off.

"Can you work weekends?" he asked.

"I can work anytime."

"Fine," he said. "You start Saturday morning."

To think, I could've ended up running a sewing machine— or handing out parking tickets! The sinks were where I needed to be!

My spirits lifted. And from the smile on Melanie's face that greeted me when I got home, it was clear she was even more elated than I was about my new job.

Saturday morning in the restaurant's dishroom, I found a guy leaning against the counter, stooped over and eating a blueberry muffin. Upon seeing me, he held out the muffin and asked, "Hey man, you want the rest of this?"

I liked him already.

"Sure," I said and took the offering.

"New guy, right?" he asked.

"Yeah."

"I'm Jeff," he said. "I'm supposed to train you—but man, I'm *so* hung over."

He rolled his eyes and shook his head to express his misery.

"You don't need to train me," I told him. "I've washed dishes before."

"What? A *dish dog*?" He straightened and then looked me up and down. "Hell, a pearl diver like *you* could probably train *me*."

"'Pearl diver?'" I asked.

"Yeah, that's an old sailors' term for dudes like us," he said.

I was flattered.

While Jeff was showing me where some of the pots were stored in the back room, he had to sit down. He looked horrible.

"You can take off," I said. "Doesn't matter to me."

"You sure?" he asked.

"Sure," I said. "I can handle it."

"Yeah, I can't tell you anything that you don't already know."

Jeff crossed to the kitchen and said something to Charlie while pointing back in my direction. Then he grinned at me as he pulled off his apron and slipped out the back door.

Not much later, the brunch crowd flooded the dining room. In turn, the busboys, like pallbearers, hauled in the dirty dishes and dumped their corpses across my counters. Though the concept here was the same as at my old job in San Francisco—resuscitate the dishes—the rhythm was drastically different. If the old job's beat had been a steady waltz, here it was some sort of Brazilian speed metal or bluegrass-funk fusion. Whatever it was, I couldn't find my rhythm.

As brunch turned to lunch, I could no longer keep the kitchen stocked with clean plates. The worrying started: if I fell any further behind, I'd get sacked. Then I'd be back to worrying again about finding a job. And as an unemployed dishwasher, I'd surely stir up doubts in Melanie about me. Yet even with so much fear to motivate me, I couldn't keep pace with the work.

What I'd forgotten, though, was that it was impossible to get the heave-ho from a dish gig. Instead of showing me to the door, Charlie phoned Jeff. When Jeff walked in ten minutes later, I couldn't look him in the eye.

"Pearl diver," he sighed. "I thought you said you had it covered."

"I thought so too," I said. "But there's just too many dishes."

"Ah, the dish dog's lament: *too many dishes*."

Jeff stepped to the sinks and saw the burnt enchilada pan I'd been scrubbing.

"Why are you bothering with that?" he asked. "That's a three-day soaker."

I handed him the baking pan that I'd just labored over for five minutes. He filled it with hot, soapy water and exiled it to a corner of the counter.

"You need some music in here," he said as he hit Play on a cassette recorder. A cacophony of noise spilled out of the little speaker.

"You into Sun Ra?" Jeff asked.

"No," I said.

"You *should* be," he said. "It's the perfect music for the dishpit."

As the vibrant sounds of free jazz echoed through the room, I realized he was right. It *did* sound perfect.

"You into Charlie Parker?" he asked.

"No," I had to say again.

"Well, Bird was a dishwasher just like me and you," he said. "Worked at Jimmy's Chicken Shack in New York. You can hear it in his sax."

Jeff advised me on the soaking time of the other burnt cookware, warned me about the worst offenders among the cooks for burning pots and pointed out the waitress to be wary of on the days when she forgot to take her medication. He was a wealth of information and I immediately fell under his spell.

Like me, he wasn't spry. Though his movements were as slothful as my own, a gracefulness to *his* sluggishness allowed him to somehow get more work done without exerting much effort. If he left the dishroom to take clean plates to the kitchen, for instance, he always carried dirty pans back to the sinks.

"Dishwashing is like chess—you always gotta think six moves ahead," he said. "But you probably already knew that."

When the restaurant closed in the afternoon, one of the cooks—Brad—came and helped us finish up.

As the two of them razzed me about my less-than-stellar first-day performance, they told some of their own first-day-on-the-dishwashing-job tales.

Brad was once christened at a job by being thrown into a dumpster by two other dishers. He had to work the rest of his shift in his garbage-stained clothes.

On Jeff's first night as a teen dishwasher, the restaurant's other disher mixed all the leftover drinks into a single concoction and made Jeff drink it. He got so sick that the cook had to dunk his head under the faucet to sober him up.

The two described other dish jobs they'd had around the country. Then Brad asked me, "You ever busted suds down in Texas?"

"Nope," I said.

"How about in Michigan?" Jeff asked. "There's some places around Ypsilanti that don't pay so bad."

Ypsilanti? One of those thousands of places I'd dreamt of going to while studying my maps? I didn't even know how to pronounce it let alone claim to have washed dishes there.

Oh, how I would've loved to be able to answer Jeff, "Ypsilanti? Sure, I busted suds there" or to have told Brad, "Texas? An easier question: where in Texas *haven't* I dished?"

But I couldn't say that. So I stood off to the side and listened to their dishwashing testimonials—while longing to join in.

Then it hit me.

I could envision it so clearly. Traveling the country, seeking out intriguing workplaces in exotic locales, enjoying the freedom of living a life consciously devoted to a lack of responsibility . . . And as I picked up and dropped dish jobs left and right, if anyone was to ever ask if I'd dished in this state or that, I'd always be able to answer, "Yes!"

The idea had only just come to me, but within seconds I was sold on it. Interrupting my two colleagues, I blurted out my plan.

"*I'm* gonna wash dishes in *all* fifty states!"

"That's great, new guy," Jeff said. "Just remember: A good pearl diver never wears underwear—it slows you down."

After that first day, I found my dishpit rhythm while working the less busy weekdays. Jeff would come in afternoons to do a brief janitorial shift that involved helping me to finish the dishes and take out the trash. As much as possible, I patterned myself after him and the way he budgeted his movements yet made each one count.

Even more than Jeff's actions, I absorbed his attitudes about work.

"Dishwashers are the least-respected restaurant workers," he told me, "yet the most important."

If the dishes didn't get washed, the whole operation broke down. No food could be served. The customers didn't eat.

According to Jeff, cooking was too much responsibility. But as employees with massive egos, cooks needed constant flattery. Anytime a cook offered him something to eat or taste, Jeff always gave the food the highest of marks—regardless of what he really thought. A rave review boosted egos and kept the eats coming.

On the other hand, the busboys, Jeff said, were the Uncle Toms of the restaurant world. Refilling water glasses and doling out bread sticks, bussers were really only waiters in waiting. They ached for the day when they could climb another rung on the career ladder to become servile waiters who smiled widely as they delivered a lousy plate of food with hopes for a pat on the head in the form of a tip.

The fact that the busboys were the ones who continuously brought us more work in the form of dirty dishes didn't help their cause.

"Take that!" one busser said as he slammed down another load on our counter.

"Argh," Jeff growled at him. "When the revolution comes, these wannabe servants will be the first to the guillotines."

"As if a revolution will be led by a dishwasher," said the busboy.

"Dish *man,*" Jeff corrected him. "Unlike a bus *boy,* I'm a dish *man!*"

•

One day, I finally got up the nerve to ask Jeff if he'd contribute something to the little dishwashing publication I still hoped to put together.

"It's a zine?" he asked.

"I don't know," I said. "What's a zine?"

Jeff explained that they were small, self-published magazines, often with offbeat contents.

"There's thousands of 'em," he said. "Come over to my place after work and I'll give you one."

Later, at his basement pad, Jeff handed me a copy of *Factsheet Five*, a zine from upstate New York that listed brief reviews of hundreds of other zines.

"You should read this, too," Jeff said. "The man tells it like it is."

He handed me a copy of George Orwell's first book—*Down and Out in Paris and London*—and then sent me on my way.

That night, completely enthralled, I read the book cover to cover in one sitting. In it, Orwell recounted the couple of months he spent in Paris in the autumn of 1929 as a twenty-six-year-old *plongeur* (that's French talk for *dishwasher*). After all his money is stolen from his room, Orwell finds himself desperate for any kind of work. So his Russian buddy Boris lines up jobs for the two of them—dishwashing for Orwell, waiting tables for Boris—at a Russian restaurant that is to open in a couple weeks.

In the meantime, Orwell takes on a one-day dish stint at a large five-star hotel. But as luxurious as the accommodations and food are for the guests, behind the scenes, for the dishwasher, slaving in the hot and humid basements is grueling. At the end of a fourteen-hour shift, Orwell is tired and drenched in sweat. He's also surprised to be offered a one-month contract. He needs the money, so he'd like to accept the offer. But, ultimately, he feels it'd be dishonest to sign on for a month seeing as he'd have to leave in two weeks to go work at the Russian place.

Boris is unhappy to hear that Orwell has turned down the contract.

"Idiot!" he yells. "Who ever heard of a *plongeur* being honest? . . . [Y]ou have worked here all day. You see what hotel work is like. Do you think a *plongeur* can afford a sense of honor?"

Boris tells him to ask to be paid by the day, sign the contract and then bail when the Russian place opens. But Orwell remains worried about the dishonesty of signing a contract he knows he'll break.

"Do you suppose they would prosecute a *plongeur* for breaking his contract?" a stupefied Boris asks. "A *plongeur* is too low to be prosecuted."

Finally, Orwell gets it.

"This was my first lesson in *plongeur* morality," he writes.

After Orwell signs the contract, he works six days a week, eleven to fourteen hours a day. During this time, he's able to pick up on other aspects of the dishwasher world.

"The food we were given was no more than eatable, but the *patron* was not mean about drink; he allowed us two liters of wine a day each, knowing that if a *plongeur* is not given two liters he will steal three."

When Orwell gets dragged into work on what's supposed to be his day off, he worries that he's too hung over to get the job done. But after working merely an hour in the basement, he realizes that his worries are fruitless:

"It seemed that in the heat of those cellars, as in a Turkish bath, one could sweat out almost any quantity of drink. *Plon-*

geurs know this, and count on it. The power of swallowing quarts of wine, and then sweating it out before it can do much damage, is one of the compensations of their life."

After a couple months at the hotel, Orwell puts in a few weeks of dishing at the Russian restaurant before he ditches that job as well and hightails it back to England. Orwell's conclusion about the profession was it shouldn't exist in the first place. He felt that restaurant dining—the cause for such crap work—was an unnecessary luxury that should've been done away with. His message: Get rid of dish soilers and set the dishwashers free. On some mornings—when I found myself unable to sweat it all out and my head was still pounding from the night before—I concurred heartily.

In the spring of 1990, Melanie planned to return to Alaska to fish as her family had done for generations. She asked me to come along and work with her. Returning to Alaska sounded great. But working on a fishing boat sounded like too much responsibility. If working on a remote island had been a dreadful thought, then working on a boat at sea definitely remained out of the question.

I accepted Melanie's offer to tag along to Alaska but told her I'd pass on any boat work. Instead, I'd stick to my newfound love: *plongeur*-ing.

When I quit my job, I bade farewell to Jeff.

"You're gonna dish in Alaska?" my guru asked. "Dude, I'm impressed."

"Keep in touch, pearl diver," I told him.

Part II

"Dishwasher Pete"

6
The Dish Master

Alaska—the Last Frontier—was, for me, the First Frontier in my new traveling dishwasher adventure. Along the three-thousand-mile drive up there, I pondered where to dish. In Fairbanks? At a national park? Maybe in some one-diner town where I could pitch my tent behind the place?

My endless fantasies were all for naught; the job found me. When we arrived in Anchorage, Melanie heard that the cannery that she sold her fish to was looking for a mess hall dishman. I called immediately and told the mess hall boss, Levon, that I was the dishwasher he was looking for. He told me to be on the next day's flight out to a fishing village in the southwest part of the state.

The only ways to reach that area were by air or by sea. No roads connected it to the outside world. That sounded awfully isolated but Melanie assured me not to worry. The town even had a pizza place, she said. Besides, she'd be out there in a couple weeks herself.

The following day, I flew on a tiny plane that seated only eight people—the pilot and stewardess included—on the one-hour flight. As instructed by my new employer, I caught a taxi-van from the airport.

"What brings you out here?" the taxi-van driver asked.

"Dishwashing."

"Yeah?" she said. "It takes all kinds, I guess."

As we crossed the tundra toward the sea, we bumped up and down and swerved back and forth for fifteen miles along a potholed road. I felt antsy. Maybe this wasn't an island, but it was definitely remote.

At the cannery, with my duffel bag slung over my shoulder, I stepped inside the mess hall kitchen. A big black guy stepped forward and gripped my hand with one of his own. With his other hand, he swatted me "hello" so hard it knocked me off balance.

"Welcome, Pete," he said.

Not until my hand loosened from his grip was I able to tell him, "Thanks."

"I'm Levon," he said. He pointed to three cooks clad in white and introduced me to each of them.

Then he asked the cooks, "Where's Sonny?"

No one knew.

Levon walked over to a wall, banged on it and yelled, "Yo Sonny! Your new dishman is here!"

Thirty seconds later, a bleary-eyed guy entered with his baseball cap on sideways.

"Pete, this is my nephew Sonny," Levon said. Then to Sonny, he added, "Give your new dishman a tour."

Sonny walked me over to the "Pantry" adjacent to the

mess hall bakery where he, Charlie the baker and Dave the cook—and now me—each had a simple bedroom and shared a small bathroom. I dropped my duffel and sleeping bags on the bed. My own bedroom? Already I felt less claustrophobic about my new job.

Then he led me through several long bunkhouses that were lined with dozens of unoccupied bedrooms and hundreds of beds. Sonny showed me the fishing boats that were waiting atop wooden blocks for the coming salmon season. He took me through the sprawling waterside cannery where, in a few weeks, the salmon would be canned or frozen. The only people in view were the dozen or so men prepping the boats and readying the cannery machinery.

Back at the mess hall, Sonny guided me through that building's maze of rooms, each of which had been tacked on through the decades as the operation grew. One room was the dining area for the office staff and tradesmen (electricians, mechanics, plumbers, etc.); another was where the college-student cannery crew ate. A third room was the domain of the Filipino workers, and the fourth dining room was a melting pot for the Japanese employees (who processed the salmon roe), the Italian-American and Native-Alaskan fishermen, as well as the Native-Alaskan cannery workers.

Sonny explained that the Filipinos and the Japanese used to eat in the same room until one meal, when the Filipinos ran out of rice. One of them grabbed a bowl off a Japanese table, which ignited a huge interracial free-for-all. Since then, the Filipinos were obliged to dine in a separate room.

The hour-long tour ended in the middle of the mess hall complex—at the dishroom. Behind stainless steel counters stood the sinks and a decades-old Hobart dishmachine. As I approached the sinks, the floorboards sagged beneath my weight as if I were walking to the end of a diving board. As I bounced up and down, Sonny warned, "Careful, lotta water been splashed on these boards over the years."

According to Sonny, this was reportedly the last cannery mess hall in Alaska that served its meals "family style." Unlike "cafeteria style"—where diners walked though a serving line—here, waitresses brought the food to the dining rooms in large serving dishes, which were then passed around each table. Throughout the meal, each waitress—responsible for four or five tables—continued refilling the serving dishes and drink pitchers. After the meal, the waitresses would clear the tables and haul all the soiled ware back to the dishpit.

I was eager to see how it went down. But first, we mess hall workers had our own dinner to eat.

We sat with Levon, Charlie the baker, the cooks and the waitresses; I plopped some salmon on my plate.

"You actually like that stuff?" Sonny asked.

Free salmon?

"Love it," I said.

"You in the right place then," he said. "We got *baked* salmon, *fried* salmon, *boiled* salmon, *steamed* salmon, *grilled* salmon, *raw* salmon—you name it."

"Really?" The canneries where I'd worked before served spaghetti and meatballs most dinners.

"You work in the mess hall now," Sonny said. "You can eat *whatever* you want, *whenever* you want."

Watching me add yet more salmon to my plate, Sonny bragged about the other fringe benefits of my new unionized job: free lodging, year-round health insurance, free air travel between Seattle and the fishing village, and—after we were laid off at the end of the summer—unemployment pay. I felt even less isolated.

•

When we finished eating, Sonny flipped a switch that blasted a loud horn from the roof of the mess hall. Suddenly, the doors flew open and a couple dozen men poured in. Dinner was on, so I fled to the dishroom.

I stood at the sinks for a couple minutes before Sonny came along.

"What are you doing?" he asked.

"Waiting for the dishes."

"Aw, man, don't worry about no dishes. There's hardly anyone here yet," he said. "In a couple weeks, there'll be four or five hundred people at every meal. You'll be seeing so many dishes, you'll be *dreaming* about 'em."

So I sat and waited. A half hour later, Sonny finally gave me a nod. He washed the couple dozen plates, the couple dozen bowls and a few racks of drinking glasses and coffee mugs. I put them away. After he ran the silverware through the machine, as instructed, I dumped the hot, wet utensils on a bedsheet Sonny had laid out on a counter. We rubbed the spoons, knives and forks dry and separated them. After we put them away, we were done.

"Told you there ain't shit to do yet," he said.

What little we did do was gratifying enough for me. Back in the Pantry, I lay on my bed, stoked to have gotten my hands on some dishes in another state. After Kentucky and California, Alaska now made it three. Only forty-seven more states to go.

The next morning at 6:30, it was back to the dishroom. I washed a few dishes the cooks had dirtied while preparing breakfast. Then I stood at the sinks waiting for more.

Sonny shuffled in, sleepy-eyed and in slippers.

"Dude, go sit down," he said. "Breakfast dishes don't even come in for another hour."

He didn't have to tell me a third time to sit. I slipped back to my room and grabbed a book. Then, in the Filipino Room, I sat and ate pancakes while I read. An hour later, I turned on the taps to fill a sink. Sonny stuck his hand in the water and shook his head.

"This ain't gonna clean no dishes," he proclaimed. "Water's *cold*!"

He pulled the plug and then refilled the sink using water from only the hot tap.

"*This* is dishwashing water," he said. "Feel it."

I watched the thick steam waft upward from the sink and thought, Is he hazing me? What next? Will he throw me in the dumpster or make me drink a concoction of all the leftover drinks?

I didn't bite.

"*You* put your hand in the water," I told him.

Without a word, he dipped his hand through the steam and into the water.

I waited for him to rip his welting hand out again like Timmy had done in Kentucky. But he didn't.

"Leave it in there," I said.

Without breaking eye contact with me, he pushed his arm deeper in the water.

"When this mess hall's full and we're working round the clock, we gotta clean the dishes in a hurry," he said. "We ain't got time for lukewarm water."

Sonny filled the rest of the sink with cold water and told me to stick my hand in it. I wanted to tell him that I'd do the dishes my own way. But I'd be working alongside him all summer and didn't want to get off on the wrong foot.

Reluctantly, my hand went in. The water was still scorching.

"Soon you'll get your arms in the hot stuff like a real dishwasher," he said.

A *real* dishwasher? Was he putting me on?

Later, after the water cooled, I was reaching for some plates at the bottom of the sink.

"You're all hunched over," Sonny said. "You're gonna hurt your back."

He pushed me aside, assumed my place at the sinks and spread his legs until his feet were about a yard and a half apart. His height dropped dramatically.

"The sink's low, so you gotta get low," he said. "See how I'm doin'? I'm gettin' lower without bending my back."

He looked ridiculous—but I didn't know him well enough to tell him so.

"Now you try," he said.

I stepped up to the sinks and spread my legs.

Sonny laughed. "Dude, you can't be serious."

"What? I'm spreading my legs."

"C'mon, man," he said. Then he kicked at my feet like a cop readying a suspect to be frisked.

My legs barely budged.

"If you can't get no lower, then your back is gonna be broke by the end of the summer," he said. "Serious as a heart attack."

I spread my legs till the muscles strained. Still, I didn't get much lower.

After we finished the breakfast dishes, Sonny took me to the food warehouse where all the mess hall's dry goods—cans of vegetables, jars of condiments, boxes of paper napkins, etc.—

were stacked high on rows of pallets. At the beginning of spring, when only Sonny and Levon and a couple others were at the plant, a ship had arrived from Seattle with all these goods. Now, we were expected to spend time each morning bringing the supplies into the mess hall as needed and making room in the warehouse for the arrival of later shipments.

"See all that stuff by the back doors?" Sonny asked. "We need to bring it up front here."

"So where do we start?" I asked.

"We'll worry about that later," he said.

He laid a sheet of cardboard over a pallet of canned pineapple juice and asked, "You play bones?"

He then proceeded to teach me how to play dominoes.

As we played, Sonny explained that his Uncle Levon had been running the mess hall for seventeen years. Not even twenty years old himself, this was Sonny's third summer in the cannery's dishpit. He came from a world very different from that of an Alaskan fishing village—a slummy part of Louisiana where he'd already fathered four children by three different women. Levon started bringing Sonny up to Alaska to provide him with an income unavailable to him in his home state.

Those first few days were mellow. In lieu of the nonstop dishing that Sonny kept warning me was in store for us, we had plenty of time to kill. When we weren't working, Sonny and I sat in the warehouse playing dominoes or hiding in one of the mess hall's many nooks, where I read my books and Sonny read his hot-rod magazines—all on the clock.

Over the following weeks, the plant accepted new arrivals every day. The fishing village counted just two general stores, three bars, that one pizza restaurant and 500 winter residents. But during the peak of the salmon season, it swelled into a boomtown of 5,000 people. By that time, the dishroom was rocking as the mess hall fed almost 500 cannery workers and fishermen each meal.

The great thing about living on-site was that I had only a thirty-second commute to work. Most mornings I was up at 6:28 a.m., had my clothes on by 6:29 and was in the mess hall by 6:30. The downside was that I could never blow off work or even stroll in late. On those mornings when the alarm couldn't rouse me, I was jolted awake at 6:35 by Levon's pounding his massive fists against the bakery wall just inches from my sleeping head.

BOOM! BOOM! BOOM!

"Pete-O!" he'd shout. "Let's go!"

Two minutes later, I'd drag myself into the mess hall.

Before the breakfast dishes, Sonny and I would stretch like athletes to limber up for our roles as the "Pusher" and the "Puller." The Pusher manned the sinks, rinsed off the dishes, loaded them in racks and then pushed a rack into the machine every 82 seconds. While the Pusher slammed a rack in one end of the machine, the Puller pulled another rack out, unloaded the piping-hot clean dishes and carried them off to the kitchen.

Our lives revolved around that 82-second cycle. We hustled to keep the machine running continuously. If it sat idle for just one second, it was one second less we'd have on our next break. While working nearly around the clock, every nanosecond of break time was vital. So if the Puller didn't return from the kitchen fast enough, at the 82-second mark, the Pusher was left barking, "PULL! PULL!" Conversely, if the Pusher was bogged down in the sinks and missed his cue, the Puller screamed, "PUSH! PUSH!"

Sonny and I were perfect dishpit dancing partners. With the 82-second cycle, we were always aware of what the other one was doing—even while our backs were turned. The trampoline-like floorboards enabled the Pusher to always know just when the Puller was about to throw one of the metal dish racks back his way. In turn, the Puller always knew when the Pusher was going to brush behind to grab the rack of dirty drinking glasses.

All the while, Sonny was converting me to the church of scalding waters. Each day, he'd increased the temperature of my dishwater, acclimating my poor hands to hotter and hotter water. Sure it fried the flesh, but damn if it didn't get those dishes rinsed.

My leg-stretching also progressed, enabling me to spread my legs wider and wider apart. Each new inch gained in width between my feet meant another tiny drop in height. Down low, I could work the sinks without bending my back.

Tossing the old metal dish racks and carrying the tall stacks of the thick plates strengthened my biceps so much that Sonny and I often had pull-up contests in the dishpit doorway: fastest to do a hundred pull-ups had bragging rights for the day.

When the work hours grew to be really long, Sonny and I skipped our morning chores. Instead, we turned off the warehouse lights and napped. Sonny liked snoozing on the stiff, flat fifty-pound sacks of flour, while I preferred crashing on the malleable hundred-pound sacks of rice.

Once, when Levon walked in and flipped on the lights, I jumped up and groggily pretended to have been shifting the sacks of rice—in the dark. Levon looked at me, laughed and cut the lights on his way out. After that, anytime he found the warehouse door unlocked but the inside unlit, he courteously left the lights off and quietly closed the door behind him.

It took me some getting used to—an authority figure who was on my side. Levon especially gained my respect because, while Sonny and I dished, he often jumped in and scrubbed the pots and pans. He seemed more *dish* man than boss man.

One morning, Levon wiped some dust off the Hobart dishmachine and said that I wasn't taking proper care of it.

"Ya gotta love your baby," he said. "Ya gotta keep her shiny and happy."

Behind him, Sonny nodded in agreement.

Levon laid his arm atop the machine and added, "Ya gotta caress Baby and give her a kiss."

He leaned over and kissed the Hobart. Sonny did the same and then said, "Go on, kiss Baby."

I looked at these two fools and told them, "*I* ain't kissin' no dishmachine!"

A week later, the dishmachine went down during lunch. The pipes were clogged, a direct result of my shoddy record of cleaning the traps. With the machine incapacitated, stacks of dirty dishes streamed into the dishpit, but few clean ones left. Chaos ensued. We were backed up for hours and missed our afternoon break.

After the cannery's plumber repaired the Hobart, I was so grateful to have my Baby back that I swore to love and adore her. From then on, each day I broke down all of her parts to meticulously remove bits of debris from all forty-eight spout holes on her four spray arms. I polished her stainless steel panels with a good rubdown. And, at the end of each shift, I followed Levon's advice by honoring Baby with a kiss.

During peak season, the fishermen and cannery workers couldn't all fit into the mess hall at the same time. So if we served a second meal exclusively for the fishermen, union rules stipulated that we earned an extra ninety minutes of premium pay. And when the cannery was running around the clock and forced us to serve a "midnight meal," we received more premium pay. Sonny and I also treated ourselves to our own premium pay by adding bonus hours to the time books we kept. For example, if we finished the dinner dishes at 9:30 p.m., we wrote down 10:30 p.m.

Levon, who had to sign our time books, took weeks to discover our added phantom hours. But when he did, he just shook his head, laughed and signed off on them. The combination of the many hours we actually worked, the union-stipulated premium pay and our own phantom bonuses meant that some weeks we were logging 110 hours of—mostly over-time—pay. It totaled over a thousand bucks a week—more than five times the typical dish wage of the time.

There couldn't have been many—if any—dishwashers in America who earned more in a month than I had that July. Still, it was a lot of work. Probably even harder than doing the work itself was enduring the claustrophobia of never being farther than a few feet away from the dishes. At around 1:30 a.m., when the last spotless dish from the midnight meal had been put away and Baby had been kissed good night, I'd charge to my room, yank off my clothes and jump in bed. If it took longer than sixty seconds to go from kissing Baby to kissing my pillow, I was dragging ass. I'd fall asleep listening to Charlie sing old show tunes as he baked through the a.m. hours. And, as Sonny had warned, a chorus line of dishes danced through my dreams all night.

When the salmon finished their run from the ocean to their spawning grounds, the employees were cut loose by the hundreds. As the plant's population dwindled, the number of brown bears in the area increased. From the back door of the mess hall, Sonny and I watched the bears migrate down from the Aleutian Range, loping along the riverbanks and scavenging for dead salmon washed ashore.

My own summer ended less gloriously than it had even for all those spawned salmon. Melanie and I had talked about using our summer earnings to make a cross-country trip together. But her born-again Christian parents had other plans. They wanted her to finish college. And seeing me as nothing but a dishwashing bum, they urged Melanie to break up with me.

Dishwashing bum? I *had* a job! A *good-paying* one, no less! Plus my skills were at their absolute peak! My hands and arms were impervious to the heat of the sink water. My bulging biceps tossed the heavy metal dish racks around like they were made of Styrofoam. And my hardened, cracked fingertips could carry the clean, still-piping-hot stacks of dishes effortlessly.

When I'd arrived in Alaska, I hadn't realized that I was still little more than a dish novice. But after a couple months of working every day under those grueling conditions, I no longer felt like a novice. I wasn't even a dish bum. I was now Dishwasher Pete—a full-fledged *Dish Master*!

Even so, that didn't help my cause. Melanie's parents were convinced that I was a lowlife who was leading her astray. Yet *she* was the one who'd picked *me* up. *She* was the one who'd taken *me* in. And *she* was the one who'd turned me on to my last two dish jobs. If I was indeed a dish bum, then they should've been pointing their fingers at her, not me!

But bum or no bum, I got the bum's rush. At the end of the summer, Melanie dumped me. I left Alaska—alone.

Though I might have lost the girl, I definitely *had* found my calling.

7

It's Journalism

A snag: Now that I'd been laid off, I was eligible to collect unemployment pay from the state of Alaska. And since those weekly $186 checks flowed in as long as I remained officially jobless, in effect, I was paid to *stay away* from the sinks. It was a beautiful concept, but one that put a crimp on my quest.

In downtown San Francisco, I took a couple of my paychecks to a branch of the bank they were drawn from and exchanged them for more than four thousand bucks in cash. I hadn't realized how wealthy this made me until I took a seat in the bank, peeled off my right shoe and sock and tried to lay the stack of hundreds and fifties between my sweat-covered foot and sweat-encrusted sock. The stack was so high, my foot couldn't fit back in the shoe. So the left foot/sock storage unit had to be employed to help carry the load.

Now bloated with loot, I splurged by spending five of those sweaty hundred-dollar bills on a white, rusted 1971 Volkswagen camper van. The road maps that I'd carefully studied for years could now be put to practical use. Those places I'd known for so long only as dots and lines and colorings on paper, I could now see in person.

I was always curious about what was down the next road or around the next street corner. And staring at a map only heightened that curiosity.

Sure, I did touristy crap—sat atop the five-hundred-foot-high Flaming Gorge Dam in Utah, rode to the top of the Gateway Arch in Saint Louis, watched the space shuttle *Discovery* launch from Cape Canaveral. But far more captivating was simply walking the streets of Los Angeles or Denver or Atlanta.

It was exciting to wake up in the van, stare at the ceiling and struggle to figure out where in the nation I was. Even more thrilling was to then recall that I was in, say, Meridian, Mississippi. I'd step out of the van and think, Imagine, a dolt like me from San Francisco, here in *Meridian*! Then it was off to see what was at the end of the block and around the next corner. I was constantly exploring, my curiosity never satiated.

What was more was discovering all the regional brands of cheap, boxed macaroni-and-cheese. I bought all that I could find and—after consuming their contents—cut out the covers so I could someday display them like big-game trophies.

Attracted by their many used-book stores, pizza-by-the-slice places and bike- and pedestrian-friendly campuses, I gravitated to a number of college towns. If I sauntered around a campus long enough, I was always bound to stumble into some meeting or reception where free food was to be had.

The lure of the suds was hard to withstand, though. In both the college towns of Austin, Texas (state #4), and Athens, Georgia (#5), I took on under-the-table dish work. But I soon discovered that working with greenbacks already in my pocket was like buying a beer while already blotto: pointless. Each job was abandoned within a week.

While passing through Kansas, the van pooped out in the town of Colby. A mechanic told me it needed a new fuel pump but it'd take days for that part to arrive from Wichita, 230 miles away. There was no choice but to wait. To pass the hours, I poked around town.

In the window of a realtor's office, local houses were listed for sale. Some homes were priced as low as $12,000. Though my knowledge of real estate was minimal, those numbers didn't sound right. What little I did know was that in my hometown, housing prices were so high—and rising so rapidly—that it wasn't just an impossibility for a dishman to buy a house there, but even renting was out of the question. In fact, not long before, as a result of the explosion in San Francisco's housing prices, my parents had been evicted from their own rent-controlled apartment of twenty-three years.

Yet each time I counted the zeros of the listed housing prices in Colby, unbelievably, the figures came out the same. It got me thinking. Between Kansan prices and Alaskan wages, maybe I could get a place of my own.

Sitting smack in the middle of America, a house in Kansas could be used as a base of operations. It could be a hideaway to retreat to after dishwashing sprees up to Alaska or around the country. It could be a place where I'd finally get around to putting together my shoestring publication of dishwashing stories. And since at some point everyone passes through

Kansas, it'd be in a perfect location to host friends—whether I was home or not.

After the new fuel pump was installed in the van, I drove out of Colby with a vow to one day return from Alaska with enough cash stuffed in my socks to purchase me one of those houses. When the van died for good in front of my friend Floater's apartment in Oakland, California, I gave it to him in exchange for letting me crash on his couch for a few weeks.

In San Francisco, my dad told me that he didn't know what to tell people about me when he was asked about his kids. For my older siblings, who all still lived in San Francisco, he could rattle off their occupations: nurse, airplane mechanic, physician, store manager. But when he got to me, he couldn't explain what I was doing with my life.

"Just tell them I'm a dishwasher," I said.

"I can't do that," he said.

I guess he was worried that dishwashing would be considered too low class. After all, in an opinion survey of 1,166 adults who were asked to rate the status of 740 occupations, dishwasher ranked #735. Only envelope stuffer, prostitute, street corner drug dealer, fortune-teller and—#740—panhandler rated lower. What appealed to me about the job—that low status—was the very thing that embarrassed my dad.

On my way to Alaska, I stopped in Arcata and tracked down Jeff at his new dish job. After his coworkers left, I helped him finish up. He'd switched restaurants, he said, because on his one-year anniversary at the old place, the owner had rewarded him with a ten-cent-an-hour raise. Jeff found the puny increase more offensive than if he'd received no raise.

"Till then, I hadn't even realized I'd been stuck at that place a full year," he told me. "So I quit."

I got to Alaska in the spring of 1991 and spent the summer switching off with Sonny as the Pusher and Puller. When the season was over, I stayed until the bitter end. After the hundreds of cannery workers and fishermen left, the plant's population counted only me, Levon and a couple of plumbers who were flushing antifreeze into the cannery's water pipes for the winter. Even Sonny had departed. He left after his five-year-old son had been wounded by a stray bullet from a drive-by shooting.

Before I departed, I put the stacks of dishes to sleep for the winter by covering them with bedsheets. Then, before laying a white sheet over her, I gave Baby a year-end kiss.

Again, I was flush with cash and could work or not work, as desired, which really meant not working. In Arcata, while walking down the street, I ran into a guy I knew, John, and his friend, Jess. John told me about his dish job at the Uniontown coffee shop, where a cook often smoked pot in the walk-in fridge. After one recent smoke-out, the clueless boss had asked John to clean out the fridge, because, he claimed, it smelled like something was rotting in there.

We happened to be standing next to a little park with a jungle gym. As we talked, I grabbed hold of the pull-up bar and, just as Sonny and I had done all summer, I rattled off the pull-ups.

I didn't know it at the time, but a couple years later I'd end up dishing at Uniontown myself (but by then the cook was smoking pot at some other job). I also didn't realize that

I'd become good pals with Jess, John's silent friend. Jess later admitted that he hadn't uttered a word that day due to being in awe of me casually chatting while doing pull-ups. I believe his exact words were "I thought you were Superman."

I got to know Jess better when I learned that he'd picked up a dish gig of his own. It was the closing shift at the same restaurant where Jeff had dished the previous year. From having hung out there with Jeff, I already knew my way around that restaurant's sinks. So I showed up with cookies for Jess's first solo night and helped him close up.

This time, instead of Superman, he called me a dishwashing saint. Afterwards, we walked around town. When I saw a penny on the sidewalk, instinctively I stopped and bent down. As my fingers stretched to grasp the loot, Jess's own fingers swooped in and snatched the coin. I was dumbfounded. In all my years of coin-finding, I'd never had competition for pennies.

"Oh, hey man, sorry 'bout that," he said. "Here, you take it."

He handed me the penny.

"No, you take it," I said. But he wouldn't take it back.

Jess was truly a kindred soul.

I bought another 1971 Volkswagen camper van that was almost identical to the one I had the year before. It too was white, rusty and broke down at regular intervals.

Three years had now passed since I'd first proposed to my pearl-diving pals that we gather dish tales in a publication. Though everyone whom I'd proposed this to thought it was a good idea, none of their lazy asses had yet written a word for it. I decided I needed to just do it myself.

So one afternoon in a Phoenix, Arizona, photocopy shop,

I was ready to put aside my procrastination and finally put together my long-envisioned zine. But first, I had to suffer a crash course in handling a photocopier. Nothing seemed to go right. Photos reproduced too light or too dark. The back sides of pages came out upside down in relation to the front sides. The paper repeatedly jammed in the machine. But through several frustrating hours, I slowly got the hang of it. The result was four sheets of paper folded over and stapled into a sixteen-page booklet. Most of the text was handwritten in ballpoint pen. And it was titled simply, *Dishwasher*.

That first issue of the zine contained the story of my attempt to interview the dish dog at the El Tovar Lodge on the southern rim of the Grand Canyon. That endeavor was thwarted by three park rangers who accosted me as I tried to locate the lodge's dishroom. They saw that among the list of questions I'd prepared for the interview was: "Is your boss a prick?"

"This your idea of a joke?" one ranger asked.

"No," I said. "It's journalism."

The lodge's dishman lived in a national park and worked barely a stone's throw from one of the world's most amazing views. Maybe he could even see the canyon from his dishpit. But did such perks outweigh having some prick squawking about spotty glassware? What *was* the downside to the job? I needed to know.

Claiming to have never heard of "dishwashing journalism," the rangers threw me out of the park. If I ever returned, they threatened, I'd be arrested.

I photocopied a grand total of twenty-five copies of *Dishwasher* #1. Fifteen of them were mailed to dish comrades I knew like Jeff, Jess and Sonny. The rest were passed out through the back doors of Phoenix's restaurants to dish comrades I didn't know. The zine was nothing fancy, just a meager attempt to entertain a few cronies.

•

In Texas, I put out a second issue. This time, I photocopied fifty copies and again mailed them off to friends and passed out the rest to at-work pearl divers. Then I traveled to northern Louisiana, and turned up unannounced at the housing project address Sonny had given me the summer before. He wasn't home, so the two women at the apartment dispatched some of the children present to find my friend. As the kids fanned out across the neighborhood, the women called around town. A small crowd gathered on the sidewalk in front of the apartment.

"What's goin' on?" someone would ask.

"Some white boy's lookin' for Sonny."

"You work for Sonny?" one man asked me.

"Not *for* him," I laughed, picturing Sonny telling his friends he was some kind of dishroom foreman. "We wash dishes *together.*"

"*Wash dishes?*" he said. "I thought Sammy was the boss of, like, twenty or thirty people in a kitchen up there."

"No, me and Sonny—" I started to say, then caught myself. "Uh, yeah, you're right. I *do* work for Sonny."

For the next twenty minutes, as a growing number of people joined in the wait, I was asked several more times if it was true that Sonny was a big shot in Alaska. I couldn't blow my friend's cover. So I lied each time and said, indeed, he was.

The crowd had grown to a couple dozen people when, after having been tracked down in a pool hall, Sonny finally arrived.

"Someone came running in saying a white boy was looking for me. They said it wasn't a cop, so I knew it had to be *your* crazy ass," he said. "I left in the middle of a hundred-dollar game."

"You shoulda finished your game," I told him.

"Couldn't do that," he said. "I was worried you'd get scared being surrounded by all these black folk."

As surprised and glad as he was to see me, he seemed even more nervous about my presence. It was as if he didn't want me knowing he'd been misrepresenting himself as the mess hall honcho while, at the same time, didn't want his friends finding out the truth from me. So after he treated me to a chili-dog-and-root-beer-float dinner at a drive-in, he said he'd see me back in Alaska. And I was on my way again.

I put out Dishwasher #3 while in Virginia and rambled all the way up to Maine. When the van died by the side of the road in southern Indiana, I didn't bother to try to revive it. I grabbed my bags and started hitchhiking.

8

The Fundamental Rule

*T*hroughout that winter, I repeatedly phoned Levon. I was lobbying for him to bring me up to the cannery as early as possible, even though he wouldn't really need me till weeks later. My plan was to work from the absolute first day possible to the absolute last one and earn enough money that year to buy a cheap house in Kansas. The pestering worked: when I arrived in early April 1992, the only people inhabiting the plant were Levon and the winter watchman.

Despite my lofty ambitions, I ran into trouble right away. As I pulled the bedsheets off the stacks of dishes and off of Baby, it felt like I had put them on only the day before. During the first two years at that job, the desire for the end of salmon season slowly mounted as the weeks passed. Now, by the end of the first day, I was already aching to go. And yet, I'd have to wait through another three and a half months of working every day until I could say my good-byes again.

I'd hoped Sonny's arrival would help distract me. But when he showed up a couple days later, his presence only fueled my yearning to leave.

"Man, I'm ready to go home already," he said before he'd even unpacked his bags. He was so serious about the latest mother-to-be in his life that he almost hadn't come to the cannery.

I, too, had left a gal behind in the lower forty-eight. I'd met K. J. in Arcata and now she was to spend the summer in Colorado with friends. In fact, every letter I received in Alaska seemed to be an outline of all the fun things various friends would be doing while I was bogged down at this job again.

For weeks, Sonny and I egged each other on by moaning and griping about missing our ladies and being stuck at the cannery.

At any other job, I would've bolted. But I couldn't stiff a boss who allowed me to sleep on the clock and pad my time book—especially after I'd badgered him to let me arrive weeks before he needed me. He'd consented in order to keep me appeased all season. But though I had only stepped off the plane, I was already unhappy.

The days eked by. No matter what we did, whether it was dishing or reading or playing dominoes at a dollar a game, Sonny and I ended up whining.

Five weeks in—when we were still weeks away from the *beginning* of salmon season, let alone its end—I got a letter from Jess.

He wrote: "Here's the scene: 2:59 p.m. I finish washing a knife and reach over to get another. I begin scrubbing—it's slip-

pery—hard to clean—next thing I know I see stars, then black-
ness for a second. I look down. 'Shit!' I'm covered in blood. It's
gushing all over my white apron and everything else."

The gist of the tale: He's now kicking back while nursing
the five-inch gash in his hand and collecting disability pay.

Lucky bastard, I thought. Getting paid to *not* work! I wished
a malady would get *me* out of working. Sure, grasping and
turning plates tens of thousands of times made my hands and
arms ache. Though the carpal tunnel syndrome may have been
severe, I didn't figure a doctor would warrant it a disability.

Then, a couple of days later, one of the bouncy floorboards in front of the sinks cracked and started to give way.

"Better watch out," Sonny said. "Fall through that floor
and you'll bust your leg."

I avoided the broken plank throughout lunch. Then,
during the afternoon break, while lying on my bed and thinking yet again about how much I wanted to leave, it all came
together: broken floorboard = broken leg = freedom!

If I jumped hard enough on that floorboard, I was sure to
fall through. And if I didn't bust a leg, at the least I'd hurt an
ankle, a toe—*something!*—and be on the next flight out.

I returned early from my break, eager to stomp through
the floor. But when I stepped into the dishroom, my ticket to
freedom was snatched from my hand. The cannery carpenter
was on his hands and knees before me, nailing a sheet of ply-
wood over the brittle floorboards.

He looked up at me and said, "These planks were so weak
I'm surprised you guys never fell through 'em."

"Yeah," I said, deflated. "Me too."

The next morning, after breakfast, Levon sent Sonny and me
around to the bunkhouses to check which rooms still needed

pillows. As we exited the second floor of one bunkhouse, Sonny was ahead of me, descending the outdoor stairs in the rain. Looking down at the steep, wet stairwell of about twenty-five wooden steps, I figured, Here's my chance.

If I slipped on that first step and fell forward, I could bounce down the stairs and onto disability pay. The stairwell's steepness and length assured that at least one bone would break. Maybe it'd be an arm, but I'd take a broken leg, too. There was just no telling what it'd be. Heck, I could even break my back or bust open my skull.

That gave me pause. Was it worth the risk? After all, a broken back could put a chill on my whole summer.

"You coming or what?" Sonny shouted from the bottom of the stairs.

What the hell was I thinking? I suddenly realized the lunacy of such an act—and realized it was obvious I had to leave, despite everything Levon had done for me.

After lunch, I told Levon, "I have to go."

"You sure?" he asked.

"I'm sure," I told him.

He tried to talk me into staying. I could pad even more phantom hours onto my time book, he said. But money wasn't the issue. He even offered to fly up K. J. and employ her as a waitress. But I knew it wouldn't help. I wanted to be elsewhere.

No matter what Levon said, it did him no good. The notion to split had hit.

But there was a hitch: The earliest date for an affordable flight out of town wasn't for another seven days. In the meantime, Levon asked me, would I not say anything about my quitting to anyone—meaning Sonny—until my day of departure? Apparently, he didn't want my abandoning the ship to give his nephew any ideas about jumping in the lifeboat with me.

I agreed to keep mum.

In the meantime, while I worked alongside Sonny, our minds were in completely different places. While he continued whining about wanting to leave, I was silently overjoyed—and feeling like a traitor for being overjoyed.

The guilt even haunted me in my sleep. The night after my conversation with Levon, I dreamt not of the chorus line of dishes, but of Sonny being sentenced to death. He was to be executed by a dishmachine—trapped inside until the scalding water disintegrated his flesh. And I stood by powerless to prevent his execution. Awaking in a sweat, I wanted to grab my stuff and flee. But that couldn't happen. I was still trapped.

This was *exactly* the scenario I'd always feared. I *knew* I never should've gotten myself stuck in an isolated job situation like this. So, then and there, a pledge was made not to let it happen ever again. Any future gigs would have to conform to a new rule—the *fundamental* rule: never work at a place where I couldn't just up and leave.

With four days to go, while standing in the dishroom waiting for the first lunch dishes to roll in, I imagined the letters I'd send to Sonny to cheer him up after I'd left.

Sonny noticed the contented look on my face.

"Hey, don't you go quitting on me and sending me letters from wherever you go," he said. "'Cause if you quit, I'm going with you."

That floored me.

"No, no," I stammered. "I wouldn't do that."

Unable to face him, I grabbed a couple of plates and made for the sinks.

•

Finally, my last day arrived. My flight to freedom was due to leave in the afternoon. After Sonny pushed and I pulled the lunch dishes, he walked to the Pantry and I kissed Baby good-bye forever. I grabbed my duffel and sleeping bags from my room and then stepped next door to Sonny's room to say so long. But, for some reason, his door was padlocked. How could that be? He *always* spent the afternoon break napping in his room. I checked the bathroom, the mess hall and all around outside. He was nowhere to be found.

Over the previous week, I'd envisioned this moment dozens of times. Yet it'd never occurred to me that I'd be unable to thank the man who'd taught me so many tricks of the trade. It was inconceivable to leave him without saying good-bye.

But the plane wasn't going to wait.

Sonny was leading 43-42 in our buck-a-game domino tournament. So I pinned a dollar bill to his bedroom door along with a note that read: "Sonny, sorry to ditch you, but I have to go. Here's the dollar I owe you from dominoes. Take care, Pete."

Sonny's wish for me not to write him letters from the outside was honored. But throughout that summer and the next few that followed, I anonymously mailed hot-rod magazines to him at the cannery. As the postmarks on the envelopes were from all over the country, maybe he didn't know who was sending them. Or maybe *because* the postmarks on the envelopes were from all over the country, he knew precisely who they were from.

9
If You've Got Time to Lean . . .

On the flight down from Alaska, I replayed over and over again in my head the image of the reception I'd get from K. J. How could it be anything less than enthusiastic? After all, I'd just bailed on a job and flown several thousand miles to be with her. But at the Denver airport, she looked disappointed.

"What's wrong?" I asked.

"Nothing," she said. Then, without much hesitation, she added, "It's just that now you'll be broke again."

She was right. A lot of what I'd earned in Alaska had already gone toward the student loan I'd received when I was seventeen. The loan had gone into default the month before so I'd paid it all off in a lump sum when I still thought I'd be lousy with money from working all summer. Now, I was not only broke, but by quitting before being officially laid off, I was ineligible for unemployment pay. Gone was my plan to come back from Alaska with enough dough to buy a cheap Kansan house.

So, in Boulder and in need of a job, I went straight to the Russian Café on Pearl Street. While passing through Colorado, a couple years before, its window flew a "Dishwasher Wanted" sign. Back then, when I stepped inside, a middle-aged Russian-looking man walked out from the kitchen.

"I'm interested in the dish job," I told him, pointing at The Sign.

He looked to where I pointed, nodded and said, "Aaah." Then with a heavy accent, he asked, "You speak Russian?"

I said no.

My answer failed to impress him because he then chatted away—in Russian. Or was it English? *Ruglish?* Whatever it was, I couldn't comprehend it.

A couple of times he interrupted his speech to bark commands—in distinct Russian—at various employees. Looking around, I considered what it would be like to work on an all-Russian-speaking staff and eat from the Russian version of the Bus Tub Buffet. My interest was piqued.

While I was lost in thought, the head Russian continued to talk at me. And I continued to nod back at him, as I assumed he was explaining the job. But he rambled on and on. How much was there to say about a simple dish gig? Soon, his talk turned grumpy, as if he was grumbling about the weather or even bitching about his wife. For all I knew, he could've been ranting about how he hated non-Russian-speaking dishwashers, but did get a rush out of butchering and cooking them.

The more he talked, the more agitated he became. The more agitated he became, the more I worried. The more I worried, the more I wanted to scram.

As he rattled on, I inched my way to the door. He followed uncomfortably close behind.

"You be here, right?" he then said in suddenly clear English as I reached the door. "You come back then?"

Apparently, at some point in all my nodding, I'd agreed to a time and date to start washing his dishes. I nodded one last time and then slipped out the door and didn't look back.

Talking to some local dish dogs, my experience didn't surprise them. The "Dishwasher Wanted" sign was a permanent fixture in that window. So for the rest of my time wandering around Boulder, I steered clear of that restaurant's street. If the Russian ever saw me, I feared, he might chase me down and show me firsthand whatever it was he'd been grumbling about.

But that'd been a couple years ago. Now, here I was, fresh from Alaska. I was confident that that The Sign in the Russian Café's window would give me a better welcome than K. J. had.

Alas, again my expectations were too high. No sign in the window greeted me. In fact, The Sign was nowhere to be found in the whole town. So I poked my head through restaurant back doors and asked around among my dishwashing comrades for any leads on jobs: again, nothing.

Finally, a wanted listing turned up in the newspaper. I called immediately and was told to come on out. When I reached the place—a deli in a vast shopping center—the boss-guy handed me an application. While I was filling it out, he looked at it and noticed my false claim to have earned eight or nine dollars an hour at other dish jobs.

"It'd be impossible to make that kind of money washing dishes around here," he said. "Normally I pay my dishwashers five bucks an hour."

"Swell," I said, too hard up to question the wage.

"But I suppose I can pay you six bucks," he said.

"Swell," I said again, earning the easiest raise a suds buster could ever expect.

So I stopped filling out the application while he described how slack a job it was.

"Lots of the time you'll just be dicking around," he said, probably not realizing he had a professional dick-arounder sitting before him. "The last guy was a lazy shit," he continued, "but he never missed a day of work and you won't find too many dishwashers in America you can say that about."

I didn't bother to tell him that he hadn't found one in me.

He finished by telling me to come in Saturday morning, adding, "But if you don't show up, it's no big deal."

I did show up on Saturday and, sure enough, he was right: the job *was* cush. After my hardcore training in Alaska, while making Colorado #6, I was able to bang out the few dishes in no time. This left me with plenty of downtime.

There's a tired old adage in the restaurant world. It's the justification mantra for busywork that goes: "If you've got time to lean, you've got time to clean." But I had my own version of the adage: "If I've got time to lean, I've got time to sit on my ass."

I dragged a chair into the dishpit, pulled a paperback from my pocket and got to work dicking around. When the boss-guy found me sitting there and reading, he suggested that I instead sweep the floor. Apparently, his definition of "dicking around" was different from mine.

So I swept the spotless floor, then resumed my sitting and reading. The boss walked in again and set a big bag of carrots on a cutting board.

"Pete, since you're not doing anything," he said, "could you chop these carrots?"

Me? Chop carrots? Cooks were people that dealt with food. The only times my precious hands touched edibles were when I was either eating it or scraping it off customers' soiled dishes (which was often at the same time).

"Chop 'em?" I asked.

"Yeah, chop them."

"Should I peel 'em first?"

"Yeah, peel them."

"Peel them like this?"

"No, don't peel away the whole carrot, just peel the skins."

"Oh, then what?"

"Then cut them."

"Like this?"

"No, that's too thick."

"Oh, like this?"

"No, that's too thin."

"Like this?"

"No, that's too thick."

"Like this?"

"That's too thin again."

It was tedious convincing him of my ignorance. But in the end, it was worth the effort. After minutes of witnessing my inability to follow his instructions, he gave up.

"Pete," he said, "just forget it."

We came to an unspoken truce. As long as I didn't sit and read, he didn't try to make me do anything remotely related to cooking. So in lieu of reading, I entertained myself by foraging through the Bus Tub Buffet. I also fooled with the radio, sprayed the spray hose aimlessly and ground up used lemon slices in the garbage disposal to make the dishroom smell nice and lemony. I made frequent pilgrimages to the drink machine to fill up on orange juice. One day I even established a personal single-shift record by drinking sixteen 12-ounce cups of O.J. (which left my scalp tingly and my brain woozy). And when all else failed, I'd sneak my book or a newspaper into the bathroom to read. Whatever the case, I always made sure to kiss the dishmachine after each shift, though I wasn't as bold as I'd been in Alaska. Here, I made sure no one was watching.

When K. J. left Boulder for college in New Hampshire, I decided to tag along. I figured New England's dishes in the autumn were a sight not to be missed.

10

A Dishwasher
for All Your Needs

Upon my arrival in Dover, New Hampshire, I hit the sidewalks looking for a trusty "Dishwasher Wanted" sign. The outing in the charming, old town was pleasant. Up and down Central Avenue and past the old nineteenth-century mills that stood waiting to someday be turned into condos or offices, I surveyed every place that dirtied dishes commercially. But everywhere I ventured, no dishwashers were wanted.

The next day, I covered the town again by foot. Again, no luck.

Repeating my stroll every day seemed an inefficient way to keep vigil for a dishman's departure. It was entirely possible that in the twenty-two-odd hours between searches, a sign could go up and another dish dog could easily snatch up the gig before I ambled by. If only I could somehow get to the restaurant owners before they even flew The Sign in the window. To let employers know that a new, available Dish Master was on the scene, I needed a direct line—*a hotline!*

So I wrote up a little flyer:

Has your dishwasher recently walked out on you?
In need of an experienced dishman?
Then call Pete
A DISHWASHER FOR ALL YOUR NEEDS
(Flexible hours/flexible pay)

On it, I listed K. J.'s phone number. In the town's restaurants, cafés and coffee shops I passed out the flyers. Most personnel accepted and read the sheet without comment.

"Is this your resume?" one woman asked.

"Yeah," I told her, somewhat flattered. "I guess so."

At the Fish Shanty—a seafood joint—I handed a flyer through the back door to an old man.

"You a dishwasher?" he asked.

"Yeah," I said.

"Aw right. Come in Friday night and I'll put you to work."

Friday night—in state #7—my new stint began as they always did: I remained silent. In any new work environment, I didn't know who was who. I didn't know who obeyed the rules and who broke them; who snitched on late coworkers and who covered for them; who kissed the boss's ass and who'd like to kick it.

I never showed my hand first. Usually I stayed clammed up until someone like Sonny revealed himself and cued me in. But here, my poker-faced routine got me nowhere.

"You're the quietest dishwasher I ever heard!" one waitress told me.

I wanted to tell her that she should've said, "You're the quietest dishwasher I *never* heard."

But I was too wary to even say that.

My coworkers were a tight-knit group. They all seemed to be related to each other. And as the foreigner in town, I remained the outsider in the restaurant, washing dishes in silence.

Most of my interaction at the restaurant was limited to the patriarch, the old man who paid me every week in a bizarre ritual. I'd stop by the restaurant during the afternoon lull. The old-timer would go to the register, count out some cash and then motion me to follow him into the corner of the dining room. He'd glance over his shoulder and scan the empty restaurant to make sure we weren't being watched. Satisfied that the scene was secure, he'd grab my hand, jam a clump of fives and ones into it and then force my fingers to make a fist around the dough.

Now convinced we were doing something that demanded utmost secrecy, I'd move my fist ever so slyly toward my pocket. It was usually when my hand was busy pushing the wad deep into my pocket that I'd remember to watch out for how he expressed his appreciation.

"Good work," he'd say and then send his hand to deliver a good-natured old-Italian-guy slap on my cheek. But he never did it right. Body parts that should've had no starring role in a good-natured slap—the side of his hand or his wrist— would box my ear or bang my temple.

In a daze, I'd wonder, Should I sock him back?

But because he smiled while delivering the blow, I had to give him a pass for being a clumsy old man.

We repeated this routine for several weeks until finally, one time, as he went to pay me, he asked, "How much do I pay you? Four-fifty an hour? Uh, no, I mean *four-twenty-five* an hour?"

His performance as an old-seafood-joint owner was usually worthy of an Oscar. But this lame attempt at ad-libbing was a stain on his career.

"It's *five* bucks an hour," I corrected him.

"Really?" he said. Then he grumbled while stuffing my hand with the correct amount. His own poor acting seemed to have thrown him off so much that he missed his cue to deliver his customary "good work" clap to my head.

One warm autumn afternoon, I sat in the sun on the front steps and enjoyed a couple beers before my next scheduled shift. As the hour grew later, I grew more and more reluctant to kill my buzz by trudging off to work.

If I walked over there right now, I thought, I could still be on time.

Ten minutes and another beer later, I thought, If I left *right now*, I'd only be ten minutes late.

Another twenty minutes passed and I thought, Leave now and I'm a half hour late.

After one more beer, I ceased thinking about being late—or even about leaving for work at all.

There were heaps of ways to flee a job. Some of them, like in the film *Scarface*, were dramatic. When the lead character, Tony Montana, starts to walk away from the restaurant where he's been dishing in Little Havana, the restaurant owner calls out to him, "Hey, wha'chu doin'? There's a lotta dishes to be washed!"

"Wash 'em yourself, man," Tony tells him. "I *retire!*"

Then Tony throws his apron at the boss.

That was one way to get an employer's attention. But for me, on this night, I remained immobile. I assumed the old man would assume my absence meant that I'd retired from the restaurant—since that's what *I* assumed.

Now freed from what little responsibility I had in the world, there was a familiar rush, the one that I could only get by quitting a job. I relished it with another beer.

Later that night, I talked to my dad on the phone. Learning that I'd gleefully dropped another job, he got upset. After almost thirty years at the same job, he was now enjoying his much-deserved and long-overdue retirement. He believed that days of leisure should be preceded by decades of drudgery, and he said so.

When I tried to explain to him that the best part of working was quitting, he told me about how he'd announced his retirement. For weeks, he'd secretly cleaned out his desk, taking home personal belongings so that on the day the notion struck, he could up and leave with minimal fuss.

Then one morning, he began clearing off the top of his desk. When his coworkers asked what he was doing, he told them he was going home.

The boss came over and asked, "You mean you're leaving at the end of the day?"

"No," my dad said.

"You're going home at lunch?"

"No, I'm leaving right now."

The boss asked him to stick around so the company could throw him a retirement party. My dad didn't want a party. He just wanted to go.

And then he did.

"Really?" I asked him when he was done telling me the story. "*You* did that?"

As his son, I couldn't have been prouder.

"You know that feeling you had when you left—that feeling of freedom?" I asked. "Well, I love that feeling so much, that's why I'm always finding new jobs—so I can quit them!"

He laughed—and I hoped he understood.

After my farewell to the Fish Shanty, a call came from a restaurant where I'd left a flyer.

The woman—who introduced herself as the chef—asked, "Can you come in for an interview this afternoon?"

"Yeah, sure," I said.

Cool, I thought, a new job to quit! But wait, what was that about an interview? Surely it had to be a mere formality. She'd ask if I want the job, I'd say yeah and we'd both be happy.

When I met the chef at the restaurant, the contrast in our appearances was uncomfortably clear. Her face was caked with makeup; she had her hair done up and she was dressed in spotless kitchen whites. Meanwhile, I was unshaven, had ratty hair and wore clothes that had almost as much hole to them as fabric.

But like a couple on a doomed blind date, we went through the motions anyway.

"Tell me about yourself," she said.

"Well, I'm a dishwasher—" I began. Then I hit a snag. What else was there to say?

"—and I can start right now," I added.

"And where do you see yourself in five years?" she asked.

"Five years?" I pondered. "Washing dishes, I suppose."

"Where will that be?"

"Wherever there's dirty dishes," I said smugly, tickled with my slam dunk answer.

But it didn't halt her persistent questioning. The inquisition soon revealed that she was more interested in a careerist for whom dishwashing was but a first rung up the job ladder. She wanted someone who wanted to be a cook someday. In short, she wanted a dishwasher who didn't really want to wash dishes.

It made no sense. If her house had been on fire and someone arrived in fireman's gear raring to put it out, she wouldn't have stopped and asked him where he saw himself in five years. She'd get the hell out of the way and let the pro do his job. I figured the same should go for dishwashing. She had dirty dishes and here I was. So what if I was disheveled, in raggedy clothes and had a stink that preceded my arrival in the room?

When she was finally done with the interrogation, I asked, "So, I've got the job?"

"I still need to talk to a few other candidates, first," she replied.

Candidates? I was looking for dish work, not the presidency.

Well, if there *had* been an election, apparently I'd failed to win her vote. After I left the restaurant, I never heard from her again.

With no jobs in town, I broke down and hopped across the border to dish at a waterfront lobster house in Kittery, Maine (#8). I borrowed K. J.'s car for the ten-mile/twenty-five-minute trip to work. Even though the drive time was shorter than my stroll-across-town commute to the Fish Shanty had been, it was exhausting to travel so far to dish. So after making the trek just three times, I returned just once more— to pick up my pay.

•

A few days later, K. J. and I were eating at a local hole-in-the-wall diner so cramped it was remarkable it was able to hold the dozen small tables and four counter stools that it did. The diner had been the first to receive my flyer since it seemed like a decent place to dish. It was cozy and oozed character. Plus, K. J. had convinced me to suspend my ban on eating out by claiming this place served portions huge enough that the leftovers were a full meal in themselves.

On this particular day, something about the diner's dish dog struck me as odd. In her late twenties, overweight and clad in sweats, she looked more like a babysitter or a Dairy Queen cashier than a pearl diver. It wasn't merely because she was female—I knew plenty of great dishgals. But there was definitely something off about her. I just couldn't put my finger on it.

While I was trying to decipher her, the dishgal suddenly stomped out of the kitchen, her face flush.

"Wench!" she yelled at a waitress. She pulled off her apron, threw it down and charged out of the packed diner.

Whoa! What panache! What timing! How could I have *ever* doubted her qualifications!

She was a *magnificent* dishwashing specimen!

Grinning, I sat admiring and appreciating the scene I'd just witnessed. Ditching the place during the morning rush, leaving a diner full of stunned customers and soiled dishes in her wake. That'd show 'em!

And *wench*? Who called anyone a wench?

She was awesome!

Then it hit me: The show had to go on.

Before anyone even had the chance to call out, "Is there a dishwasher in the house?!" I stood and crossed the diner. Right inside the kitchen doorway, the boss-guy was hunched over the sinks, already busy with the dishes. I could've kept my mouth shut and watched him sweat it out. But my need for work outweighed my need to see him suffer.

"I'm a dishwasher," I told him.

He looked perplexed.

"You . . . want to work?" he asked.

"Yeah," I said.

"How do you know we need a dishwasher?"

"I just saw what happened," I said, pointing in the direction of the front door where the Dish Mistress was last seen.

"And you say you're a dishwasher?"

"For Christ's sake, Alex!" yelled one of the two cooks who were frantically manning the stoves. "Just hire the guy!"

"Okay," the startled boss said. "Job's yours."

He handed me an apron. In less than four minutes, I went from customer stuffing my face to employee busting the suds.

Diving right in with the dishes was no problem. Following the lead of the two cooks—Danny and Ricky—was more challenging. They moved so swiftly, and we shared such a small dance floor, that I kept bumping into them. But, little by little, I learned all their steps and got into the swing of the place.

But then an order came in and Danny called it out to Ricky. Danny repeatedly shouted, "Waffle! Waffle!" until Ricky turned to me and said, "Dishwasher, you gotta make the waffle."

"I don't know how to make waffles," I said, playing my ignorance card.

Ricky pointed to the waffle-maker next to my sinks.

"Just pour the batter in and close the lid," he said.

Since he wouldn't take my word for it, I had to prove it to

him. For the next few hours, each time a call went out for a waffle, I'd pour the batter in and close the lid. Sometimes I'd open the lid too early and serve up the waffles gooey, or I'd open it too late and make sure they were burnt.

But this strategy backfired. The cooks either threw out the waffles or sent them out to customers—who, in turn, often sent them back. Stuck redoing waffle orders meant that instead of making no waffles, I was forced to make twice as many.

At the end of that first shift, Danny and Ricky and the three waitresses invited me to join them at the bar next door for their usual postshift drinks. After the unexpected day in the suds, I could use the refreshment. Danny bought me a beer, commended me on my sink-work and joked, "But we won't talk about your cooking."

The two cooks, it was revealed, were married to two of the waitresses. The third waitress wasn't related by blood or marriage to the others, yet she was still considered kin.

"We're all like family," Ricky explained to me as he spread his arms out to indicate everyone at the table—including me.

Unlike at the Fish Shanty—where my status as a foreigner in a small-town family restaurant branded me an outsider— at this place, by simply being an employee, I was considered a member of the clan.

On this occasion, though, the family only wanted to bitch about the black sheep—the departed Dish Mistress. They described her with terms like "fucking nuts" and "crazy bitch" and tried to convince me that the terms were fitting. But I couldn't bear to hear anyone denigrate my heroine. So after drinking just the one beer, I told them I'd see them in the morning and then split.

•

After that, I was dishing for them almost every day from six a.m. till three p.m. The occasional waffling was offset by the quirky kitchen, the decent cash and—especially—the food. Danny and Ricky encouraged me to forgo the Bus Tub Buffet and order whatever I wanted from the menu. So every day I went to work with the goal of gorging enough food to not have to eat again until I was back at work the following day. And if I didn't work that next day, then I really needed to sock it away to hold myself over.

For example, on one shift I managed to consume: a garlic bagel with cream cheese, a bowl of cereal, apple juice, three strawberry-topped pancakes, a slice of cheesecake, orange juice, a Swiss/tomato sandwich, a bowl of fruit, a banana, a blueberry muffin, grape juice, a pineapple-walnut muffin, two brownie sundaes, a plain bagel with cream cheese, a plate of French fries, cranberry juice, milk, plus many hand-fuls of blueberries, walnuts, chocolate chips, chopped bell pepper, broccoli and hunks of cheese. Like a squirrel stuffing his cheeks with nuts to bury in the ground to get through winter, I'd stuff my face with grub to bury in my stomach. And it always got me through the next workless day.

The only thing I never ate was waffles, because I'd have to make them. And I was still dragging ass on that front. In addition to under- and overcooking the waffles, I took to purposely spilling the batter all over the counter so that, by midmorning, we'd run out of the goo and waffles would be eighty-sixed from the menu.

I also began just ignoring the "Waffle!" command. Five minutes after the rest of an order was ready to be sent out, when Danny would ask, "Pete, where's that waffle?" I'd say, "Waffle? What waffle?"

Since they were convinced that I was plain stupid, the cooks seemed to get more frustrated than angry. But that didn't prevent them from still yelling "Waffle!" a couple times a day. If anything, it only made them yell it louder.

That was, until one busy Saturday morning when Danny received a ticket and called it out to Ricky.

"Mushroom omelet! . . . potatoes! . . . wheat toast! . . . waffle!"

I cringed.

But then Danny added, "Scratch that, no waffle!" To the waitresses, he shouted, "Eighty-six the waffles—*Pete's* working today!"

And that was that. Without using physical force, real or threatened—just good old-fashioned civil disobedience—victory was achieved. From that day on, I never made another waffle.

I was still expected to join the postshift jaunts to the bar next door, though. But after nine hours of slaving over the sinks and forcing myself to eat as much as possible, come closing time, my mind was fixed only on lying down. Besides, after working alongside my coworkers all day, the last thing I wanted to do was rehash with them—in painstaking detail— all of the day's events. So every afternoon, I opted out of the bar invitation via some excuse: didn't feel well, had to make a phone call, K. J. was waiting for me. . . .

But each excuse was met with an offered compromise: Take an aspirin, use the restaurant's phone, invite K. J. along. . . .

Come November, the pressure really mounted. My coworkers were planning a huge after-hours Thanksgiving dinner to be held right there in the restaurant. My presence was expected.

"C'mon, dude, you don't have any family in New Hampshire," Danny said. "Ya gotta come."

But I didn't gotta and I didn't go.

If indeed I was a member of this restaurant family, then I played the same role in it that I did in my own. I was the quiet and disappointing son who gladly stuck around for the free eats but who didn't stick around any longer than he had to.

11

Snowed In

U pon hearing that some far-off ski resorts in the Rocky
Mountains were so desperate to attract dish dogs that
they paid almost double the minimum wage plus provided
free room and board, I'd added "Rocky Mountain Ski Resort"
to my new To Do list of places to work. Then my pal Colleen
happened to land one of those jobs at a Montana ski resort
and sent me an invite to come dish alongside her. In addition
to the perks, the job location was high in the Rockies, out in
the great outdoors, away from civilization. . . . It sounded
like a nice change, so I wasted no time getting there.

Leaving K. J. in California with a box of the "Dish Master"
T-shirts I'd been silk-screening and sharing with fellow pearl
divers, I told her I'd be back in a couple months. The 36-hour
bus trip got me as far as Bozeman. In a borrowed pickup
truck, Colleen drove me the remaining thirty miles up to

where the road dead-ended at the ski resort in the Gallatin Mountains of Montana (#9).

Since employee lodging cost $150 a month per person, Colleen and I decided that I'd just crash in her room—without informing the resort's authorities—and split her rent. After I dropped off my duffel and sleeping bags in Colleen's room in the employee housing, I was eager to stretch my legs and explore my new surroundings. Colleen pointed me in the direction of the main lodge. I walked alongside the road for a couple minutes, reached the lodge and poked about in the lobby. Adjacent was the building that housed the ski shops and restaurants and the cafeteria where I'd be working. I tried to mosey around outside some more but found it difficult. There were only a couple of short, wet streets lined chest-high with plowed snow. When vehicles sped past, they came with a gust of icy, wet air.

Back at her room, I asked Colleen where was a good place to walk.

"Yeah," she answered. "There really isn't any place to walk here."

"What do people do then?"

"Ski," she said.

The next day at the cafeteria—where skiers stopped for a sandwich and a beer between runs—Colleen showed me the ins and outs of the job. She taught me how to pinch food and beer (a backpack was enough to do the trick), how to punch in/out another employee's time card (to pad a friend's work hours) and where to hide out for unofficial breaks (the seldom-used upstairs dining area was best).

But Colleen couldn't enlighten me on how to avoid the gig's major drawback: bussing tables. Though the bussing didn't entail much—just rounding up cafeteria trays and bus tubs of dishes about once an hour—it did bring me in direct contact with customers. If my dish guru Jeff had seen me out there breaking my rule about never bussing, his heart would've snapped in two. And as bad as it was to have to come into contact with customers, worse, these customers were wealthy snobs.

During that first shift, I nearly collided with skiers as I carried trays across the dining area. It happened three different times. I had the right-of-way, each time, yet was cut off by a customer (males in their forties or fifties). To avoid a collision, I had to slam on the brakes.

I didn't understand. Did these rich arrogant pricks really expect me to meekly yield to them? Did they also expect me to curtsy while I was at it?

Colleen told me I wasn't crazy; she'd also had near-misses while bussing. That being the case, from then on I vowed to bus with a vengeance. During my second shift, I yielded to no one. Anyone who thought to cross *my* path ran the risk of being bulldozed by a slothful-but-determined dishman.

While I was bussing tables early one morning, some lady asked me what time the shops outside the cafeteria opened. I told her I didn't know.

"You work here and you *don't know*?" she asked.

"Hey," I said, "I'm too busy *working* to go shopping."

She reacted with a look on her face that said, *"Well, I never!"*

Then, a couple days later, some other crabby rich lady accosted me while I was gathering trays in the dining area.

"Where are my gloves?" she asked me. *"Where are my gloves?!* I left them on that table a minute ago!"

On the table indicated sat no gloves.

"I don't know." I shrugged and then started to walk away.

"They were on *that* table! Where are they?!" She said it as if *I'd* taken the gloves.

"If you left them on that table and they're not there now," I told her, "then I don't know where they are."

"You don't understand, they're *leather* and *very* expensive," she said. "I want them back!"

She repeated the description as if to prove she could describe the gloves I'd apparently stolen. After telling her to talk to the manager, I retreated to the sanctuary of the dishpit.

Twenty minutes later, I was back in the dining area. Lo and behold, I found a pair of expensive-looking leather gloves. Normally, I wouldn't have given them a second glance. But because she'd done such a convincing job in selling me on these gloves' expensiveness and leatheriness, I pocketed them. Within hours, they were mailed to K. J.

What I liked about traveling was wandering through neighborhoods, looking at the regional architecture and discovering what made the places unique. But what made this place unique to me was its inability to allow me to explore. Outside, there wasn't a lot for me to do except look longingly at the unwalkable expanse of snow-covered mountains. Who'd have thought the great outdoors could be so constraining? It was no wonder why the ski resort was so hard put to attract dishers!

Actually, everyone else in the cafeteria's kitchen—the other dishwashers and the cooks—took every advantage of the job perk that was totally useless to me: the free ski pass. If Colleen dished in the morning, she brought her ski gear with her to work. Then, within minutes of her shift's end, she was suited up and on the ski lift to spend the rest of her day on the slopes.

I had no interest in skiing. Or, more accurately, I had no interest in buying—or even renting—the necessary ski pants, coats, boots, gloves, goggles, cap, poles, skis, boards, etc. My desired activity required me to have nothing more than any old pair of shoes and a suitable surface on which to use them.

Other options for spending my leisure time were extremely limited. I could hang out in Colleen's room and read. But spending a couple hours cooped up in that tiny, poorly lit space always got old fast.

Or, in the main lodge, I could try to read in the lobby. But if I hated the presence of the customers while I was on the clock, then worse was trying to enjoy my free time while the snoots clomped about in their ski boots and vulgar outfits.

Twice I used a day off to hitchhike the thirty miles down to Bozeman. But between the brief winter daylight and my poor luck with rides, those trips were of little satisfaction. One morning it took two and a half hours of pacing and shivering before I got picked up. By the time I reached Bozeman, I had only a couple hours to frantically wander. Then I had to make my way back to the town's outskirts, where I paced and shivered while hoping to catch a lift back up the mountain before it turned dark.

Eventually I developed my own ski resort pastime and it required no wearing of expensive, specialized gear. It didn't even require shoes. At the end of my shift, I'd slip a few beers out of the cafeteria and sneak over to the outdoor Jacuzzi. There, I'd crack open a beer, strip down to my drawers and hop in with the snobs. If anyone was aghast, all the better.

●

After being snowed in on the job for almost four weeks, I was met at work one morning by the boss-guy. He was grinning. I braced myself for whatever chicanery he had up his sleeve.

"Pete," he said, "how'd you like to be a cook?"

It was bad enough I was bussing tables. Now this?

The night before, two ski-bum cooks had bolted for some slopes in Colorado. Now shorthanded, the boss-guy was looking at me with the reassuring smile of a con man who'd found an easy mark. But I was nobody's patsy.

"No thanks," I told him and started to make for the dish-pit.

"You sure?" he asked. Then he cooed, "It *pays* more."

No matter what the bait, it was still a trap—more responsibility.

"I'm a *dishwasher*," I said. "*Not* a cook."

He was stumped when I walked away from the deal. Hopefully he was even more so when, a couple days later, I walked away for good.

After loitering in Seattle for a few weeks, I made it back to California, excited to tell K. J. about my growing To Do list for tackling the dishes of the nation. I wanted to hit a dude ranch in Wyoming. Then maybe I'd head farther east to sleep on some of the couches and floors that'd been offered to me—"Dishwasher Pete"—via letters from the increasing number of readers that *Dishwasher* was gaining.

But when I arrived in Arcata, K. J. was far less passionate about my plans than I was. In fact, I arrived to find that she'd moved my box of "Dish Master" T-shirts from her closet to the apartment of some friends.

"And that's where you can stay while you're in town," she said.

That's how I learned I'd been dumped. Apparently my traveling dish act didn't quite fulfill her needs. And in my absence, she'd met a better player. He had his own place, stayed put in town and had a steady job—as a cook.

To numb the pain, I went to the movies. A friend who sold tickets at the theater let me slip in for free whenever she was working. So each night I took solace by watching *Dragon—* the film about Bruce Lee.

In the flick, after the young Lee emigrates from Hong Kong to the United States, he's hired on as a dishwasher in a Chinese restaurant in San Francisco. When a comely waitress comes on to Bruce, it drives the jealous head cook crazy. He can't understand why the waitress would be interested in an ignoble dishwasher. Tensions in the kitchen rise until Bruce is forced to fight the cleaver-wielding, four-man cook crew—all at the same time! In the alley behind the restaurant, our hero ends up kicking some serious ass.

At the 7:05 p.m. showing, this scene would begin at 7:28. So every night I'd arrive at around 7:26, be let into the theater for free, sit down and watch Bruce fight back in the name of pearl divers everywhere.

After the scene, I'd exit the theater thinking maybe that's what I needed to do. Maybe I needed to kick some serious cook ass.

But in the film, Lee doesn't get the girl. (Then again, in real life, he hadn't washed dishes upon his arrival in the United States; he'd *waited tables!*)

Even if I couldn't emulate the dishman from the film, I wasn't too worried about the girl. I had other things on my mind: another forty-one states to complete my mission.

12

Biscuits, Hush Puppies and Deep-Fried Everything

I didn't make it to the dude ranch. But in Saint Paul, Minnesota (#10), I did dish at a coffee shop. Then in Dayton, Ohio (#11)—where Larry Flynt once busted suds at an Italian restaurant—it was at a hospital. To get myself hired on at the hospital, my urine had to be drug tested. So when it was time to quit, I thought it fitting to call the boss and tell him in my worst druggie voice, "Bro, I'm totally high right now."

He was supposed to tell me to get lost.

"It's okay," he said instead. "What you do on your own time is your own business."

Huh? What'd I have to do to get fired?

"But like, I'm seeing *sounds* and smelling *colors*," I added.

Still, he wouldn't can me.

"Don't worry about it," he said. He insisted I come to work. So I was forced to end my work relationship a more conventional way: I hung up the phone. With that, I'd quit.

When I rolled into Hattiesburg, Mississippi, I had my heart set on working in some dumpy shack diner that served grits, biscuits, hush puppies and deep-fried everything. I wanted a place where catfish was caught from the kitchen window and the bathroom was just a hole in the floor. Sure, they were clichés. But they were what I craved.

While wandering the streets of Hattiesburg, though, I didn't find a single "Dishwasher Wanted" sign. Some towns fly The Sign and some don't. For example, a few months before, in Boston, Massachusetts (#12), I'd only just left the bus station and was meandering along Newbury Street on my way to my friend's apartment when I saw The Sign flying in a café window. I popped in, got the job and was asked to start that night. Then I continued on my way and, within minutes, saw *another* sign. But not wanting to be *too* gluttonous, I left that second job for some other pearl diver to pick up.

Though in Hattiesburg I didn't find a sign downtown, I *did* find plenty of neat old buildings that were vacant, crumbling and forgotten. While the buildings were great to explore and lounge about in, their condition was depressing. Obviously, their best days had long passed.

One day I picked up applications from fourteen eateries. None of them were exactly shack diners. And the one bar where the urinal *was* a hole in the floor? They said, maybe not surprisingly, that they had no use for a dishwasher.

The following day, I sat down to fill out the applications.

First, though, my story. I had to figure out how to explain who I was, why I was in this town, why I'd left my last job, etc. Was I a happy-go-lucky ass-kisser? A scowling transient? An impoverished family man in a jam?

While I was staring at the stack of blank applications and pondering my identity, the phone rang. It was the fella from the Chinese restaurant. When I'd asked him for an application the day before, instead of handing me one, he just asked for my name and number. And why not? Any other information (experience, references, education, etc.) about a dishwashing applicant was superfluous.

"You dishwasher?" the voice asked.

"Yeah," I said.

"You want job?"

"Yeah."

"You hired."

The next afternoon at the Chinese place, Milton—the boss—explained that a couple days earlier, his dishwasher was caught trying to supplement his income by robbing a nearby restaurant. Off to jail he went, and into his job I followed.

For less than an hour, I putzed around the dishroom with the lunch dishes before I was told it was time to eat. The dining area was deserted—the afternoon lull—but the lunch buffet was still set up. After following the cooks through the buffet line, I sat at a small table with my book.

"No," Milton said. "You sit here."

He pointed to an empty seat at a larger table where the rest of the crew sat.

One of the cooks leaned over and said, "In Chinese culture, it's rude to eat alone."

Well, I figured, when in Mississippi (#13), do as the Chinese-Mississippians. I moved to the big table.

"Where you from?" one of the cooks asked.

I told the truth. "San Francisco."

My answer got the attention of everyone at the table. I quickly learned that to Chinese immigrants in a place like Hattiesburg, Mississippi, San Francisco—home to a massive Chinese community—was Mecca. No one present had yet made the pilgrimage, but they all hoped to do so someday.

"A lot of Chinese restaurants there," Milton said.

"Oh yeah," I said. "Hundreds of them."

When he asked how the food at this restaurant compared with the chow at the Chinese places in San Francisco, I didn't lie to him.

"This is better than any Chinese food I've ever had in San Francisco," I said.

Since I'd never worked in a Chinese place, and because I didn't eat out, I'd actually never dined in any Chinese restaurant in San Francisco. But the food was free, so I felt obligated to praise it.

That night, Milton walked into the dishpit, reached for the pot I was busy washing and said he needed it.

"Let me just rinse it first," I told him.

"Not necessary," he said and then grabbed it.

"Yeah, but—"

He made off with the soapy pot and, a minute later, started making soup in it.

Later, he told me I was spending too much time scrubbing pots. They needn't be rinsed after they'd been washed. He then pointed to a rack of water glasses waiting to be run through the dishmachine and said, "Don't need to wash these."

Milton picked up the rack and carried the glasses back to the dining room.

Now normally, a request to work less couldn't have fallen

on more sympathetic ears. But this kitchen—and everything in it—was so filthy and greasy that my professional genes couldn't let the cleaning slide.

In the days that followed, Milton kept a close eye on me. He was quick to inform me if he thought I'd spent too much time pot-scrubbing. Therefore, in his presence, I had to swab the pots and pans ever so casually. But as soon as his back was turned, I'd scrub furiously. And before I ever dared to run the water glasses through the machine, I had to peek around to make sure no one witnessed my subversive act.

Actually, there was never a moment when I was truly alone; I shared the dishroom with a cockroach colony. Roaches—and rodents, too—had a keen appreciation for free grub that challenged even my own. In almost every American restaurant, they're snacking away. Though some restaurants are better than others at keeping the vermin out of view of the customers, the critters are there nonetheless. Any restaurant owner that claims otherwise is lying and diners should avoid the place. But at a restaurant where the owner does cop to infestation, though it may seem an unappetizing idea, one shouldn't hesitate to dine there. It may be infested, but at least the owner is honest—and that should count for something.

At this Chinese joint, all around me the cockroaches scuttled, scampered, skipped and scattered. Before I arrived on the scene, they'd had free rein to brazenly eat whatever they wanted. But now there was a new sheriff in town. I soon spent much of my time tracking, trapping and slaying them. Or, at least, trying to.

Once a cockroach clung to a plate I'd pulled from a bus tub. Before I could hose him off the plate and down the drain, the roach leapt onto my shirt. I tried to brush him off, but the surly critter maneuvered much too fast. My hands scrambled to catch him as he ran laps around my torso.

Then I felt something on my pant leg. Another roach was trying to pull me down. A third dropped from the ceiling onto my head. It was three-on-one—*unfair!* As we jostled and wrestled, my body spun across the room and crashed into stacks of dishes. They knocked me off balance and to the floor I went. Two of them held me down while the third slapped me senseless. In bitter defeat, I mumbled, "Uncle." Each roach dragged a bus tub of dirty dishes off to a dark corner. To the victors went the spoils.

That may not be exactly how it happened, but that was how it ended. If anyone, it was *I* who was the intruder—the pest. The cockroaches were there before I arrived and would be there long after I left. They could skip and scamper to their heart's content. I admitted defeat and, in the vermin wars, officially proclaimed my neutrality.

The job provided mountains of fortune cookies. And when my fortune read "Work expands to fill the time available," I knew that it was time to move on. Then again, if I'd really wanted to, I could've culled a fortune that would've prompted me to stay. But this particular fortune turned up on the very afternoon that the restaurant's previous dishman finally made bail. Upon his release, he came straight to the restaurant. After catching up with the cooks, he entered the dishpit.

"So you're the new dishwasher, huh?" he asked.

Shy about discovering how an armed robber might react to an opportunistic disher who'd nabbed his job, I answered reluctantly, "Um, yeah."

But in this restaurant, I discovered, he was no armed robber. He was a dish dog. And so was I. Though he didn't know me from Adam, almost instantly he showed off his new jailhouse tattoos of his kids' names.

Then the old disher hung out and told me about how, at his hearing, the presiding judge openly disapproved of his interracial marriage.

"The judge about shit himself when I told him we have kids!" he said as I scrubbed a pot. He started putting the pots away without first rinsing them. Watching him work, I realized that, as a mere itinerant, I'd just been keeping the dishwater warm for him during his absence. And judging by his failure to rinse off the soap, I knew the quality of dishwashing would again decline to a level satisfactory to the boss. It was clearly time to pass the scrub brush back to him.

At the end of my shift, I quit, telling Milton I was leaving town.

"Yeah, you a big-city guy," he said. "There's nothing for you to do in this town."

There was some truth in what he said. While traveling around the country enabled me to see all the places I'd dreamt about, it also provided me with the opportunity to window-shop for possible places to live if I were to ever settle down after the quest. Any possible new hometown would need to be somewhere where I could wander the same streets year after year. And not only was there a limit to how much exploring could be done in a town as small as Hattiesburg, but many of its walkable streets were being replaced by sidewalk-less, strip-malled boulevards.

Unfortunately, it was a typical story. Even Milton pointed it out to me.

"Here, for entertainment, people go to Wal-Mart," he said. Instead of strolling the streets, they strolled the store's aisles—even if nothing was purchased.

For weeks, the talk of the town had been the closing of the

old Wal-Mart and the opening of the new, farther-out-of-town, superenormous Wal-Mart. Around the restaurant, as well as around town, the question on everyone's lips was the same: "Have *you* been yet?"

I hadn't been yet. So I went to see what all the fuss was about. While following the sidewalk-less boulevard out of town, I got a bad feeling as I lumbered past all the big-box stores and drive-throughs. After finally reaching the store, within minutes of entering I became disoriented, developed a rare headache and had to flee. Though my first Wal-Mart experience lasted no longer than six or seven minutes, it made a deep impression on me. If municipal strolling was limited to this monstrosity's aisles, then I knew I wouldn't be able to stay settled in a town like this for long.

I liked what I saw of what the town had been; feared what it was becoming; and agreed with Milton: small-town life here wasn't for me.

After he paid me, I filled a bag with enough fortune cookies to last me a month.

According to my meticulous records of *Dishwasher* correspondence (hundreds of names and addresses scrawled chronologically into a large book), a *Dishwasher* reader lived in this town. So I sent him a postcard.

"Hey, this is Dishwasher Pete. I'm in town," it read. "Let me know if you wanna hang out and swap suds stories."

Minutes after my final shift at the chowmeinery, the phone rang. It was a friend of the person I'd written to. She'd actually been the one who'd found a copy of *Dishwasher* #9 at a bookstore in Atlanta.

"Can I take you to breakfast tomorrow and pick your brain?" she asked.

"If you're paying," I said, "you can pick whatever you want."

The next morning, while I scarfed diner fare, the woman—Cheryl—asked the usual questions about my quest. How did it begin? What states had I hit? Where was I headed next?

To that last question, I answered, "I don't know yet."

"Louisiana!" she exclaimed. "You need to do Louisiana next."

She'd just finished a master's degree in creative writing and was in the process of moving back to her boyfriend's place in New Orleans.

"You gotta come down and stay with us and wash dishes there," she said.

New Orleans? I'd heard identical accounts from two different white guys who'd unsuccessfully sought dish work there. White employers, they claimed, hired only blacks for those jobs. In both accounts, the narrators had left that town without busting any suds, saying it was impossible for a white boy to dish in New Orleans.

I accepted Cheryl's offer, gung ho to prove those chumps wrong.

13

Head Dishwasher?

In New Orleans, I hoped to dish in a stereotypical place. So I explored the French Quarter and scoured the windows of every Cajun-y and Creole-y restaurant for *"Plongeur Wanted"* signs. Not seeing any work advertised in the French Quarter, I took to walking into places and asking for applications. No one showed any interest in hiring me, though. But then again, I suppose I didn't show much interest in *being* hired. Restaurant managers sought enthusiastic desperation in their applicants, a *"please* hire me" expression on their faces. In my case, whenever my application was reviewed, I usually slouched in a chair and yawned and scratched. Not even the creative list of references on my application—a circus midget, a retired pederast, a future astronaut and even the southern Indiana judo champion—caught their attention.

While pounding the pavement looking for work, I covered a lot of ground and saw a lot of the city. The architecture of so many of the old shotgun shack houses in both well-heeled and decrepit neighborhoods was captivating. But what held my attention even closer were those neighborhoods' sidewalks. In a lot of areas, the pavement was uneven, pushed up by tree roots and/or from decades of neglect (that is, where there *were* sidewalks and not just dirt paths). If a stroller wasn't careful, he could (or in my case—*did*) trip and land on his face.

Because I was so busy watching where my feet were stepping, my eyes were diverted from searching for The Sign or seeing the passing houses. But the diversion proved beneficial—it helped to hone my coin-finding skills. Pay phones, newspaper machines and especially the sidewalks of the nation were awash in currency if one was patient enough to look for it. My burgeoning skills—like being able to distinguish between a nickel and a slug from fifty feet off—came in handy. In fact, they were so useful, they helped me find change *eleven days* straight.

But my coin-finding luck remained better than my job-finding luck.

"This is Pete," *Cheryl said,* introducing me to some guy at a party she dragged me to. "Pete's a writer."

"Oh yeah, what do you write?" he asked.

"Well, I'm *not* a writer," I said.

"He's a writer who happens to wash dishes," Cheryl said.

I didn't agree. An air-conditioner repairman who complains about a restaurant's crappy eats is not a food critic; he's an air-conditioner repairman. A schoolteacher who allows her husband to snap nude photos of her is not a porn star; she's a schoolteacher. And a dishwasher who writes about washing dishes is not a writer; he's a dishwasher—and a damn proud one.

"I'm a dishwasher," I told the guy, "who happens to write."

"Well, mister-dishwasher-not-a-writer," he said, "where do you wash dishes?"

"Nowhere right now," I said. "This is a tough town for a dishman."

"That's 'cause you're too *white* for the job," he said. He claimed that at every place in New Orleans that he'd worked as a waiter, whites waited and blacks dished.

"That's a myth," I said. "Any place that needs its dishes washed will hire any willing dope to do it—regardless of race."

He claimed it was racist of me to want to dish in New Orleans.

"You're taking a job away from a black person," he said.

If, according to his theory, certain jobs were for whites and certain ones for blacks, by eschewing my "white job" (as a banker or lawyer or whatever) to work a "black job," wouldn't I be freeing up my "white job" for a black person?

Racism, I told him, was assuming that shitty jobs should be reserved for blacks.

Regardless, it would take more than rumors about racism to keep me out of the sinks. After canvassing the town proved fruitless, I stooped to combing the newspaper classifieds. But each time I answered an ad, I found two or three other (usually black) job seekers already there, filling out applications. I never got hired.

There were other classified ads for dish jobs out in Metairie, the suburb bordering New Orleans to the west. Not long before, Metairie had distinguished itself by electing the asswipe David Duke—former Ku Klux Klan grand poobah—to a seat in the Louisiana House of Representatives. Oddly enough, it was dishwashing that turned Duke into a racist. In his autobiography, he described watching a dishwasher at a coffeehouse in Delhi, India, in 1971:

> *Cleanliness was not one of his finer points, for he looked as though he moonlighted as a gravedigger. Crusty black dirt trimmed the tips of his long fingernails; the lighter spots on his face and neck, on closer inspection, turned out to be streaks where sweat had washed off some layers of muck. After hundreds of swabbings from the same filthy water, his dishrag resembled what I imagined were mummy wrappings.*

Duke's dainty sensibilities were so offended that by the end of the day, he had a revelation: "It was at that point that I realized who I am. I am an Aryan."

Looking at all the openings listed in Metairie, I had to wonder, Did I really want to try to dish out in a place that had elected a well-known bigot to office?

Well, the question was moot; I didn't want a job located farther than I could comfortably commute by foot or by bike. And there was no way I was walking or cycling out to Metairie every day. Especially since I was already within walking distance of hundreds of New Orleans restaurants.

Besides, I remained confident I could find a job in town. After all, when Levon Helm, drummer of The Band, quit Bob Dylan's first electric tour in 1965 because he was tired of the audiences' booing, he fled to New Orleans and got a job dishing at The Court of Two Sisters restaurant. (Never mind that he was fired after a day and a half when he was caught eating an entrée.) And when Alex Chilton (of the Box Tops and Big

Star fame) dropped out of the music scene, he also wound up dishing in the Quarter. If those two white boys could do it, why couldn't I?

My faith began to waver. After all, there was that time in San Diego several years before when I had searched high and low for dish work. At a couple restaurants that flew The Sign, the managers wouldn't even give me an application. In fact, they both offered me instead a position as a *waiter*! And not one, but two boss-guys straight out told me they only hired Mexicans to wash their dishes. One explained he had "less trouble with them"—meaning it was easier to keep them in their place. Raises and promotions were neither asked for nor offered. But because I was white, it was assumed I'd skip out on them within weeks, when a better opportunity came along.

Well, it was true—I would've skipped out within weeks. But it wouldn't have had anything to do with better opportunities, just the same opportunity in some other restaurant in some other town.

Then it happened. I got a call from a chef at a restaurant in the French Quarter. When I'd handed him an application the week before, he'd shown no interest in hiring me, despite my concerted effort to not yawn or scratch (the slouching was unavoidable). Now he was saying to come in, that he had a job for me.

As I trekked down to Decatur Street, I was pumped with excitement. The naysayers and myth-perpetuators were going to be proven wrong. A white man *could* find a dish job in New Orleans.

In his office at the huge restaurant, the chef grinned as if he was as thrilled as I was about the job.

"You'll be in charge of the other dishwashers—six to ten of them on any given night," he said.

I didn't understand.

"You'll be head dishwasher," he explained.

Head dishwasher? Me? I barely managed to be the head of myself, let alone heading anyone else. Besides, as a suds buster who hated authority, was I really expected to push around my fellow workers?

I was stunned silent.

The shock continued as he gave me a brief tour of the dishrooms located on two different floors. Indeed, all the other dishers were black. Why hadn't he promoted one of them? They obviously knew the setup better than I did. Instead, he hired a white guy to be the head of a bunch of black guys.

"Yeah, this'll work out great," he said as he glanced at my application again. "You say you're a hard worker, so this'll be a good job for you."

That socked me like a punch in the gut. Never in my life— not in the deepest darkest moments of sarcasm, not as a practical joke and especially not as a story line on an application—had I ever called myself "a hard worker." If anything, I took great pains to never sell myself as a hard worker. This dude was clearly delusional.

Still, it *was* a dish job. Deeply confused, I said nothing. As I left, the chef told me to return the next afternoon at five o'clock to begin head-dishwashing.

The following day was spent agonizing over what to do. Still desperate to dish in New Orleans—to make Louisiana state #14 in my quest—and in need of cash to get traveling again, here was my opportunity. As five o'clock approached, I started walking—not to the Quarter, though. Instead, I wandered through Mid-City, resuming my search for the all-important window signs. And it was a good walk. That liberating feeling of discarding a job, I discovered, could be achieved without even ever gaining it. Then, to top it off, in three different spots along a one-block stretch of South Carrollton Avenue, I picked up nine coins—37 cents total. Not too shabby!

A couple days later, a listing appeared in the want ads of the *Times-Picayune*:

Dishwashers wanted for one-day jobs
Cash $$$ paid per day

Now *that* was the gig for me. I was so impatient to get started that instead of hoofing it, I bummed a ride from Cheryl. When we pulled up to the listed address, Cheryl looked at the seedy characters in front of the building. They were lounging on the sidewalk and drinking brown-bagged booze.

"You're not about to sell your plasma, are you?" she asked.

"No," I said. "At least I don't think so."

I got out, skirted the sidewalk loafers and reached through a steel gate to knock on the door. A rough-looking mug opened the door and gruffly asked, "Yeah? What d'ya want?"

The whole scene felt clandestine, so I said, "The newspaper ad sent me."

"Oh, all right." His scowl softened. "C'mon in."

He unlocked the gate, introduced himself as Terry and led me into the office. He explained that this was where companies involved in shady work like asbestos removal found their cheap labor. Now the operation was expanding its labor pool to crack the dishwashing market. Since us dishers often shook off our jobs without notice, this place was assembling a crew of dishmen. Now jilted employers would have a place to pick up last-minute replacements. As the hopeful laborers waited for job assignments, they hung around in the hiring hall and out on the curb.

The plan was captivating. I could already see my role: the on-call, troubleshooting pearl diver—wherever and whenever dishes needed washing, I'd be there (though, inevitably, I'd be late).

It reminded me of the scene in Charles Bukowski's book *Factotum*. The author's alter ego, Henry Chinaski, gets hired at a downtown Los Angeles employment office to answer the phone and hire the dishwashers. On his first day, he needs four dishwashers from among the forty bums waiting outside the office. So he throws four pennies in the air. Whoever retrieves a penny, gets a job. Then , as Bukowski writes:

> *Bodies jumped and fell, clothing ripped, there were curses, one man screamed, there were several fistfights. Then the lucky four came forward, one at a time, breathing heavily, each with a penny.*

"Where do you need me today?" I asked.

"Nowhere," Terry said. "We need to sign on the dishwashers first before we can start offering to hire them out."

In the meantime, he said, he could assign me other jobs. I gave Terry—word for word—the same reply I'd overheard another dishing applicant give only minutes earlier:

"Nah, none of that heavy labor stuff for me, just dishwashing."

•

The next morning, I awoke full of confidence from having found a job. But the thought of sitting around a hiring hall wasn't nearly as enticing as the prospect of poking around a place I hadn't yet explored. While considering whether New Orleans could ever serve as my permanent home, I figured— if so—it'd be fun to live near a ferry route. So I caught the Jackson Avenue ferry across the Mississippi River to Gretna. The town, with its runty cottages, was pleasant. But it was too quaint to justify living in just to ride a ferry every day. I didn't get around to calling the hiring hall until late in the afternoon. Terry answered and reminded me that in order to be hired out, I had to either be at the hall in person or I had to call in the morning.

"And no," he said. "There ain't no dishwashing jobs yet."

The next morning I caught the Algiers ferry across to the neighborhood of Algiers. Though it was sleepier than even the most drowsy of New Orleans neighborhoods, its ferry sailed straight to the French Quarter. So it won my vote for most-likely-place-for-me-to-live-in-New-Orleans because it was just a short ferry ride from so many potential dish jobs.

After my venture into Algiers, I called Terry. He yelled at me, "Look! You ain't gonna get any jobs by calling in the afternoon!"

My morning-time strolls and late-afternoon check-ins persisted one more day. That last time I called, Terry didn't bother answering my question. Upon hearing my voice, he hung up. My career as the on-call, troubleshooting pearl diver was over before I was ever called upon to shoot a single trouble.

Now I was really in a pickle. As summer neared and the punishing New Orleans humidity increased, I became hell-bent to get out of town. But I had no money for a bus ticket. So, to pick up some cash lickety-split, I guinea-pigged it. At a research clinic, drugs were put in my mouth and in my veins as doctors and nurses sat around to see if I'd get a fever. I was one of the lucky ones; there were no reactions to note. I survived the placebo with enough dough to get myself moving.

Cheryl, her boyfriend and everyone else I knew in town rubbed it in. This white boy still hadn't dished in New Orleans. Louisiana wouldn't be conquered state #14 after all.

I left town defeated.

14

Fumes

I stepped off the bus in Little Rock, Arkansas, walked out of the bus station and found the house rented by Jim, a dish dog I'd met briefly in California. Jim had told me to look him up if I ever passed through Little Rock. Because it was only six in the morning, I decided to wait a couple more hours before officially looking him up. In the meantime, I crashed on a beat-up couch on his porch.

When Jim woke me a few hours later, practically the first words out of his mouth were: "Have you found a job yet?"

Of course I hadn't. Not only had I been in town for just a couple of hours, I still had a few dollars in my pocket from the New Orleans drug study. I usually didn't look for work until I was flat busted. Knowing more dishing loomed once I hit that no-money mark, I could stretch those final few bucks for weeks. But, like surrogate parents constantly wondering when I'd get off my ass and get a job, well-meaning friends often suggested places for me to work. Actually, it was helpful. Otherwise I would've ended up broke and cadging money from them. My parents would've been happy, had they only known that so many people were out there trying to keep my butt in line.

"Let's get some beer," Jim said, "and go find you a job."

Several hours and miles and a couple of six-packs later, while we were walking up Kavanaugh Boulevard, Jim struck gold—The Sign in a restaurant window that'd been so elusive in New Orleans: "Dishwasher Wanted."

"Perfect!" he said.

"Great," I muttered.

Jim pushed me into the restaurant. I asked for the job and was hired.

"Two things," the chef said. "Don't show up to work drunk and don't drink on the job."

Apparently he didn't smell the fumes, because he then asked me to start right away.

Since I knew all too well how painfully slow the work hours dragged whenever I started a shift plastered—and since I was already close to that state—I told him, "I'll come back in an hour."

That was now another rule of mine: Never start drinking until at least halfway through a shift, when the end was in sight (a rule I'd adhere to every night at that job).

An hour later and slightly more sober, I returned. A few minutes behind me, Lonnie—the other disher—arrived and trained me.

"Chef Dumb hired you?" he asked.

"Yeah," I said. "Why's he called Chef Dumb?"

"'Cause he's dumb."

Four minutes after it began, the training was complete.

"Now you just find yourself a chair," Lonnie said, "and make yourself comfortable."

He pulled a chair for himself into the tiny dishroom. I slapped together a makeshift seat by placing a new mop head atop a five-gallon bucket.

Sitting was a familiar position for us here. Despite its efforts to be an upscale eatery, even on the busiest weekend nights, the place attracted mostly yuppies-in-training who drank at the bar and ordered little from the kitchen. The upshot: few dirty dishes. Everyone else—bartenders, barbacks, wait staff, bussers and even the cooks—were constantly busy, but there was barely enough work in the dishpit for a lone dishwasher, let alone a two-man crew. So I sat on my ass and read my book while Lonnie sat on *his* ass and listened to the radio.

Arkansas was now #14.

During that first night, while I was standing over the sink and scrubbing a few pots and pans, Lonnie pulled down his pants and showed me all the entry and exit wounds from when he'd been shot in both legs. As he told the story, I started to feel dizzy, as if still plastered from the beers of hours earlier.

Lonnie then pointed his forefinger and fist at my face to describe the revenge he'd exact on his nemesis: "I'm gonna blow his head off."

My own head was now clouded and felt like it could blow away.

"Yeah, but won't prison suck?" I asked.

"I'm not gonna get caught," he said. "You know why? 'Cause no one will know who did it."

"Oh," I said, "I hadn't thought of that."

Queasy, I looked at the steamy fumes I was inhaling from

the sink and asked, "Hey, man, what'd you put in this water?"

"All that stuff," he said, pointing to several plastic jugs beneath the sink. They were the very cleansers, detergents and bleaches whose labels warned against mixing them with other cleansers, detergents and bleaches.

On the verge of passing out, I tore through the kitchen, through the dining area and out the front door. On the sidewalk, I finally breathed fresh air.

Over the next few nights, though I was able to convince Lonnie to be less ambitious with the cleaning agents, the air in the dishroom remained acrid. Sniffing around, I figured out that some sort of noxious fumes were emanating from the locked utility closet adjacent to the dishpit. What the gas was—or what it was used for—I had no idea. All I knew was that it made me teary-eyed and nauseated. When I complained about it to Chef Dumb, he vowed to look into it.

Lonnie dealt with the gas issue by hanging out in the kitchen and bullshitting with the cooks or by hanging out at the bar and bullshitting with the bartenders. Preferring reading to bullshitting, I'd remain in the dishpit with my book until my concentration dulled or my vision blurred. Hanging out elsewhere in the restaurant may have meant breathing cleaner air, but it also meant encountering Chef Dumb and his empty promises. Or worse, encountering the customers.

Unfortunately, I couldn't completely avoid the creepy patrons. Employees and customers used the same bathrooms. There, I had to endure lushes in suits practicing their dance moves, suggesting pickup lines and pissing on the floor. It was enough to make a dishman stay in the pit and whiz in the empty sink.

Though I never ran into Little Rock's very own Bill Clinton, who was president at the time, while in town I did meet a native named Chip. He told me about the time when Hillary and Chelsea came into a place where he was working. Hillary ordered a sandwich. Chip plucked a booger and added it to her dish. Hillary ate the sandwich.

The Bus Tub Buffet paid off well at this place. At cheap diners where the portions were larger, very few leftovers made it to the dishroom. But at fancy places, customers paid bundles for puny portions and then often left much of their meal untouched. This restaurant was no exception.

Because a bus tub's yield is random, I never knew what would be next on my menu. That, in itself, could be both exciting *and* perturbing. Eating whatever came my way meant gorging on superrich cake, then some mushy green beans, then maybe a fruit tart dessert with the teeth marks still in it. Then cold chicken, soupy pasta, more cake, oily potatoes and so on. Though it could add up to a lethal combo in my stomach, no matter how much my gut implored me not to, I always shoveled in more grub. The result: a bellyache—but a good bellyache, one from too much stuffing as opposed to those horrible nothing-in-the-gut bellyaches.

The main drawback to the Bus Tub Buffet was the damn smokers. There was nothing worse than reaching for something like a choice hunk of chicken parmesan only to find a cigarette butt stamped into it. Only the most heartless of customers could mistake leftovers for ashtrays. Hopefully they weren't so careless as to also use their leftovers as repositories after successful nose-picks. Putting boogers in the food was something best left to the professionals.

•

Meanwhile, *the gas from the* utility closet continued to be a nuisance. One night, I pressed Chef Dumb on the matter. He swore, "It'll *definitely* be fixed by tomorrow."

When I arrived the following night, the dishpit was still as gassy as Chef Dumb's promises.

A dishwasher in a situation like this wields little power. That is, with the exception of one teeny maneuver. It's a move that requires almost no effort, energy or planning. In fact, even proclaiming the two words to express the maneuver was sometimes itself too much to bother with. Really, this tactic required nothing but to do nothing.

As I stood in the dishroom doorway considering my next move, Chef Dumb seemed to read my thoughts.

"*Please stay,*" he begged. "Go hang out at the bar, have a drink, read your book. Then just come do a load of dishes, then go back to the bar."

He was so desperate that he was willing to break his own rule by having me drink on the job. I was tempted to see what other bribes he might have in store. Free meals on my days off? A raise? Better yet, a decent chair in the pit?

But I couldn't do it. He'd promised to fix the gas leak— and he hadn't done so. And I didn't want to let him get away with it.

"No thanks," I told him. Then I added those two crucial words: "I quit."

To make sure he didn't gas even more dishwashers, I was prepared to do the unthinkable: snitch to the authorities. But it was 5:30 on a Friday afternoon—the health department was closed for the weekend.

It turned out I never had to make that call.

I left Little Rock that night. While passing back through

town a week later to pick up my paycheck, I entered the restaurant and found Chef Dumb sweating it out at a table as a couple of health inspectors read off the violations. I was glad to hear the dishroom gas leak made the list, along with improper food storage, improper food handling and vermin infestation. The last violation was a surprise to hear considering I hadn't seen any of the rascals myself. But then again, as a bystander in the vermin wars, I hadn't been looking for them.

While Chef Dumb was busy getting reamed, I wandered into the kitchen. A prep cook told me that on the night I'd walked out, Lonnie did the same only an hour later. A few hours after that, a cook went out in grander fashion: he threatened to return and shoot Chef Dumb. But instead of following through with his threat, a few days later he called the health department—and talked.

After the health inspectors left, Chef Dumb ceased wetting his pants long enough to retrieve my paycheck. In the meantime, I panicked about my pay. What would I do if he tried to screw me on what he owed me? I had no leverage. I'd already quit; the health department had already been alerted. What could I do? Order a gigantic meal, eat it and not pay?

When Chef Dumb handed over the check, I was both surprised and relieved to discover that it was accurate.

"So, what d'ya say?" Chef Dumb said, smiling nervously. "Ready to come back to work?"

He looked like a rejected lover who refused to accept that it was over. And I didn't know how to break it to him. I muttered something indistinct and then split for good.

15
Plenty of Crumbs

A week later, while in Albuquerque, New Mexico, a reporter and a photographer from a local daily newspaper asked to interview me. They wanted the story of my fifty-state dishwasher quest. More and more, similar requests from other journalists had been arriving in the mail. I'd consented to a couple of interviews. One result—an awful "hey-look-at-this-wacky-guy!" article—was so hokey that other newspapers around the country ran it as well.

In another article, the sloppy journalism by the reporter led him to claim that the name of the zine was *Dishwasher Pete*. He alleged I'd dished in Fairbanks, Alaska (never had), and Alabama (hadn't yet). He further claimed, "Dishwasher Pete could be to restaurant kitchens what Sinclair Lewis was to butcher shops." I could've been wrong, but I believed the nitwit meant to compare me with Upton Sinclair and his work in changing conditions in the *meatpacking industry*! (Which, of course, I wasn't.) In total, the article contained forty-six errors.

Another newspaper writer, after listening to me explain why I wasn't interested in being interviewed, had the gall to use our off-the-record phone conversation to write his article.

One journalist asked me, "What makes Dishwasher Pete run?"

Questions like that, I thought, make me run—*far away!*

So I told the Albuquerque newspaper duo that though I was flattered by their interest, I wasn't interested. They then argued that I needed them for the publicity. But I wasn't seeking recognition. Besides, *Dishwasher* already had the greatest publicity machine in the world: the word-of-mouth recommendations of its readers. In fact, with production and distribution happening on the road, the zine was already more than a handful for me—without any added publicity.

When I passed through San Francisco weeks later, my dad told me that a producer from CNN had somehow tracked down his phone number and had been calling my mom and him three times a week for nearly a month. The guy had been pestering my parents to get me to call him. And now my dad was begging me to get this guy off their backs. My dad figured I'd gotten myself into some sort of mess, like when I was a teenager and he'd received phone calls in the night for him to come pick me up from the police station. He didn't understand why any television producer would want to talk to me about my inability to hold down a job or stay put.

So I called the producer. He said CNN wanted to tape a

profile of me. As usual, I was skeptical. I gave him the speech about my apprehension toward the news media, how I didn't want the publicity, how TV is evil, etc. During the second of two 45-minute conversations, he began to take my arguments personally and became defensive. He claimed he was (in his very own words) "down with the cause." He hadn't always worked for "The Man" but was forced to because he had a mortgage to pay, a family to feed and—get this— needed to put shoes on his children's feet. He actually implied that if I didn't consent to an interview, his two daughters would go barefoot!

I'd had enough.

From then on, I stopped responding to all inquiries from the media. Any envelopes on official letterhead from New York or Los Angeles that showed up in my trustworthy post office box went straight into the garbage—unopened. To make it clear, in the next issue of *Dishwasher*—#12—I added a message: "A Note to All Major-Media Types: Don't bother trying to call me because obviously I have no phone. And don't bother writing me either because whatever you have in mind, I'm not interested."

A week later, while talking to my pal Jess—the dishman I'd met in Arcata—I told him about the CNN incident.

"Oh man!" he said. "I can't believe you told them no!"

He admitted it was his dream to appear on television and be seen across the nation.

"Hey, Pete," he said, "next time you're asked to be on TV, let me go in your place, okay?"

His desire to be on TV seemed to outweigh my desire to not be, so I said, "All right."

"You mean that?" he asked. "You promise?"

I couldn't really foresee any further TV invites so it seemed harmless to give him my word.

"Sure," I said. "I promise."

Before I even arrived in Portland, Oregon, I pretty much knew it was a prodishwasher town. After all, I'd traveled there the year before to attend the Dish Fest—a "wage slave rave" at the old X-Ray Café. Dish Mistress Melody hosted a gathering of pearl divers who played music to dish by, competed in dish Olympics and tested their knowledge in a dish-trivia competition (which, for the record, I won by answering the final question correctly: "What is the proper temperature for a rinse cycle?" 180 degrees Fahrenheit, of course). I'd left town after the Dish Fest knowing that Portland was a place I needed to return to work.

Now I was back for the Northwest Tour—to make Oregon, Washington and Idaho #s 15–17. In a single day, I rambled around and poked my head through the back doors of a few restaurants; met some interesting suds busters; was told about the dishman who had the Hobart logo tattooed on his arm; heard a new story about a hazing ritual (rookie dishers were sent through a cold-water cycle in the machine); and even landed a couple of jobs for myself. Then I ran into a friend who told me another convincing story. A few hours earlier, upon seeing the Dish Master T-shirt she was wearing, a stranger had exclaimed, "I'm a dish *DAWG*!!" The way she mimicked his drawled *"DAWG!!"* settled it for me: Portland was indeed a town for dish dogs.

I felt like Lorry, the character in Edward Dahlberg's 1930 autobiographical novel *Bottom Dogs*. After rambling around the country, Lorry arrives in Portland, where "he had to get a job, even if it was one of those stale jackass businesses draining greasy dishes under a scalding faucet, wiping 'em, washing 'em; always those goddam dishes till he thought his nerves, for the ache and fidgetiness they caused him, would drive him insane."

I needed some "stale jackass business" myself and found one at an immense German Oktoberfest held at a decrepit amusement park on the edge of town. I reported to the cook tent, where an army of cooks stirred the hot tub–sized vat of sauerkraut, spun roasted pigs over open flames and grilled hundreds of bratwursts. The boss-guy, Nigel, explained that I was to shuttle the sheet pans, banquet pans and cooking utensils on a pushcart to the dishroom in a building on the far side of the amusement park. He then led me over to the pit.

"It's just over this way a bit," he said. We walked. And walked. "You have to make your way through the crowds but it shouldn't be a problem."

We walked. And walked. And walked some more, until we finally reached the dishpit.

"Now, that's not a bad walk, is it?" he asked.

He seemed concerned that I'd balk at the job because it involved so much legwork. There were a thousand petty reasons why I might have bailed. But being asked to push around a cart outside, without any supervision, was definitely not one of them.

Not long after I started shuttling my dish passengers across the park, I began to research all the possible routes through the crowds: along the river, past the rides, past the booths and side stages. Periodically, I'd stop by the hub of the festivities—the vast circus-tent beer hall. Lederhosen-clad oompah bands performed on two large stages at opposite ends of the tent. In between the stages sat long rows of Oktoberfesters who swung their beers aloft and swayed in sync with the waltzes and the drinking songs. Far too often, one of the bands would break into the chicken-dance song, which sent the crowd into chicken-dancing frenzies—and sent me on my way again.

The first day passed rapidly, as did most of the night. I developed a steady pace, balancing my time between mingling in the crowds and dishing in the pit. But when the park closed for the night, I was drowned in soiled cookware. Stacks and stacks were brought to me. I tried to keep up, but Nigel kept bringing me even more.

"I'm rounding up some more guys to help you out," he claimed a couple of times.

The reinforcements never materialized. Soon, even Nigel stopped showing up. Still, I scrubbed and scrubbed until finally, after too many hours of backbreaking work, I wanted nothing more than to leave. So I stopped washing—and started hiding the remaining dirty dishes atop the drying racks and under countertops. When I finally departed, the amusement park was completely deserted except for the night watchmen.

Later that same morning, when I returned to the amusement park, Nigel apologized for the lack of help the night before.

"I've made some changes that I think you'll appreciate," he said. The alterations were a newly recruited dishman and—to help haul the dishes back and forth across the park—a motorized cart.

Excited about having someone to roam around the park with, I found my new Oktoberfest friend in the dishroom.

"Hey," I said. "My name's Pete."

He looked at me with disgust, then spat with a twang, "*I* ain't washin' dishes all day. One way or another, I'm gonna be outta here by this afternoon."

So much for seeing the sights together, I thought. Since I sensed he'd be no fun to roam around with, I suggested we rotate positions—while one washed, the other could drive the golf cart.

"Boy, that ain't no *golf cart*!" he scoffed when he saw it. "That's a *John Deere*—the finest blah blah blah . . ."

In addition to not wanting to stroll with him, I immediately realized I didn't even want to listen to him.

When Country Boy seemed to be done lecturing me about my ignorance of automotive matters, he insisted there'd be no role-switching. *He* would drive. *I* would wash. End of story. Then he shoved a wad of chewing tobacco in his mouth. Salvation: his words were so garbled that I was saved from his nonsense.

Screw him, I thought. Here I'd made a perfectly reasonable offer and he rejected it out of hand. For a blowhard to disrespect dishwashing so readily, I figured the best thing to put him in his place was a healthy dose of elbow-deep suds.

"*I'm* driving," I said and then explained that it was a complex task—specific routes to be followed, other stops to be made. After convincing him to remain in the dishroom, he pouted as I drove off.

Every time I returned to the pit, Country Boy whined about the deal. Several times he marched outside and defiantly sat in the driver's seat. The more he tried to intimidate me, the less I empathized with him. Still, each time I coaxed him out of the cart, I'd follow up by helping him wash a few sheet pans. That is, until he crossed the line.

Now, as a Dish Master, I'd stuck my hands and arms in every variety of uneaten, half-eaten, half-digested, wholly digested, pre- and postconsumer waste. No greasy, grimy, gloppy gloop had ever fazed me. It was part of the job. But when Country Boy spat tobacco juice in my dishwater, I gagged. It was a discourteous, unprofessional and just plain disgusting act. I pulled my arms out of the sink and, without a word, walked out. The motor cart and I took an extended tour of the parking lots.

When I eventually returned with another load of dirty pans, I was pleased to find—true to his initial pledge—Country Boy had deserted his post. With a man AWOL, Nigel instructed the cooks to reuse the cookware. That way, I didn't have to wash it so frequently. Now I had even more time to drift about.

When the Oktoberfest closed that second night, the pots and pans that'd gone unwashed for hours suddenly came to me all at once. Even after Nigel brought over a couple of guys to help, it was exhausting trying to finish up. We didn't realize how late it was until we took a break outside and noticed everyone else had left. So we drained the sinks and stashed the unwashed pans with the ones I hadn't washed the night before.

When we finally left, not even a night watchman was in sight.

After a quick bike ride home and a few hours' sleep, I was back in the well-stocked dishpit. A guy wearing an apron loitered by the sinks.

"All right!" I said. "Are you gonna wash dishes with me?"

A puzzled look came over his face.

"It ain't a bad job," I added.

The look on his face grew even more confused.

I thought for a second and then asked, "Mexico?"

"Meh-hee-ko!!" he erupted.

Poking myself in the chest, I said, "My name's Pete."

"Pete?" Then, pointing to his chest puffed out with pride, he said, "Ephrem!"

Though the language barrier hindered us from fully understanding each other, it didn't prevent us from conversing—me in English, he in Spanish—as we washed that first round of dishes. Afterwards, I tried unsuccessfully to get Ephrem to drive the cart. So I drove while he washed for a while. Then I fixed up a couple of plates of food for us. After eating lunch in the dishroom, Ephrem tried to convey some urgent message to me.

"You wanna drive the cart?" I asked.

I pointed at the cart. He shook his head no.

"You want more food?"

I brought another plate of bratwurst and sauerkraut back from the cook tent. He waved it off. He grew more anxious as I ran out of ideas. Acting as if I was crazy for not understanding his apparently simplest of requests, Ephrem returned to the dishes. I gave up and left the dishroom.

A half hour later, after wading through the crowds, I ran into Ephrem in the cook tent. He grabbed my arm and led me over to a row of Porta Pottis.

"Baa troom!" he exclaimed.

"Oh."

To equip me for future reference, he taught me the Spanish word for *bathroom/Porta Potti,* which I immediately forgot. I tried to get him to forgo the English word *baa-troom* in favor of *can.* But this language lesson only led to another round of us both scratching our heads.

The rest of the day passed smoothly until the motor cart ran out of gas behind the roller skating rink. A security guard who happened upon me and my stalled vehicle offered to retrieve some gas for us. But why, he wondered aloud, was the dishwasher shuttle so far from both the dishroom and the cook tent? When I was slow to come up with an excuse, he correctly guessed that I'd been joyriding through the parking lots. He then promptly abandoned us. I hiked back to the cook tent, pronounced the fate of the motor cart and handed in the keys.

I was back to using the pushcart.

The next morning, I found three Hispanic-looking guys lounging in the pit. Upon seeing me, they jumped up and bustled around the sinks though there was nothing yet to wash.

"Hey, what's up?" I asked.

No reply. Since none of them spoke English, I tried to assure them that they didn't have to do any busywork in my presence. I wasn't The Man. But my message was lost on them. So I sat down and indicated they should do the same. They wouldn't fall for that one either.

In New Orleans, I'd rejected the head dishwasher position because I didn't want any power of authority. But this was even worse. I wasn't even the head dishwasher. Yet, no matter how hard I tried, they acted as if I had authority—power that I couldn't turn off!

Then, in a curious development, Ephrem popped in cheerfully pushing a cart full of pans. If Ephrem was shuttling the goods, and more than enough pearl divers were manning the sinks, then what work was I supposed to do?

I ventured over to the cook tent to get a bite and nose around. While I was talking with one of the cooks, he asked me to stir the vat of boiling sauerkraut. I politely declined. Another asked me to help tend the hundreds of brats on the grill. I responded by excusing myself from the cook tent.

It wasn't yet noon, and I was scheduled to work past midnight. How was I going to fill the time? I wasn't needed in the dishroom and didn't want to be needed in the cook tent. Worst of all, I had no book with me. Wandering around, watching the crowds, the oompah bands and the damn chicken-dancing would have to do.

A couple of times, I stumbled across Country Boy. Each time he saw me, he spat and then said, *"Sucker!"* I followed him once to see what new job he held. But all he did was traipse about. Then again, that's all *I* ever did. So technically, he *still* might've been a dishwasher.

Wanting to go on the rides but having no money, I rummaged through the confetti of torn tickets on the ground for an unused one. While the search did kill an hour, I failed to turn up a single ticket. So I decided instead to barter. In the cook tent, I loaded up a paper plate with brats, sauerkraut and a giant pretzel, then offered it to the ticket-sales girl in exchange for ride tickets.

"Can't do it," she said.

"Oh well," I said and handed her the food anyway.

That gave me an idea. Many of the employees were working twelve- to sixteen-hour stints, yet they were issued only one meal ticket per shift. These folks were in need of free eats. So I loaded plates of grub in the cook tent and then handed them out to the old man sweeping up cigarette butts, the guy checking IDs at the beer garden, the girls selling T-shirts and so on. Everyone appreciated the free food. But more important, the hours passed so fast that it was almost possible to forget that I was being paid to wash dishes.

When I brought food over to the dishpit crew, none of them would sit down and eat in my presence. So I left them to chow down in private and walked. I walked around until my feet were sore. Then I sat. I sat around until my ass was sore. Then I walked again, to the cook tent. I fixed another huge meal for myself and retired with it to some stairs hidden behind a dumpster. I stretched out and shoved one last oversized pretzel in my mouth. Ahhh . . .

When I awoke, the stars were out and pretzel dough was pasted to the inside of my mouth. Groggy, I had no idea how long I'd slept. I dragged myself into the cook tent, where I was again asked to stir the vat of sauerkraut. So I dragged myself over to the dishroom, where I was again treated like a boss. So I just shuffled around the park some more, unsure of where to go or what to do. I had already spent over ten hours doing no work. Trying to occupy myself turned out to be far more exhausting than actually washing dishes.

When a costumed chicken came up and tried to teach me the freakin' chicken dance, without thinking, I barked, "Get away from me!" Then, through the chicken's beak, I saw a dejected teenage girl. What a jerk I am, I thought, and apologized to her. Despite the fact that there were still more hours of pay to earn by doing nothing, yelling at six-foot chickens was a clear indication that it was time to go.

I searched for Ephrem to say *adios* but couldn't find him anywhere. Hoping he'd found a choice hiding spot of his own, I headed for the exit. To cheer myself up about knocking off early, I reported my morning arrival time a few hours earlier than it actually was and then rode my bike aimlessly through the night, still unsure of where to go or what to do, but with a smile on my face.

Portland was a comfortable town, a place where bus drivers actually waited until riders were seated before lunging forward. A place where old men lingered in the parks, looking for opponents in rounds of horseshoes (I was always happy to oblige). A place where more floors and couches were put at my disposal than I was able to accept.

It was also a place where I received numerous invitations from dishwashers, bartenders and wait staff to stop by their workplaces. Sometimes the invites were for me to use the front door; sometimes the back door. Sometimes it was for during open hours; sometimes for after hours. Regardless, the result was always the same: free food and/or free beer were pushed my way.

And everywhere I roamed, pennies—if not fancier denominations of coins—awaited my discovery. The coin-finding record was absolutely shattered here as I booked success on *thirty-three days* straight! On one of those days, in twelve different finds, I plucked from the ground a total of thirty pennies! The streets of Portland were truly paved with copper.

Portland was unmistakably a dishwasher's town. Indeed, when the city's eccentric previous mayor—Bud Clark—had retired from politics, he'd proclaimed, "I could wash dishes the rest of my life and still be happy."

In Portland, I felt the same way.

My friend Melody, the hostess of the Dish Fest, asked me to come work where she'd been dishing for years—at an exclusive women's club for the crustiest of Portland's upper-crust old ladies. When Melody ran this idea by her boss, he was open to it on one condition: he wanted to meet me first.

On my way to the meeting, I grew suspicious. Melody casually mentioned that the boss had read her copies of *Dishwasher*. If he knew of my tales of slothful work habits, sticky fingers and contempt for authority figures, then why would he want me anywhere near his establishment? Maybe he was setting me up. In the name of employers nationwide—bosses who were sick of lazy, thieving malcontent dishers—was he going to ambush me? Would it be verbal abuse or could I also expect fisticuffs?

As it turned out, neither. The guy actually just wanted to regale me with tales of his own swashbuckling days. He, too, had once been a young, lazy, malcontent dish stud. And because he couldn't regale his wife with such stories, he did what increasingly more dish alumni were doing via letters: he shared them with the one person he figured could appreciate them—me.

Since the boss-guy knew what he was getting into when he hired me, he shouldn't have been surprised when I called in sick. So what if it was supposed to be my first shift? The day before, a friend had snuck me into a wine-and-cheese distributors' convention. Eight hours of guzzling free wine and gobbling free cheese had left me unable to work. The boss suggested I come in late. No, I told him. There'd be no working for me that day, just lying in the park and resting my head.

A few nights later, I finally did arrive at the ivy-covered mansion where, after playing rounds of bridge, the club members ate their meals. At least that's what I was told. I never actually saw any of the society gals myself, owing to the fact that, when I wasn't in the dishpit, I always stuck to the servants' lounge, the servants' corridors and the servants' entrance. It was through that very same servants' entrance that each night I snuck out pieces of the fancy china. By the time I quit—a few weeks after I began—I had a complete, four-person set to ship to my buddy Colleen in Montana for her birthday.

The boss, I figured, would've been proud.

•

The Northwest Tour's next stop in Portland was at a seafood restaurant. When I first asked about work there, the cook said he already had dishwashers, but took my name and number anyway.

"'Cause you never know," he said.

A few days later, he came a-calling to say his night disher had arrived drunk, then disappeared. The cook found him slumped out back, just conscious enough to announce his two-week notice. The pearl diver stumbled to the dishroom and then, a few minutes later, out the front door. The cook caught up to him down the street and asked what was up.

"I can't wait those two weeks," the boozehound replied. "I quit now."

And now, here I was. Easily the best thing about the place was that the dishpit was completely sealed off from the kitchen, the dining area and the bar—a sanctuary where I could turn up the radio and dish in peace.

In peace, that is, with the exception of the odd shrieking noise that came from beneath the sink. At first, I figured it was simply the groaning of the garbage disposal or moaning of some pipes. But when the noise persisted, I turned down the radio and investigated. Beneath the counter, behind the garbage can, I located the source: a shoebox-sized mousetrap. I picked up the metal box. Through the cracks, some mice could be seen frantically looking for a way out.

Though I was officially neutral in the vermin battles, I had no desire to dish to the death throes of these prisoners of war. If anyone had a beef with the mice, or vice versa, then they all could hash out their differences after I was no longer at the helm of this pit.

I grabbed a knife and pried open the trap. Three mice

scampered out and disappeared among the room's clutter. I broke the trap's spring mechanism and, while I was at it, also replaced the lethal pellets on the floor with croutons and fresh shrimp. (Judging by how often I would need to replace the shrimp, mice really dig shellfish!) For my remaining weeks at that job, the only sounds in the dishroom were the drone of the dishmachine, the screech of the disposal and the hum of the oldies station on the radio.

In one nightspot that I wandered into to ask for work, the waitress told me that since lunch was pretty slow there, they had no day dishwasher—she did the dishes herself. I proposed to her that I wash her lunch dishes and she feed me lunch. She was game. From then on, I'd stop by afternoons, dish for an hour and then eat my lunch. She was working less, I was eating more—and everyone was satisfied.

When I happened to ask the waitress about herself, she told me that she was a writer.

"Oh yeah?" I asked. "Hey, I'm a dishwasher who happens to write."

"What do you write about?" she asked.

"Dishwashing," I said.

My answer killed the conversation. She left the kitchen and said little more to me that day—or in the days that followed.

Then, one afternoon, I stopped by after having just received a couple weeks' worth of mail forwarded by a friend from my post office box. When I was done washing, I sat down to eat my lunch and open envelopes. There were the usual requests for copies of *Dishwasher* from, among others: a grandmother in Kansas; a self-described Minneapolis "gutter punk"; a University of Georgia college student; a policeman in Denton, Texas; a disher-turned-lawyer in Ithaca, New York; a Puget Sound housewife; and a teenage Mexican dish dude from Tucson. There were letters from comrades updating me on their latest on-the-job exploits and also mail containing clippings about dish dogs in the news and references to dishers in pop culture. And, inexplicably, there were even a couple of letters from restaurant owners inviting me to work for them. (The boss from the women's club apparently hadn't gotten word out to them yet.)

Standing over me and surveying the envelopes, the waitress asked, "What's all this?"

"My *Dishwasher* mail."

I tried to convince her that people like a good dish tale. But she failed to comprehend why so many folks would write to me. After all, she was the writer and I was just the dishpit dipshit who worked for food.

Then she pulled an envelope from the pile and recognized the name on the return address.

"You know him?" I asked.

"He's only my *favorite* author," she said.

"What, he writes books?"

"Yeah," she said and then stared at me. "So why's he writing *you*?"

I shrugged and said, "Lotsa people write me."

She studied me for a moment longer before asking, "You want to come over to my house and read some of my writing?"

I liked to read, among other things, so I said sure.

When her shift was done, we caught the bus out to her place. I sat on the couch and opened more mail while she changed out of her work clothes (black top and black skirt) and into her nonwork clothes (black top and black skirt). She sat down beside me on the couch and asked if she could open some envelopes.

The more mail she opened, the closer she inched toward me. By the time she asked if she could keep the letter from her favorite author, we were sitting thigh-to-thigh. My heart was racing.

"Sure," I answered, thinking, Dishwashing can really pay off.

Then I noticed the photos scattered around the room—photos of her with a guy.

"Who's that?" I asked.

"Him?" she replied as she inched away from me.

It took another few minutes of persistent questioning before she admitted that he was her boyfriend.

I left, never having read her writing.

I ditched that gig a couple weeks later and then worked more jobs around Portland—a couple of days here, a few shifts there. I covered some shifts for friends and dropped in on others to lend a helping hand.

My friend Kerry told me I could pick up some of his shifts at a diner. While showing me around the pit, Kerry introduced me to the diner owner.

"He's the one I told you about," Kerry said to him.

"You that guy who writes that dishwashing thing?" he asked.

"Yep," I said.

"No, no, no, no, no," he said. *"You're* not working here."

Over Kerry's protestations, the boss-guy ushered me to the front door. I took no offense in being fired before I even began. Finally, a boss who was familiar with my work had an appropriate reaction.

Though he didn't care for the likes of me, others did. Several times strangers singled me out of the crowd—while I sat on a park bench, on the bus, on my bike—and asked if I wanted a job. Why me? 'Cause I looked penniless? Or because I looked gullible? Whatever the case, the offered jobs and their descriptions of heavy lifting and lengthy hours were always rejected.

One offer, though—made while I waited for a bus on SW Sixth—was for a dish job. I accepted without hesitation. But then the guy mentioned something about uniforms.

"Uniforms?" I asked.

"Yeah, but don't worry," he said. "They're *nice* uniforms, with tasteful colors."

Uniforms might have been handy when uniformity was necessary—like for knowing who to shoot on a battlefield. But I didn't need to be uniformed—*I* flew solo.

"Sorry," I said, explaining another rule of mine: "The company colors don't fly on *my* back."

When the Northwest Tour *finally* moved beyond Portland's city limits, I went up to Seattle, Washington (#16), and worked at the old anarchist Black Cat Café. It was owned and operated by a seven-member collective. Everyone was the boss, or, better yet, *no one* was the boss. They solicited volunteers to do the dishes in exchange for hefty amounts of tasty grub, a share of the winnings from the tip jar and veto power over the music selection. To spread the opportunity around, one was only supposed to volunteer a couple of times a month. But since the collective members figured out who I was, they allowed me to abuse the system. I worked every day.

Well, "work" is too strong a word. With the laid-back atmosphere, no boss pushing me around and shifts that lasted only three hours—it hardly felt like work. Even so, it wasn't enough to keep me in Seattle.

The Washington leg of the Northwest Tour was cut short when I got sucked away by the continued allure of Portland. I tried to take the Tour back up to the Rocky Mountains of Montana. But once there, I immediately remembered how I hated being trapped atop a snowcapped mountain and, within twenty-four hours, retreated back to Portland. As for Idaho, I never even tried.

The weeks and months passed in Portland. I hadn't stayed in one place for so long in years. Constantly spoiled by all the couches and floors and food and beer at my disposal, it was hard for me to leave. It's like the legend that's told of an old Seattle restaurant. The place was so filthy the cockroaches that got stuck to the sticky trap paper grew fat where they lay—that's how many crumbs fell their way. Plenty of crumbs fell my way in Portland. I grew fat. But that's not bad. I liked crumbs. I *loved* crumbs. I just had to unstick myself, once and for all, and resume my mission.

16
Letterman Jumped Back

The cross-country bus trip was typical of how I liked to travel. I'd arrive in cities early in the morning, run errands and wander around all day, then get back on a bus that night. In Salt Lake City, I drank a couple beers with an old retired dishman who'd often sent me letters about his dish days of decades past. In Omaha, I hand-delivered zines to three people who'd each sent me orders for them. One of them worked at a copy shop and stuffed my duffel bag with freshly photocopied *Dishwashers*—on the house. In turn, I lightened my load in Chicago by dropping off a few hundred zines at Quimby's and a couple other book and record stores. In Cleveland, I had no specific errands to run, so I hawked zines to passersby on the downtown streets. In total, I sold twenty-one copies to strangers that day. And for years afterwards, I received letters that began with something like, "You probably don't remember me, but I once bought a copy of *Dishwasher* from you on the streets of Cleveland. . . ."

Within minutes of arriving at New York City's crowded Port Authority bus station, I felt a hand root through my coat pocket. Even though the book in that pocket was being mistaken for a wallet, I was extremely flattered to be greeted by a genuine—though pitiful—pickpocket. And because I was done with the book—Tom Kromer's *Waiting for Nothing*—I pulled it out and offered it to my greeter. He turned down the offer and quickly disappeared into the crowd. Still, I felt welcomed.

Like Burt Reynolds, Robert Duvall and Richard Gere, who'd each arrived in the city and washed dishes as a first step toward their dreams of acting in New York, I hoped to wash dishes as a first step toward my dream of, well, washing dishes in New York. After all, according to the song, if I could dish here, I could dish anywhere. Therefore, it was absolutely imperative I dish here, given that my plan was to dish *every*where.

From the moment I stepped out of the bus station, the search was on. All day, every day, I prowled the streets looking for my kind of work. I trekked through all five boroughs. I hiked the entire length of Broadway from Inwood down to the Battery. I trudged from Manhattan out to Coney Island and back. I walked until my feet bled (bad timing for breaking in new secondhand shoes). And when I wasn't walking, I was riding. I clocked hundreds of miles, going back and forth on the entire length of all twenty-five subway lines.

With my insatiable appetite for seeing cities and their old neighborhoods, I was in heaven. The job-search expeditions became so intense that even when I did see "Dishwasher Wanted" signs, I kept on moving. Getting pinned down in some formal job would've only left me with less free time to meander—and too tired to meander in the free time I'd have left over.

I looked up everyone in town who'd ever written to me, which led me to explore neighborhoods and streets I hadn't gotten to yet and meet people who were, for the most part, pleasantly surprised to find me on their doorsteps. Many of them would go on to invite me over for dinner or have me apartment-sit or dog/cat-sit for them while they were out of town.

One such dinner was on Staten Island. Returning from the meal on the Staten Island Ferry, I took in the ride and the view, thinking that if I were to ever settle in New York after I was done with the quest, I'd live on Staten Island just so I could ride the ferry every day.

After a couple weeks of expeditions to look up people and to scare up a job, I received a letter with the return address *Late Show with David Letterman*. I went to toss the letter in the trash, but then, recalling my promise to Jess, reconsidered. Actually, the more I thought about it, the more I liked the idea of him standing in for me on television. Not only would it allow my friend to fulfill his lifelong dream of appearing on TV, but he'd also get to fly to New York for free, we'd get paid and—most appealing of all—we would eat an unimaginable amount of free food backstage. I say "we" because if there was going to be free food, then *I* was going to be there too.

I called Jess, told him to call the show as "Dishwasher Pete" and gave him carte blanche to say or do whatever he wanted in my name. The show's staff was thrilled to get his call. Every day for a week, Jess was on the phone with a producer. They discussed more than a single appearance; the producer talked up the idea of having "Dishwasher Pete" appear as a recurring guest, checking in from his dish jobs around the country.

Then the producer called and told Jess to be on a plane that very night. He'd be filling in for a canceled guest the following day. Jess rushed to catch the red-eye from San Francisco. When he arrived at the Rihga Royal Hotel on West 54th Street, the desk clerk tried to squeeze a room deposit out of him. The hotel wanted a credit card, but he didn't have one. They wanted $150 cash; Jess didn't have that either. After much resistance, Jess eventually agreed to a $20 cash deposit.

By the time I met my pal at the hotel, he'd already heard from Letterman's people that they didn't need him for that day's program after all. So we sauntered around the city all day and all night, returning to the hotel as the sun rose.

Ten days later, Jess flew to New York again. This time, I met him at the airport and we rode into Manhattan in a stretch limo. And this time, our reception at the Rihga Royal was less than welcoming.

"Oh yeah," the desk clerk grumbled. "I remember you."

Jess told the clerk that if he wanted a deposit, he'd have to get it from Letterman—my alter ego wasn't forking over a dime this trip. When the desk clerk called the show, whoever was on the other end, while agreeing to cover the deposit, apparently explained that Jess washed dishes for a living.

"Oh, is *that* what he does?" the clerk snorted.

Before we went upstairs to our suite, I emptied the front desk's candy dish into my pocket.

That night, we hung around the hotel and turned on the TV right in time to hear Letterman announce the next night's guests: "Ron Howard, Alison Krauss and Dishwasher Pete."

Hearing my name announced was surreal. My gut tightened and I began to wonder if I really wanted to bother going through with the plan. I turned off the TV. Jess wasn't so sure either. To get our minds off the show, we roamed the hotel in our complimentary pillowy white bathrobes and raided the leftovers from room-service trays abandoned in the hallways.

In the morning, I went to a friend's apartment downtown and picked up my disguise: a suit. When the lender of the suit finished tying my tie, he stepped back and said, "There! Now you look like a suave Italian banker!" The figure in the mirror looked more like a forlorn Mormon missionary to me. Either way, I felt safely disguised; it was only the fourth or fifth time I'd ever worn a suit.

I moseyed back to midtown, pausing to use my tinkered-with Radio Shack gizmo that afforded me free long-distance calling. Every couple blocks I'd stop at a pay phone to call Cheryl, Colleen, Jeff and other friends around the country. The message was: Watch Letterman tonight.

"You're really gonna go on that show?" was the common question.

"Watch and see" was my standard response.

I couldn't tell them what they'd see; I wasn't sure myself.

When I called my dad, I explained that I'd be on—or rather, *not* be on—television that night.

"But the TV listing in the newspaper says 'Dishwasher Pete,'" he said.

"I know, but you just gotta see for yourself what happens."

He didn't like the sound of it, but agreed to tune in.

●

When I returned to the hotel room, Jess was pacing anxiously. He'd just learned that the TV show had a researcher on my trail. Since we didn't know what the researcher had uncovered, we didn't know what Jess might have to answer to. Even worse, we didn't know if they'd dug up a photo of me. If they had, then we needed to be able to explain why Jess was "Dishwasher Pete." So we grabbed a few beers, snuck up onto the roof of the fifty-five-story hotel and, for an hour, developed various stories.

Satisfied with our many alibis (and hungry from fasting all day in preparation for the free eats), we descended from the roof. Waiting for us at the hotel entrance was a limo, a thick-necked chauffeur and a thicker-necked bodyguard— and the most bizarre car ride I'd ever taken. The Ed Sullivan Theater was right around the corner from the Rihga Royal Hotel. By foot, the theater could be reached in two or three minutes. Despite my penchant for checking pay phones for quarters and my habit of picking up stray scraps of paper, even a slowpoke like me could've made the trip in five minutes. Yet, with midtown Manhattan's traffic locked in rush-hour gridlock and all the one-way streets working against us, the several-block trip by limousine lasted an agonizing half an hour.

At the theater, a small crowd of celebrity hounds huddled around the limo, expecting a star to emerge. I suggested Jess appease the autograph-seekers with signatures like "Jacques Cousteau" or "Jesus Christ." Instead, he sprang from the car and bolted through the crowd—like a real celebrity!

Inside the studio, an assistant showed us around the stage while that evening's musical guest, Alison Krauss, ran through her sound check. When Jess was invited to sit in Letterman's chair, I was playing my role—tagalong friend "Jerry," a graphic designer from SoHo—so low-key that I didn't even step forward to snap a photo of Jess at the desk, lest I unwittingly focus any unwanted attention upon myself.

Upstairs in the dressing room, the assistant asked if we'd like a beer.

"Sure," Jess said.

"How does a bunch of *imported* beer sound?"

The offer was supposed to impress us. And the sad truth was—we were terribly impressed.

"*Sounds good!*" Jess said.

"And what would you guys like to eat? I'll go down to the deli and get whatever you want."

We'd expected to be greeted by a full spread of food, so— caught off guard—we weren't prepared to give orders. When Jess voiced his meager request, I nearly screamed.

"A cheese sandwich," he said.

Anything! We could have *anything* from the deli!

"And a cheese sandwich for you too?" the assistant asked.

"Yeah," I mumbled. "But, you know, with a lotta stuff on it."

"Yeah, a lotta stuff on mine, too," Jess added.

As soon as she left, we closed the door, relieved to have successfully cleared the first hurdle. A few minutes later, a woman walked in, introduced herself as Diana—the talent coordinator—and then said to me, "Pete?"

I shook my head and pointed to my friend. Diana shook Jess's hand but then looked back at me.

"Wait a minute," she said. "*You're* the guy in the photograph."

Damn! Not only *had* they dug up a picture of me, she even recognized me in my disguise!

"He just poses for the photos sometimes," Jess said.

Diana continued staring at me.

"*He's* Pete," I said. "My name's Jerry."

"Really, guys," she said. "What's going on here?"

Simultaneously, Jess and I babbled conflicting stories. Despite having come up with a half-dozen explanations, we'd never decided exactly which one we'd use. So while Jess told some convoluted story about how we were an amalgamation of a character called "Dishwasher Pete," I told some convoluted story about a mix-up with the photograph. This wasn't good. The whole mission was on the brink of doom—and we hadn't even gotten fed yet!

Amazingly, our gibbered explanations somehow managed to confuse her so much that—with showtime fast approaching—she resigned herself to remaining ignorant.

Changing the topic, Diana asked Jess why an earlier invitation had gone unanswered (it must've been tossed out unopened). She also told "Pete" how excited the staff was to have him on the show, especially considering they'd been told it couldn't be done.

Meanwhile, trying my best to avoid her interest, I remained silent, stared out the window and yawned.

When Diana finally sat down, she chose to straddle the arm of the couch, which minimized her miniskirt even more. Revealing all that leg appeared to be no accident. Diana's chitchat with Jess turned flirtatious. She was obviously trying to calm his nerves before his national television debut. But instead of putting Jess at ease, all her flirtatious attention only made him nervous. He started to sweat.

When the much-anticipated food and beer finally arrived, Diana split. We didn't get much chance to enjoy our free eats in peace, because in walked Daniel, the segment producer. Straight off, Daniel let it be known that he didn't like what Jess was wearing. Jess thought he looked nice in his suit. Too nice, thought the producer. He tried to convince my stand-in to go down to the wardrobe department and put on something a bit trashier to make him look more like a dishwasher. Jess initially refused but then compromised by removing the tie that the producer thought was "too loud."

Daniel then showed Jess a list of six questions Letterman might ask and six prepared replies the host could expect to hear.

"Say he asks you question number three," the producer said. "How you gonna respond?"

Suddenly, Jess was rehearsing lines for his upcoming "impromptu" chat.

All the while, I quietly ate my sandwich, swigged my beer and watched Letterman and Ron Howard backslapping on the monitor. When Jess departed for the makeup room, Daniel stared at me.

"You look familiar," he said. "Do I know you?"

"No," I answered a little too eagerly. I shook my head, shrugged my shoulders and then hid my face behind my sandwich. I must've fooled him, because he then turned to the monitor and actually began laughing at Letterman's lame jokes.

When Jess returned from the makeup room, he showed off his freshly painted face and said, "Pretty weird, huh, Pete?"

Thankfully, the verbal slip eluded Daniel, who was busy expressing his concern over how much beer Jess was consuming. The producer then persuaded Jess to drink a cup of coffee.

"Tough luck!" I told my friend, as I commandeered the remaining beers.

Then Daniel led us downstairs to the tiny green room beside the stage, where we sat with a couple other people and watched the show on a monitor for a few more minutes.

"Okay," the producer announced. "It's time."

Jess rose, winked at me, then disappeared.

I looked around. Under my couch cushion I found a quarter! Then I made quick work of devouring the strawberries and grapes from the fruit bowl. As I was moving in on a plate of gourmet cookies, the television screen came back to life. Suddenly, there was Jess, without the obligatory stroll-across-the-stage entrance, already sitting next to Letterman (who'd never busted suds, unlike his rival Jay Leno, who had at Boston's Playboy Club).

"Folks," Letterman said, "our next guest has spent the past ten years"—he was wrong; it was actually *six* years—"working toward his ultimate goal: to wash dishes in every state in the union. Here he is, a true American patriot, Dishwasher Pete."

I dropped my cookie and laughed so hard I slid off the couch.

One of the two other people in the green room asked, "Is that your friend?"

"Yeah!" I cried between fits.

"And that's really his goal, to wash dishes in all fifty states?"

"Yeah!"

"That's . . . very strange."

"Yeah!" I said. But wait, this bozo was calling Jess strange. No, he was calling *me* strange. I was momentarily confused until the sight of Jess on the screen overwhelmed me once again. Laughing like a madman, I no longer cared.

Much of what Jess said came more from his own experience as a dishman, except for his answer when Letterman asked, "When will you complete this task?"

"Well, I'm in no hurry," my proxy replied. "I'd hate to finish this whole thing—my life's dream—by the time I'm thirty-five because there'd be nothing left."

It was the same lighthearted, yet honest, answer I gave whenever I was asked this same question.

"Yeah," Letterman added. "Once you've climbed Everest, man, it's a long way down."

I laughed nonstop through most of the interview until I realized Dave was steering Jess toward doing his Fire Hand trick. Though Jess had lobbied the staff for two weeks to let him do this stunt, they remained so skeptical about the trick that I was sure they wouldn't actually allow him to perform it.

Letterman: Now, Pete, as I understand, to sometimes while away the lonely hours in the kitchen you've taught yourself kind of a little trick.

Jess: One of the tricks that I learned—well, after an accident I had when I sliced my hand open, I don't know if you can see it, it's a five-and-a-half-inch scar, it's from slicing my hand open and I had nerve surgery and my hand is dead, but . . .

Letterman: So the story has a happy ending then!

Jess: But I can light cigarettes and cigars by catching my hand on fire and putting it up to the—

Letterman: He can catch his hand on fire! May we dim the lights, please?

The lights dimmed. Letterman put a cigar in his mouth. Unlike the countless viewers who later pointed it out to me, Dave failed to notice that Jess lit his *right* hand, not the left one scarred in the knife-washing accident years before. Dave was probably too distracted to notice because he was more concerned with the flames Jess was thrusting at his face. Letterman jumped back in fright, his cigar unlit.

Before I knew it, the show was over and I was alone in the green room. I pounced on the refrigerator, but it held no beer. In fact, there was nothing else edible in the whole room except for the gourmet cookies.

I was searching for a container for the cookies when Jess poked his head through the door just long enough to say, "Hey, let's get outta here!!"

"But wait, Jess!" I yelled. *"Cookies!"*

I grabbed as many cookies as I could cradle in my arms and caught up to Jess at the elevator. Up in the dressing room, I grabbed the rest of the beers and we rushed down the stairs. Outside, Jess led the charge through a much larger gauntlet of fans. He knocked aside at least one autograph book held out for him to sign. A pack of frat boys pushed toward Jess and shouted, "Pete! Pete!" Terrified, Jess dove into the limousine and slammed the door.

On the way to the airport, we sat back and enjoyed our cookies and beers. After putting Jess on the plane to San Francisco, I rode the subway back into Manhattan. When the train stalled for over an hour beneath the East River, I loosened my tie and took a long-overdue nap.

The following day, while wandering through the Columbia University campus, I stumbled into a ritzy reception that had the kind of fancy spread I'd expected at the Letterman show. As I gobbled my way up and down the buffet table, one of the food servers gave me a dirty look. Sure, I was the only person in attendance who wasn't dressed up or socializing. But if only she'd seen me the day before—*wearing a suit and all!*

"I'd be in a suit, too," I told her. "But I'm a Mormon missionary and today's my day off."

She turned her back on me. I stared at her cautiously while using both hands to stuff my mouth. I felt relaxed. After the chaos of the previous couple days, my life was now back to normal.

•

A couple weeks later, I was talking to my dad on the phone. Apparently, the day after the broadcast, several well-meaning friends called the Letterman show demanding to know why they let an imposter pretend to be Dishwasher Pete.

"You mean that wasn't Pete?" came the response.

Reports of our shenanigans were now being reported in various newspapers and magazines. Over the phone, my dad was antsy to read me the article that ran in the *San Francisco Chronicle*.

"'A spokesman for the Letterman show said they had no idea they were dealing with an ersatz Pete,'" he read. Then he asked, "You know what *ersatz* means?"

"Nope," I answered.

"It means: cheap imitation," he said. "They're calling your friend a cheap imitation of you."

Then he laughed. He liked being in on the joke. And he even seemed proud of me.

When Jess called the Letterman show collect to ask where his $500 appearance fee was, the talent coordinator told him, "I know you're an imposter." Before hanging up on him, she added that her job was "in jeopardy."

Right on time to pay Jess's rent, the $500 check did arrive. But we never heard from Letterman again. The show made fun of the guests, audience members and regular people on the street, yet Letterman and his staff didn't seem to laugh when the joke was on them.

17
Dishwashers, Unions and New York

A couple weeks after Jess had left town, I was sitting on a street corner in Brooklyn eating pizza with two friends. A big brute covered in tough-guy tattoos approached us.

"Is one of you Dishwasher Pete?" he asked.

I didn't know who he was, so I peeped not a word and just took another bite of my slice. My two friends, though, wasted no time in fingering me. Almost in unison, they announced, "*He's* Pete."

Oh shit! I thought.

Was he some rabid Letterman fan who couldn't take a joke?

When he stepped forward and thrust out his hand, I cringed, convinced he was going to sock me.

Instead, he smiled and offered me his hand to shake.

"My name's Billy," he said. "I heard you were in the neighborhood and wanted to meet you."

Oh.

He said he was a lapsed dishman and urged me to come dish at the place where he was now cooking.

I said okay.

I followed Billy around the corner to a dinky, storefront Mexican restaurant where he introduced me to its charming owner, Suzy.

"You need to hire this guy," Billy told her, "'cause he's the most famous dishwasher you'll ever meet."

Being a famous dishwasher, she said, deserved a free burrito.

While she made the burrito, we discussed the possibility of me busting her suds. I said that since I was busy devoting my time to roaming the city looking for The Sign, I wasn't really in the market for a formal job. She said that since her restaurant was so small, she wasn't really in the market to formally hire a dishwasher. So we struck a deal: I could drop in at any time on any night and wash some dishes in exchange for some cash and loads of food—no strings attached. In fact, the arrangement was so casual that I didn't even consider counting it as my official New York job.

After not eating all the next day, I showed up the following night famished from my walk. I was ready to scrub some dishes and eat loads of food.

After I dished for half an hour, Suzy asked, "Hey, Pete, you want a beer?"

"Sure."

"Good, then you have to go to the store to get it! *Ha! Ha!*"

Billy and the waitress joined in the laughter as Suzy

handed me a twenty and told me to buy a twelve-pack. Crossing the street to the corner bodega, I figured if being the butt of the joke meant taking breaks to go buy beer, then I'd like working there.

And indeed, I had such a good time dishing there that even though my presence wasn't mandatory, I stopped by every night. The boss usually bought the beer, the food always satisfied me and the dishes never piled too high. Before I started hanging around, Suzy or Billy or the waitress had to wash the dishes in addition to cooking and/or waiting. Now, with me running the sinks, the others enjoyed a surplus of free time unknown at most restaurants, where busyness was next to godliness. Suzy even let me display on the eatery's walls my growing collection of laminated macaroni-and-cheese box covers (now numbering 127).

One night, when the place was quiet, I looked around for something to wash. Lying atop a refrigerator was a grease filter—a screen that usually sat in the hood above the stove to catch grease. I had picked it up and started carrying it to the sink when a moving brown mosaic came to life on the screen. I'd interrupted a cockroach feast in progress and immediately dropped the screen. It hit the floor with a thud. Dozens of cockroaches bounced off the screen and landed across the kitchen floor. In shock, I looked at them. For a second, they looked back at me. Then they started to scatter. Without thinking, I grabbed a spatula, swung wildly and flattened cockroaches left and right. With every blow, I was betraying my neutrality in the vermin wars. But because the pests kept running, I kept chasing. Until Suzy grabbed my arm.

Through clenched teeth, she said, *"Not in front of the customers!"*

On the other side of the counter, several diners stared in disbelief.

Meanwhile, those feisty little buggers were getting away! So I grabbed the grease filter, threw it in the dish sink and filled it up with scorching hot water. As dozens of roaches scurried out of the nooks of the screen, I watched with perverse satisfaction while they quietly succumbed.

Afterwards, when my bloodlust dissipated, I granted immunity to the survivors and resumed my neutral stance.

When not wandering or dishing, I was in the New York Public Library tracking leads on dishwashing history, culture and lore. Once, while poking through some issues of a 1930s communist newspaper, I came across an article about a strike. It was staged by a radical culinary union in New York in 1934; the strikers had attacked the hotels and restaurants that they were picketing. My curiosity piqued, I checked the *New York Times* for their version of the protest. A brief article described twenty-four-year-old Ramon Bolasquez, a striking dish dog from West 144th Street.

On February 12, Bolasquez was one of 1,500 culinary workers who marched through midtown Manhattan and clashed with police in front of the picketed hotels. In the days before, windows had been smashed at some establishments. The Waldorf-Astoria Hotel installed shatter-proof windows on its ground floor. Bolasquez did the Waldorf-Astoria one better by using a slingshot to take out windows on the hotel's upper floors. He also hit the windows of the Savarin Restaurant. While he was taking aim at the Hotel Lincoln at Eighth Avenue and 44th Street, the police nabbed him. A struggle ensued as the strikers tried to free the suds buster. In the end, the cops hauled him off and charged him with carrying concealed weapons.

Mesmerized by the image of pearl divers taking to the streets to fight for their rights, I marched from the library up to the Waldorf. On its façade I taped a piece of paper that read:

**On this spot in 1934,
dishwasher Ramon Bolasquez
smashed the windows of the Waldorf-Astoria
during a strike by culinary union workers.**

The Bolasquez story led me to think about the heritage of dishers in New York and their involvement in radical unions. I spent countless hours squinting at roll after roll of microfilm. By scouring these copies of old labor, anarchist, socialist, communist and mainstream newspapers, I learned about the various unions that had attempted to organize the "unskilled" restaurant workers that the mainstream Hotel Employees and Restaurant Employees International Union scoffed at.

It wasn't surprising that dishers would take to the streets to fight to improve their pay and working conditions; the standards for both were horrendous. For instance, during World War I, dishman Walter MacGregor wrote to the anarchist journal *Freedom* about his job:

> *I was walking along Sixth Avenue in the vicinity of Forty-Second Street when I espied the "banner" in the window. "Dishwasher Wanted," it announced. Now I had often heard that dishwashers are the very lowest scum of humanity. I entertained at that moment the conviction*

that I, being jobless and hungry, belonged to that lowest scum; and beside that, I had a genuine curiosity to find out why dishwashing is considered so "low" a calling.

. . . The heat and stink of that place on a warm day! The stench from the enormous garbage can mingled with the smell of grease, even the most acclimated old-timer stuck his nose to the door occasionally for a breath of fresh air.

Thompson's being both a popular and low-priced lunch room, there is never a let-up in the mountainous pile of dishes that comes pouring through the cubby-hole onto the dishwashing table. There is never a moment all day long to rest or sit down, and even if there were, one could not sit, for no convenience is provided for this purpose.

When I went to wash dishes for Thompson, I expected hard work, but what stunned me was to learn the hours and the pay given as compensation. Thompson's works its dishwashers twelve hours a day, seven days a week.

I received eight dollars a week and I was told by a fellow worker that if I "stuck" I was "supposed" to get a half day off every other week.

"But," he added dryly, "there's so many comin' an' goin' all the time, y'll be lucky if y' ever sees a half day off."

In 1929, one dishwasher, working twelve hours a day, six and a half days a week at a large chain cafeteria, wrote of the conditions he endured:

The dining room of this place is clean and white. We are forced to keep everything spotlessly clean. The

*menus and walls boast of cleanliness and service ren-
dered the patrons. It is advertised as a place where everything is sanitary and the food wholesome—pure food
health place. But if the customers took one look into the
kitchen they would never come back. There, everything
is as dirty as it is clean in the dining room. The floors
are always sloppy. The shoes of the kitchen workers are
always wet and most of us suffer from perpetual colds,
catarrh, rheumatism and we all had the flu during the
winter but did not stop working until forced to go to bed
and returned to work long before we were well. And the
health authorities wonder how these diseases spread so
rapidly during an epidemic.*

*Nothing is wasted. Any piece of food that can be used
for hash, stews, pudding, etc. is fished out of the garbage and saved. If the boss or his lickspittle manager
sees any of us throwing away a piece of meat, butter, or
bread, we are bawled out and warned we will be fired if
we do it again.*

In 1930, a few dishwashers took matters into their own
hands. A radical culinary union newspaper reported on this
protest:

*On 44th Street and 5th Avenue is located one of the
biggest "Happiness Restaurants" of the Loft Corporation. But "Happiness" in that particular restaurant is
only for the boss and not for the workers. In fact, the
name of this restaurant should be "Happiness" for the
bosses and "Misery" for the workers.*

*The management of this restaurant was the first to
introduce the wage cuts in the Dining Room as well as
in the Kitchen Departments. But this was not enough, it*

went as far as to cut out the meals of the workers (the "left overs") altogether.

One bright morning the manager received an order from their central office to increase the profits and decrease the expenses. The efficient manager used and abused his "noggin" and finally found his way out. He posted an order notifying the workers that, from then on, all employees must get their meals from outside. Any employee caught eating on the premises of the Happiness restaurant would be discharged immediately.

When the clock struck twelve, the dishwashers, the lowest paid of all the workers in the restaurant, who receive $12 a week for a 12-hour continuous grind a day, stopped the machines and left the restaurant in a body and went to get their lunch. The manager tried to stop them at the door but the workers told him they could not work the machines on an empty stomach.

Twelve o'clock is the busiest hour of the place and if the waitresses and cooks would have followed the example set by the dishwashers and come out and come up to our union headquarters to organize for the fight, today the Happiness restaurant would be a union shop.

After the waitresses and cooks practically scabbed on the dishwashers, when the dishwashers got back from their lunch, the management told them they could have their meals back.

The bits of history that I was uncovering fascinated me. Decades before I ever picked up a scrub brush, pearl divers were in the streets battling for their rights and—intentionally or unintentionally—for the rights of the dishers of future generations. Absolutely remarkable! Their legacy needed to be honored. So to shed light on the suds busters' participation within radical culinary unions, my poking around in the library eventually led me to write an eight-thousand-word article for the zine titled "Dishwashers, Unions and New York City: A History."

On the hottest day of the summer of 1995, while apartment- and cat-sitting in a non-air-conditioned residence, I found myself battling Koko the cat for the apartment's lone cool spot: the chair that caught the breeze from the two fans.

I lost that battle and fled the apartment.

Out on the street, the humidity was so stifling, I couldn't conduct my job search or even concentrate to scan the sidewalk for coins. So I hopped on the subway and rode in air-conditioned luxury for the rest of the afternoon. Come evening, I was on the L train as it headed toward the burrito joint's station. When the train arrived at the stop, though, I didn't budge. Even on cool nights, the restaurant's kitchen sweltered. I couldn't imagine how hot it'd be in this heat wave. And, frankly, I didn't want to find out.

Remaining on the subway, I realized that this was the first night I wouldn't be dishing there since it'd become my hangout. At formal jobs with scheduled days and assigned hours, I was rarely on time, when I bothered to show up at all. Now, with this informal arrangement and its built-in freedom, I hadn't missed a single night of work when I was in town.

That's why I liked the job so much. I could stroll away in the middle of a load of dishes and no one would complain. I could bop across the Hudson River to Hoboken, New Jersey (#17), to put in a few shifts at a Washington Street restaurant and Suzy wouldn't feel like I was cheating on her. I could even leave town—go down to Philly or Baltimore, up to Connecticut or upstate New York. After a few weeks, I could hightail it back to New York City, step off the bus or train and ride the subway straight to the burrito joint. Showing up with an empty stomach, I could jump right back on the dishes while a meal was prepared for me.

It was an awfully plush deal. So plush, it spoiled me. For a while, at least.

That winter, after being out of town for several months, I showed up unannounced at the burrito joint. I had a hunger in my gut and a hankering to dish. With a line of customers out the door, the place was jumping like never before. Pushing my way through the crowd, I found Suzy busy in the kitchen. Business was good, she said. So good, in fact, she pointed to a guy at the sinks—*my* sinks.

Immediately, I got the message. In my absence, the chore of washing dishes had become a formal job, which meant that I was out of an *in*formal job.

Feeling stupid for assuming that those dishes would always wait for me, I bumbled about Brooklyn, not sure what to do. I entered a subway station and walked to the far end of the platform. I watched a mob of rats rummaging through the debris along the tracks. Several trains passed. I stood there and realized it was time to finally work a formal job in New York—one with assigned hours, specified duties and a set wage.

A couple days later, I found myself in the massive kitchen of a huge catering firm in the Financial District. Employees bustled around me as I waited for the head chef to return so he could lead me to the dishroom and I could start my new gig. Not having worked in an operation as huge as this in a long time, I was disoriented by the blinding fluorescent lights and the shiny stainless steel surfaces. Dozens of kitchen workers hustled to and fro in their white shirts and salt-and-pepper pants, while I slouched in my street clothes, hands in pockets.

When twenty minutes passed with still no sign of the chef, I presumed he'd forgotten about me. Setting out to find the pit myself, I ventured down corridors and peeked around corners. While failing to discover the dishpit, I succeeded in stumbling across the back exit.

"Just leave," a voice in my head urged.

"No, stay," the other voice argued. "I need a real job—and the money."

"But this place is giving me a headache."

"Come on, stick it out. It's just an eight-hour shift."

"Eight hours? There are so many other things I could do for eight hours!"

"Oh, don't be such a quitter."

"Quitter? *Quitter?!* I'll show you a quitter."

These internal debates were little more than formalities since the outcome was always the same.

I slipped out the back door and made a break for it.

A couple hours later, while I was resting on a bench in lower Manhattan, an office worker on his lunch break sat down. When he asked me what I was up to, I told him I'd just walked off a dishwashing job.

"I quit a dishwashing job once," he said.

"Oh yeah? What happened?"

"The owner came in the back and I said, 'Git the fuck outta here!' And then I walked outside and jumped in a cab."

I told him I liked his style.

"Well, good luck on finding another job," he said.

"Yeah," I said.

Maybe I wasn't so much like Burt Reynolds or Robert Duvall or Richard Gere, I thought. Maybe I was more like

Joe Buck—the character from *Midnight Cowboy*. He'd left his dish job in Texas and caught the bus to New York to follow his dream. When Joe Buck found himself contemplating a "Dishwasher Wanted" sign in the window of a pancake house in Times Square, he said, *"Shee-it!"* And walked away.

Then again, Joe Buck's dream was actually to be a male hustler. *My* dream was just to dish in New York City. And as a matter of fact—formally or informally—I'd already accomplished that. State #18 was done. It was time to move on.

18

Unconquered Territory

W hile traveling along the West Coast, I drifted back to
Portland and did volunteer work at Reading
Frenzy—a cozy, downtown book and magazine shop that
sold *Dishwasher* and had even held an exhibition of my
mac-n-cheese box collection. The work consisted mostly of
sitting around and reading the store's offerings in between
ringing up the occasional customer. Periodically, one of them
would ask if there was a new issue of *Dishwasher* for sale.
Feeling too shy to admit to strangers that I was its creator, I
usually answered, "I hear number fourteen will be out in a
couple weeks."

But I felt guilty about being so sly. After all, these strangers were fans of my quest. So I decided to make a concerted
effort to be more open with them.

The next time the issue arose was when a twenty-year-oldish dude came in and asked, "You have any of that *Dishwasher* guy's Dish Master shirts for sale?"

I was finally going to "out" myself to a customer by explaining how, the coming week, I hoped to make a newly designed Dish Master shirt using the hundreds of used T-shirts purchased from the pay-by-the-pound Goodwill warehouse.

But before I had a chance to utter a word, the customer spoke again.

"I sent that guy *five bucks* for a shirt six months ago," he moaned. "And I *still* haven't gotten it!"

I kept my mouth shut. The pledge about coming clean to the customers was rescinded. Anonymity had its advantages.

A couple days later, a woman strode into the store and immediately grabbed two copies of "Music to Wash Dishes By." Her good taste caught my eye. The record was my doing. Four bands had each contributed a song about dishing. In between the songs, I added some narrative from the 1960s training film "Mr. Dish Machine Operator." The result was a seven-inch vinyl record and accompanying booklet.

As the woman continued to browse the shelves, I grew nervous that she might ask me about the record. Sure enough, when she approached the counter, the first words out of her mouth were "What do you think of this record?"

I wanted to give her a noncommittal shrug. But at the same time, after years of discussing this project with Jess, I was proud to have actually completed it and wanted to sing its praises.

So, attempting to be honest, yet remain anonymous, I answered, "I think it's the best record ever."

She squinted through her cat-eye glasses and asked, "Are you Dishwasher Pete?"

My instinct was to lie and deny. But she was cute. And that threw me off.

Too flummoxed to fib, I meekly admitted, "Yeah."

She smiled and introduced herself. She was Lara from Chicago. Not only was she familiar with the zine, she'd even written me a couple letters in the past. Now Lara was returning to Alaska to work another summer as a fisherwoman. She hung around the shop and chatted for an hour until my shift ended. The next night, in the downtown storage room where I was crashing, she helped me silk-screen a hundred Dish Master shirts. When we were done, she didn't leave. She was scheduled to fly out later that day but—with this sudden turn of events—instead delayed her flight till the end of the week.

Later in the week, at the last minute before Lara left town, I decided to escort her—via the bus—the 125 miles to the Seattle airport. At the airport, as she was checking in, she asked the woman behind the counter how much a second ticket would cost. Upon learning of the amount, Lara counted out a few hundred bucks from her wallet and then said, "Come to Alaska with me."

"What?" I said. "Right now?"

"Yeah," she said. "I've got just enough cash to buy you a ticket."

I didn't have much time to answer. Her plane was beginning to board. Alaska?! While it would've been romantic and impulsive to have just jumped on the plane with her, I only had the clothes on my back. I hadn't even locked the storage room door back in Portland. So I felt kind of square to decline her offer.

"But we'll stay in touch," I said.

Not long afterwards, I floated through the Southwest, dished at a bagel joint in Albuquerque, New Mexico (#19), and then ended up back in New Orleans. After Cheryl picked me up from the bus station, as we drove to her house, she pointed out the restaurants in her new neighborhood.

"There's an Italian place up on this corner and a Creole place down that street," she told me. "That restaurant over there doesn't seem bad. . . ."

I found the tour odd. Cheryl knew damn well that I didn't like eating in restaurants. But I said nothing and politely looked to wherever she pointed.

Then she said, "I'm not letting you leave New Orleans *this time* until you get a dishwashing job."

She did have a point. Louisiana remained unconquered territory. After that failed attempt a couple years earlier, I'd passed through town a number of times without even trying to crack the New Orleanian dish market. But this time around, I was nearly broke. To reach any next destination, I had to drum up some cash by making Louisiana #20.

A few days after my arrival, while ambling along Banks Street, I saw a flyer tacked to a tree:

NOW HIRING:
Food Service Personnel
* Daily Work
* Daily Pay

Daily dishing for daily cash? No waiting weeks while my paycheck was held hostage against me quitting? Ideal! But it sounded eerily similar to Terry's hiring hall, where I'd tried without success to be the on-call troubleshooting dishman.

The next morning, I set out for the flyer's Canal Street address. But first I had to find a pecan pie. Not a whole pie, mind you, just one of those tart-sized ones to put me in the right mood for working. Yet, despite its being the height of pecan season, after a thorough search of a dozen corner stores, I was still pieless. Then a woman passed me on the street and asked, "Would you like to buy a pie?"

I took a few steps before I realized what she'd said. She was holding a box full of *homemade, tart-sized pecan pies*! I saw this as such a good omen about my new job that I spent my last five bucks on three pies.

The pie search set me back timewise; I didn't reach the hiring hall until midafternoon. I was glad to see it wasn't Terry's company but was surprised to find the place already closed for the day.

I sat on the curb and ate my pies. Not wanting to make the same mistake I'd made at Terry's, I vowed to return early the next morning.

At nine a.m. the next day, I was at the hiring hall, ready to work.

Bring on the dishes, I thought as I stepped inside.

Seeing an empty waiting room, I smugly figured I was the first laborer to arrive. I told the guy behind the caged counter that I was looking for a dish job.

"You late," he said. "Jobs all taken."

"Already?" I asked. "It's only nine o'clock."

"Guys start getting dispatched outta here at *five* o'clock," he said. "Last one left about an hour ago."

"But all I want is a dishwashing job."

"We got plenty of those. You just gotta be here at five."

Five a.m.? Who the hell needed their dishes cleaned that early in the morning? Schools? Hospitals? Restaurants where the previous night's dirty dishes still awaited washing because the disher had scrammed mid-shift? Aching to find out firsthand, I signed up.

Before leaving, I read the dozens of signs covering the walls of the hiring hall. Employees were warned not to forge time cards or paychecks, screw around on the job or sneak off mid-shift. Cursing, drinking and fighting were prohibited in the hall. Bathing, on the other hand, was encouraged. The underlying message was: "We're on to you."

I studied every sign and then left determined to return earlier on Monday morning. Five a.m.? That wouldn't be so tough. After all, I'd risen at five a.m. seven days a week for seven years as a paperboy.

Monday at five a.m. found me still prone on the couch, out of shape from my paperboy days. The same thing happened on Tuesday. On Wednesday, I tried to stay up all night. At five a.m., though, trudging off to the hiring hall to work came in a distant second to trudging over to the couch to sleep.

Later Wednesday morning, Cheryl woke me up and said she'd seen The Sign at a nearby restaurant. She urged me to call the place.

"I've already got a job," I told her, "down at that day-labor place."

She rolled her eyes and pushed the phone at me. "Call the restaurant."

"But the day-labor office is counting on me," I protested.

She picked up the phone, dialed and stuck the receiver in my face. I could hear the ringing.

"Take it," she said.

A stern voice answered, *"Hello?"*

I hesitated, then grabbed the phone.

"I was calling about the dishwashing job."

"You have any experience?" the voice asked.

"Plenty," I said.

"Come over this afternoon then."

That afternoon I walked over. The restaurant was closed so I pounded on the front door. The stern-faced old man who opened the door matched the stern voice on the phone.

"I'm here for the dishwashing job."

"You have experience?" he asked again.

"Yeah," I said. "I've washed a lotta dishes."

He led me inside, showed me to a table and said he'd be right back. I took a seat and surveyed the joint. It looked pretty swank: plush red furniture, chandeliers, wineglasses set out on table-clothed tables. The décor was something else. The wall to my left was covered with military paraphernalia: medals, banners, flags and autographed glossies of generals sporting sadistic, satisfied grins.

Several of the photographs prominently featured the old man in a Marine's uniform. He must've been some sort of career officer who retired from the service to open his own restaurant. I couldn't help but wonder if the dining room's military theme carried over into the kitchen. What if he ran the place like a drill sergeant?

"Come on, you stoop-shouldered maggot!" I could hear him screaming. *"I want those dishes so shiny I can see my reflection in them!"*

I squirmed in my seat.

Then I noticed that the wall to my right was plastered with guns, bayonets and daggers. That was the clincher: I was in the wrong place. Working at five a.m.? Far more appealing than working here.

I stood and made for the side exit, but the door was locked. I turned and headed for the front door, only to run into Colonel Restaurant Owner. He held out an application. I looked down at it.

Broke and still needing to lick the dishes of Louisiana, I hadn't much choice. Reluctantly, I grabbed the application and returned to the table. This time, though, I sat with my back to the weapons.

When I was finished with the application, I handed it back to the Colonel. Without bothering to take a look-see at anything I'd written, he asked, "So, you have experience?"

His hang-up with "experience" was really beginning to irk me. Sure, I was a Dish Master, but anyone with ten minutes in the suds could claim to be experienced.

"Yeah," I answered for the third time.

"All right, let me talk to the chef."

He disappeared through the double doors. In the kitchen, shouting ensued. Someone was upset about something, but I couldn't quite hear what. Suspecting the argument concerned my application, I inched myself nearer to get a better listen. Before I could decipher anything, the shouting abruptly stopped. Suddenly, the Colonel punched his way through the double doors. His face looked even more stern, like he was going to yell at me.

Instead, he said, "You start in two hours."

I left, crossed the street to a park and sat on a bench. Getting this New Orleans job had been way too easy. Of course, landing dish jobs was *supposed* to be easy—it's why I dished. But I'd begun to believe the naysayers who claimed I was "too white" to find a gig.

A couple hours later, I returned to the restaurant and noticed that the hostess, waiters, waitresses, back-waiters, barbacks, bartender and even the few customers already seated were all white. In the kitchen, too, there were nothing but white faces. As I checked out my accommodations, I wondered why the Colonel skipped the whole white-in-front/black-in-back thing. Maybe the old man flat out refused to hire African Americans in a city whose population at the time was almost 70 percent black.

The dishpit was nestled in an L-shaped alcove: a virtual dishcave. At my disposal were a Hobart machine and, in the back corner, out of view from the rest of the kitchen, three sinks. There was plenty of room, plenty of counter space and plenty of privacy. The setup showed promise. I decided to stick around.

For an hour, no coworker small-talked me or even bothered to ask my name. I kept a low profile and dished in peace until the Colonel sauntered into the dishcave with some dirty glasses. Without so much as a "How ya doing?" or *"Attenshun!"* he rattled off a racist joke. Now I knew why he didn't hire blacks. Before I could react, he turned and left.

I put down the dishes. There were better uses of my time and energy than by providing them to some racist asshole. I made up my mind to go. While I was untying my apron, in walked the other pearl diver—Bernard. He was black. His presence wrecked my argument that the Colonel was too racist to hire blacks. I retied my apron and decided to stay. It took a few more minutes of dishing before it hit me: the lone black man was *washing dishes,* which only confirmed the original claim of institutionalized white-in-front/black-in-back racism. I was untying my apron again when Bernard sidled up to me and said, "I wanna show you something."

He led me to the rear of the dishcave and pointed to a

bucket in the corner. He'd filled it with ice cubes and cans of beer. The scales tipped again. I retied my apron and then broke my own rule about not drinking until the second half of a shift by opening a beer.

Since this was my first night and Bernard's first week on the job, I was suspicious about why the Colonel seemed to have trouble holding on to dishwashers. It felt like at any minute, the Colonel would run us through boot-camp drills or slam us with dishes. But after that one joke, the boss said nothing more to us. In fact, the dishing was so breezy, Bernard and I had ample time to hide out and drink our beers. So the Colonel's lack of long-term dishers was just chalked up to our profession's penchant for quitting.

The next night, everything changed. The dining room was seething with dish-defilers; the kitchen was packed with pot-burners. From the start, Bernard and I were swamped. The previous night's luxurious beer breaks were a distant memory.

When a ruckus erupted out in the kitchen, I stepped up to the front of the dishcave to see what was going on. Not surprisingly, the disturbance was caused by the head chef. By that time in my "career," I'd witnessed dozens of temperamental cooks throw hundreds of tantrums. But this sorehead was in a class of his own. Over the course of several hours, he put on an impressive performance. While a lot of cooks were only good for one or two outbursts per shift, the relentless Chef Tantrum unleashed one tirade after another. He snipped at his cooks. He snapped at the wait staff. The guy never let up.

Later, when a waitress had the audacity to claim Chef Tantrum had screwed up her order, he flipped his wig. Everyone—Bernard and me included—stopped working to watch him yell and scream. He threw spatulas on the floor. He hurled whisks across the kitchen. Then Chef Tantrum came around from behind the line, marched up to the waitress and shouted in her face, "It's all *your* fault!!"

The waitress burst into tears and fled into the dining room.

"Don't talk to her!" Chef Tantrum screamed at us onlookers. "*Nobody fucking talk to her!!*"

"Man," Bernard whispered to me, "I need a beer."

Bernard wrapped a couple beers in his apron and hotfooted it upstairs to the bathroom. Having seen enough myself, I retreated to the far recesses of the dishcave and started knocking out the mess that'd been piling up.

Now I finally understood why dishers didn't stay. It wasn't the Colonel—it was Chef Tantrum. Who'd want to stick around for all that yelling? And more important, why hadn't the Colonel court-martialed that knucklehead? I'd seen other tantrum-y cooks keep their jobs because they were indispensable to the restaurant. But Chef Tantrum was anything but indispensable. He'd surely chased off a slew of competent employees. Those who stayed were forced to tiptoe around him. And from what I'd sampled from the Bus Tub Buffet, his cooking wasn't all that great.

It was almost closing time when Bernard returned drunk from his break. Desperate to finish up and leave, I surveyed our mess and said to Bernard, "Let's take care of this."

"Yeah," he agreed. "Let's bust 'em out."

With a valiant effort, we put a dent in the stacks. But that mattered little—at closing time, we were hit by a tidal wave. The cooks brought us all their cookware from the kitchen.

The busboys brought us all the dishes from the dining room. Everything came at us at once. When the counters reached capacity, stacks sprouted on the floor around our feet. Mounds of dishes grew into hills, and hills grew into mountains. The dishes only stopped coming at us when all the other employees finally went home.

As Chef Tantrum was leaving, he called across the kitchen, "Good night, Dad!" My ears perked up and I turned around. The farewell was directed at the Colonel. *Aha!* Now it all made sense! Chef Tantrum could scream at the employees with impunity because dear old daddy was the owner.

Not wanting to work under such nepotistic conditions, I decided that once the night's dishes were clean, I'd collect my pay and leave for good.

We worked our asses off but made little progress. No matter how much we attacked the stacks, they just wouldn't shrink. I was baffled.

Then, from my post at the sinks, I happened to look over and see Bernard searching for a clear space to park a rack of clean dishes. All the counters were full, so he set the rack down beside the dishmachine. Then, apparently without thinking, he pushed the rack in the machine and washed it—again.

I assumed that he was suffering from dishpit battle fatigue. But minutes later, after the Hobart's cycle finished, I watched him again searching for a place to set down that same rack of clean dishes. And again he just slid the thing back in the machine to be washed. He was more smashed than I'd suspected.

Though I now knew why the mountains of dishes weren't eroding, I wasn't sure what to do about it. Even if I could've magically sobered up Bernard, it would've still taken us hours to finish.

When Bernard grabbed a couple of beers from the bucket and stumbled up the stairs to the bathroom, I didn't object. With Bernard holed up in the bathroom and the Colonel reading the newspaper in the bar, waiting for us to finish, I was now alone in the kitchen. It was time to act.

First, I needed order. I combed through the piles, pulling out the trash and the silverware. I stacked all the like-sized plates and dishes together. I gathered up the pots and pans and carried them back to the sinks. After twenty minutes of organizing, the dishcave was still a disaster area.

Since it was going to take hours just to clean the pots, I decided they'd have to wait for some other day to be scrubbed. I filled them with hot water and stashed them under a counter. With those out of the way, I started grabbing pans, utensils and other things that could wait.

I was crouched down on the floor, cramming dishes under a counter, when the Colonel walked in. Clueless as to what I was up to, he told me there was to be a large brunch in the morning.

"I expect you two to be here at eight a.m.," he said.

Without waiting for my response, he returned to the bar and his newspaper.

Eight a.m.? It was now one-thirty in the morning. Did he really expect us to work even later, sleep a couple hours, then return?

I already knew that to really get a boss's attention, it was best to jettison a job during peak hours like the Dish Mistress had done in New Hampshire or the Happiness Restaurant dish crew had done back in 1930. But since the Colonel's place wouldn't hit its peak for hours to come, I did the next best thing: continued stashing the dishes. After all the nooks under the counters in the dishcave were filled, I started hiding dirty dishware throughout the kitchen: under more counters, on shelves and—as a very last resort—in the ovens. After everything was stashed, I rinsed out the sinks, wiped down the counters and kissed the dishmachine. The dishcave sparkled when, right on cue, Bernard stumbled back in from his hour-long visit to the bathroom. It didn't faze him in the least that we were suddenly "done."

The Colonel took a quick glance in the dishcave.

"Well done," he said. "You guys'll be back at eight o'clock, right?"

"Yeah," we both replied.

Out on the sidewalk, I told Bernard not to return in the morning because there were piles of dirty dishes hidden across the kitchen.

"Don't I know it," he said. "That place is just filled with dishes."

For a moment I worried that he was too drunk to understand not to come back the next morning. But as I watched him weave his way down the block, I realized he was so shit-faced he didn't even know he was expected to work at eight a.m. He'd be all right.

I departed picturing the next day's scene. Chef Tantrum, while trying to prepare the big brunch, was going to uncover one cache of dirty dishes after another. He'd go ballistic. The Colonel would curse having hired a dishman with so much experience.

Oh, to have been a cockroach on the wall when all that went down! I enjoyed my walk.

It was almost three o'clock when I arrived at Cheryl's. In need of a new job, I decided to stay awake and hit the day-labor office at five o'clock. But then it dawned on me: when the Colonel and/or Chef Tantrum discovered the devastation in the dishcave and their dearth of dishmen, what else could they do but make an emergency request to the day-labor office for on-call troubleshooting dishers?

It was obviously best that I steered clear.

Later that morning, Cheryl claimed that since I didn't get paid at the Colonel's, it shouldn't count as my having held a job in Louisiana. She was as determined as ever to see me finally cross it off my list, and though I hated to admit it, she had a point. While I had no fixed rules about what constituted working in a state, the most basic requirement should've been at least to have received pay for my labor. After all, even at the job in Kentucky (#1), though I'd crashed and burned after only ninety minutes, the restaurant had mailed me a paycheck worth almost four bucks. So to properly proclaim Louisiana as #20, I had to either face the Colonel, Chef Tantrum and their wall of weapons to demand my pay—or find a new job altogether.

19
Seafaring

While hunting for a new job a few days later, I was offered one. The job wasn't in New Orleans, though. Lara invited me to dish on the fishing boat she was working on in Alaska. The offer was tantalizing. It was a chance to return to Alaska, to watch Lara ply her trade as a fisherwoman and to fulfill a growing ambition to dish off-shore.

For a couple of years, I'd been carrying around an application to dish on a paddleboat that sailed up and down the Mississippi and Ohio Rivers. I'd been also considering adding seafaring cruise-ship dishing to my To Do list. And while in Vancouver, British Columbia, I'd met a dish dog (or rather, a dish *pig,* as we're known north of the border) who bragged about his sweet gig busting suds on the ferries that sailed between the mainland and Vancouver Island. His description of his lax position made me reconsider my pooh-poohing of offshore jobs.

But, of course, I hadn't yet pursued any of these kinds of jobs due to the Fundamental Rule. That granddaddy of all my self-imposed work-related rules still prevented me from working gigs where I couldn't leave the moment the notion struck. And if the notion struck while on Lara's boat—and I deep-sixed the job while at sea—leaving would be difficult. I'd be at the mercy of the short-tempered skipper to be put ashore. For talking him into hiring a dud like me, the skipper would blow up at my gal. Things between Lara and me would be less than shipshape. Through all that anger and tension, I could be left stuck on the boat for days or weeks, pining for the mainland.

The job had major potential to be a massive disaster. Before I set foot on the boat, I had to know for sure that I could survive breaking the Fundamental Rule.

For a few days, I fretted about what to do. Then, while looking through the *Times-Picayune* for a New Orleans dish job, I found the answer. Dishwashers—or galley hands—were needed to work on oil rigs on the Gulf of Mexico. Working a job like that could serve a threefold purpose. I'd master Louisiana. I'd earn enough money to get me to Alaska. And, most important, I'd test the Fundamental Rule under circumstances with less dire consequences. If I couldn't hack it on an oil rig, and the Fundamental Rule proved unbreakable, then I'd forget about the fishing boat. But if I survived, a whole new genre of dish work would open up to me: riverboats, cruise ships—and my sweetheart's fishing vessel.

A couple miles upriver from New Orleans, in the town of Harahan, the company that supplied galley hands for oil rigs had its offices. I took a bus there and after filling out a bunch of paperwork was stunned to meet the interviewer. I couldn't help but gawk at him. He was a dead ringer for Bill Clinton. In his office, the Clinton-clone said I needed to take an exam and then proceeded to quiz me about things like honesty and integrity and employee theft.

"If you knew a coworker was stealing from the company," he said, "what would you do?"

Robotically, I replied, "I'd tell my supervisor immediately."

The exam was a cinch. While I fed him the obvious answers ("All hail The Company! The Company is my friend! I shall not steal from The Company!"), I remained distracted by the Clinton-clone's remarkable resemblance. He had those same puffy cheeks, that same dimpled chin and the same haircut. Hell, he even had that same shit-eating smirk Clinton had when he'd gut welfare, push NAFTA and increase military spending while musing to himself, "To think, liberals love voting for me!" Except this guy's smirk seemed to say: "You think I look like Clinton and you're just *dying* to ask me about it."

He had me pegged. I *was* dying to ask. But how many thousands of times had he heard, "Did you know that you look *exactly like* Bill Clinton?" Even if I'd tried to be witty ("Hey, did you know that you look like Spiro Agnew?"), he probably would've heard it before. So I said nothing about it while I pondered why he was here, interrogating prospective galley hands, when he could've been shaking his ass in Vegas as a celebrity look-alike.

When the exam ended, the Clinton-clone tallied up my score.

"How'd I do?" I asked.

"Not so good," he replied dourly.

Not good? He had to be kidding.

"In fact," he added, "you flunked."

Flunked?! How could I possibly flunk some asinine honesty exam?

"Can I see that?" I asked, reaching for the test sheet.

"I can't let you do that," he said. "But hang on, I'll be back in a minute."

He left the room with my test.

It made no sense. I couldn't possibly have flunked. But then again, I hadn't listened closely to many of the questions, being so distracted by the presidential resemblance and all.

That was it! It was all a ruse! The company employed this celebrity look-alike to administer the exam as a way to purposefully trip up applicants!

"It'll be okay," the Clinton-clone said when he returned. "See the receptionist to make an appointment for your physical."

Huh? So I hadn't flunked after all? What the hell?

As he ushered me out of his office, I wondered if he told all prospective galley hands they'd flunked. That way, the applicants—grateful to be hired at all—would tone down any possible on-the-job dishonesty.

Or maybe, I *had* flunked. But, as was the case with lots of employers, the desperation for a dishman made the Clinton-clone overlook my *plongeur* morality.

The next day's physical exam was quite thorough. At a medical complex that specialized in job-related patients, I moved along—assembly-line style—from one room to the next. A dozen doctors and nurses took turns poking and prodding, X-raying and EKG-ing me, hammering me and having me look that way and cough. Evidently, the company wanted only the primest slabs of meat washing their dishes. And I proved a willing slab; I broke another of my rules by allowing myself to be drug-tested for a job.

At the company office the following day, the receptionist told me I'd passed the physical. Next hurdle: the orientation meeting, where a company representative explained life on an oil rig to a half-dozen prospective galley hands and cooks. He told us what we could expect and what to bring. Though there were no women in our group, he also gave a lengthy, apparently mandatory, speech about the procedures for female employees to file sexual harassment complaints.

The company rep then spent a good fifteen minutes trying to convince us what great jobs these were. The more he poured it on, the more I smelled B.S. Stuck on an oil rig for weeks at a time? Working twelve hours a day, seven days a week for minimum wage? Nothing worth boasting about. Though I had my own perverse reasons for doing this, I didn't know why others would subject themselves to such punishment. But when the rep admitted that the annual turnover rate among galley hands was 90 percent, I felt better. For whatever reasons others were submitting themselves to this, it was extremely unlikely that they'd be doing it for very long.

When it finally was question time, I piped right up.

"So how do we go about quitting in the middle of our hitch?" I asked.

The rep fidgeted. We'd only just been rounded up and now he had to tell us how to split.

"I'm sure none of you will," he said unconvincingly and then explained that if we did quit, we couldn't leave the oil rig until a replacement arrived.

"How long would that be?" I asked.

"A day or two," he said.

A day or two, I thought. When the notion struck, a day or

two could be a long—a *very* long—time. I shouldn't have been surprised that I trembled at the thought. After all, the Fundamental Rule existed for a reason.

After the meeting, the Clinton-clone called me into his office and said I hadn't given the make and license plate number of my car on my application.

"I don't have a car," I said.

"You don't? Why not?"

"I guess I don't need one."

"You need one for *this* job," he said. "In fact, owning a car is the most important qualification for being a galley hand."

"I have to own a car to wash dishes on an oil rig?"

"That's right. When you're on-call and the dispatcher tells you to be at the coast in three hours, you have to be there. We can't wait for you to borrow a car or to find someone to drive you."

"Well, in that case," I said, "I *do* own a car."

"Great. What kind?"

"It's a . . . station wagon."

"And what's the license plate number?"

"Uh . . . I'm not sure."

"You don't know your own license plate number?"

"Well, I'd have to go outside and check."

"You go do that then," he said.

I stepped outside and wrote down the license plate number of a car that I hoped wasn't his. He accepted it and, minutes later, I was issued a hard hat, safety glasses and two work shirts. Another rule—no company garb—fell by the wayside. I was now officially on-call.

I didn't drive my imaginary car back to New Orleans. Didn't even take the bus. Instead, the rest of the afternoon was spent meandering back to the city, soaking up my last fleeting moments of freedom. The Fundamental Rule was on the verge of being broken and I feared the worst.

When I finally reached Cheryl's house, the phone was ringing. A booming Cajun voice on the other end of the line asked for me. I said I wasn't home. Or rather, I said "he" wasn't home. It was the dispatcher. He had a job for me and it was important that I called him as soon as I got in. I assured him that I would.

This was happening much too fast! I wasn't ready to abandon the security of the mainland. For an hour, I paced around the house. The phone rang again. Again, it was the dispatcher. I still wasn't in.

Before the phone could ring once more, I decamped to my friend Tanio's house, where I sometimes stayed. It wasn't long before Tanio's phone also rang. It was a dispatcher. Somehow, I'd listed Cheryl's phone number on one part of the paperwork and Tanio's on another. They were calling both numbers. I couldn't hide. That night and the next day, it was so torturous that I jumped every time a phone rang.

By the second night, the stress had worn down my resistance. I finally picked up the ringing phone and said I was good to go.

"That's what I like to hear," the dispatcher said. "Be at the heliport at six o'clock tomorrow morning."

I woke up Cheryl in the middle of the night and she drove me to the coast. We left early enough to make the two-hour drive through the bayous in time for me to catch my flight. But when we arrived at the coast, we got lost. Even though there were only a couple of roads where the bayou met the Gulf, we couldn't find the heliport. So we stuck our heads out the windows until we spotted a helicopter and followed it to the heliport. We finally arrived, over an hour late. I had no idea if my flight had been held up for me or if it had departed, leaving me jobless.

While Cheryl waited in her car, I entered the heliport. A man at the counter handed me a clipboard and asked me to sign in. I wrote down my name, the name of the rig I was destined for (Shell149), and, like everyone else who'd signed in before me, I checked the Yes box beneath the question: "Have you flown in a helicopter before?"

Unlike an airport, the heliport didn't have regularly scheduled flights. It operated more like a taxi service, taking passengers as they checked in. So I hadn't missed my flight after all.

Outside I thanked Cheryl for the ride.

"I don't want to see you for two weeks!" she said before driving off.

Because I was the only one headed for Shell149, and was nothing but a lowly galley hand, there was no rush to fly me out. So I did my waiting in the waiting room by pacing around. Some guys waited by sleeping in chairs; others slept on the floor. Out on the balcony, guys watched helicopters come and go. Every five or ten minutes, a helicopter would land and a couple guys would hop out, a couple others would hop in, and away the helicopter would go again. Everyone looked so suave, dashing in and out of the helicopters. It was as if they all possessed some inside knowledge about flying in copters—knowledge I didn't have.

I marched straight back to the counter, grabbed the clipboard and changed my answer. No, I told the guy, I'd never flown in a helicopter.

"What happens now?" I asked.

He didn't know. He conferred with the other two behind

the counter. They weren't sure either. As far as they knew, I was the first person who'd ever answered no to a question that was a mere formality. They discussed the issue among themselves and then led me into a back room. I sat on a couch while one of them put on a safety video and another made popcorn for me. As I watched the presentation—which focused largely on what to do if the helicopter plunged into the sea—the heliport employees looked on and added comments like "That's news to me" and "I never heard that one before."

The warning about not chopping off one's face by stepping into the helicopter's tail rotary wing made a strong impression on me. So did the warning that I should expect to vomit. I hadn't even considered vomiting. So, for the next few hours, my pacing around the heliport now included worrying about puking in the helicopter.

After four hours of watching everyone else come and go via the blue morning sky, I finally heard my name called. When I ran out to the helicopter, I gave a wide berth to the tail rotary wing. I tossed in my duffel bag and hopped in the copilot's seat. I strapped myself in, put on the radio headset the pilot handed me—and was still scouting for a good place to vomit when the pilot asked, "All set?"

With control panels on all sides of me, the only reasonable place to upchuck was between my legs, onto the windowed floor of the bulbous front end of the helicopter.

"All set," I said.

The engine revved and the blades whirled. My gut tightened and I spread my legs wide in preparation for vomit. As we lifted off, I watched the ground drop from beneath my feet. The sensation was so much more surreal than nauseating that I didn't shower the floor with partially digested popcorn after all.

•

We flew over the heliport, over the bayou and out over the
Gulf of Mexico. We cruised for twenty minutes before the oil
rigs came into view along the horizon. As we approached the
rigs, I studied them intently, wondering which would serve
as my survival camp for the next two weeks.

We passed one platform after another until a colossus
came into view.

Oh, no, I thought. Let it be *any* of them but *that* one!

On a structure so mammoth, hundreds of rig hands would
need to be fed. They'd run me ragged at the sinks. It'd be hell.
I tried to psychokinetically veer us toward any of the other
rigs, but it didn't help. We made a beeline for the big rig.

As we got closer, I could see why this rig made a great impression. While the others were single platforms, this rig
consisted of three platforms connected together.

The helicopter landed on the roof of the tallest building of
the middle platform.

"So where can I find the galley?" I asked the pilot.

"Go down the stairs and someone will show you," he
said.

I took off my headset, put on my hard hat and safety
glasses, grabbed my duffel bag and hopped out. Reluctant to
break my link with the outside world—with freedom—I held
the door open.

"So . . . where'd you say that galley was?!" I shouted over
the roar of the whirling blades.

"Just go down those stairs!" the pilot shouted back. "*Now,
shut the door!*"

I shut the door, ran across the roof and down a few stairs.

Then I stopped. But right as I was considering running
back up to the roof, the helicopter revved up and took off.

My link with freedom was broken. The Fundamental Rule was broken. There was nothing to do but face the consequences.

Down the stairs, I popped my head through an open door and asked a guy which way to the galley. Go this way and that, he said, down these stairs and those.

"Can't miss it."

I followed his directions and found myself out in the middle of the platform, surrounded by cargo containers and huge pipes and assorted industrial junk.

"You passed it," a voice said. "The door's back that way."

A man in a porthole of one of the cargo containers pointed back the way I'd come. So I searched, but couldn't find a door. Were these asswipes sending the tenderfoot all over the damn rig as a gag? I cursed myself for having let the helicopter leave without me. Then I noticed a handwritten sign scrawled on a piece of cardboard.

KEEP OUT!
THIS MEANS YOU!
WET FLOOR!
—Redneck

The sign hung from what I realized was a door handle. I tugged and pulled and turned the handle every which way but couldn't get the stinking door to budge. I was too green to even unlock a simple latch. Then, almost magically, the door popped open from the inside. In front of me stood the guy I'd seen through the window.

"Fuck it, son!" he said. "Don't just stand there playing with yerself. *Come on in!*"

He introduced himself as Redneck, the galley steward, my boss.

I stepped inside and asked him where the galley was.

"Man, yer standing in the motherfuckin' galley!" he scoffed.

He had to be putting me on. Even though there was a tiny kitchen, the whole space was barely large enough to be considered a small break room.

"Where's everybody eat then?" I asked.

"Right fuckin' there!" Redneck said, kicking one of the two benches that faced a counter along one wall.

Of course, a hundred employees couldn't fit on those two benches. But since he obviously figured the newcomer was gullible, I played along.

"Yeah, okay," I said.

Acting as the official welcoming committee, the rig clerk arrived right behind me. He instructed me on what to do in case of an emergency.

"If there's an explosion," he said, "run to whichever platform isn't burning."

Explosions? Burning platforms? The company rep hadn't warned me about any such calamities.

After the rig clerk's brief speech, he handed me a sheet of paper and told me to sign it. A single paragraph stated that the signer knew how to swim and that the company was not responsible if the signer drowned. I read the paragraph several times as the pen remained poised in my hand.

"What's wrong, can't you read?" the rig clerk said. "Just sign it."

I looked at him and said, "No one told me I needed to know how to swim to be able to work out here."

The clerk and Redneck exchanged looks. I got the impression that the clerk wasn't about to show me an instructional video on how to swim; he was different from the nice fellas at the heliport. So I went ahead and signed the paper.

Redneck (he insisted on the name) then introduced me to the other galley hand, who was busy mopping the kitchen.

"Cuz," Redneck said, "show your partner to his new home-away-from-home."

Though working this job meant breaking many of my rules, it didn't break them all. The rule about working a short distance from where I slept held true here. Cuz led me about thirty paces across the platform to another cargo container—our quarters.

Sandwiched inside were two sets of bunk beds, four lockers and a bathroom. I put my duffel bag in the lone empty locker, threw my jacket on the bed beside it and asked, "So Cuz, how long you been a galley hand?"

Before he could answer, a voice from the bunk below mine screamed, *"Get the hell outta here!"*

We scrambled for the door.

"And turn out the damn light!"

Outside, Cuz said, "You just met Cookie, the night cook."

Back in the galley, Redneck doled out the job assignments.

"Pete, you're gonna be in the galley with me, working the dishes," he said. "Cuz, you're the BR."

"What's the BR?" I asked.

"The BR's the bedroom hand," Redneck said. "He's the motherfucker that makes all the fuckin' beds and cleans the fuckin' bathrooms—does all that housekeeping bullshit."

Making beds? Wait a second! There'd been a fifty-fifty

chance that I could've gone through all that trouble, traveled all that way and broken the Fundamental Rule just to end up *making beds*?! Shuddering at the thought of how close I'd come to failing to rack up Louisiana yet again, I praised my good fortune.

My job instructions from Redneck were simple: "As long as you keep them fuckin' dishes clean, there ain't a mother-fucker on this rig who can give you shit."

Kinder words I'd never heard.

After a brief tour of the little bitty kitchen, Redneck showed me my sinks. I stepped up and assumed my preferred dishing stance, legs spread wide like Sonny had taught me. Looking straight ahead, I saw heaven. Above the sinks, right at eye level, was a porthole that looked out at the Gulf of Mexico's endless expanse. Though there wasn't much to look at—a whole lot of sea, a whole lot of sky and dozens of rigs off in the distance—the small window already put me at ease.

My gaze out the porthole was broken by Redneck's saying, "Eh, Pardner . . . eh, Pardner."

I didn't recognize my new nickname.

"Eh, Pardner," he said, "you don't fuckin' cuss much, do ya?"

"No," I answered. "Not really."

"Well, fuck it," he said. "I'll have to motherfuckin' cuss for the both of us then."

And he did.

Then it was time for lunch.

I expected the cramped, two-bit galley to be mobbed, like the mess hall in Alaska had been, when the mealtime horn would blow and four hundred fishermen and cannery workers would storm in. Here, though, there was never any rush.

Redneck explained that despite the three platforms' being attached, the crew was actually pretty small. The middle platform—where the galley was—stood over a drilled well that was pumping oil back to the mainland. Most of the crew worked in alternating twelve-hour shifts drilling a well under the platform to the south of us. The northern platform was still being built, though only a half-dozen guys were working at it. Altogether, there were about thirty people to be fed. Because their meal times were staggered, never more than five or six workers were in the galley at any given time. This meant there was always something for me to wash but never a hurry for me to wash it.

At lunch that day, nearly all the rig hands spoke with Cajun accents. Occasionally, they lapsed into French, which made it difficult for me to follow the conversation. One topic I could make out was whether the Company Man—the rig's head honcho—had stopped at the bordello on his way to the rig earlier that morning. Conventional wisdom held that when the Company Man visited the bordello on his way off-shore, he was tolerable. When he didn't, he was an ass.

When the Company Man finally came in for his lunch, Redneck wasted no time asking, "How was the cathouse?"

The others paused from their meals to hear the Company Man's answer.

"Aw," he grumbled, "I didn't have time to mess around with that this morning."

An uneasy silence hovered in the galley. Then one of the rig hands started telling a joke about Pierre and Clotilde that soon slipped into French.

●

During lunch, a grinning rig hand approached this *plongeur* and asked, "How's it going, brah?!"

"Okay." I shrugged and then resumed washing the dishes and looking out the porthole. He stood there for a moment as if waiting for something, then grew irritated and stomped away.

"What's that quiet-ass motherfucker's problem, Redneck?" he asked.

"He likes looking out that fuckin' window," Redneck told him. "What can I say?"

I didn't understand. I was keeping the dishes clean, just as Redneck had instructed. Otherwise, all I did was look out the porthole and mind my own business. Why would anyone have a problem with that?

Over the next couple of days—and after several similar encounters—I finally realized what my job entailed. After gritty shifts of roustabouting and roughnecking, the rig hands expected the galley hand to act like a court jester and provide comic relief. They wanted to be greeted in the galley by a witty remark or a joke, maybe even a song and dance.

What they got instead was me washing dishes and staring at the sea. Well, that was their tough luck. If I'd wanted a job shucking and jiving for diners, I would've become a waiter long before. My mission was to dish—and dish I did.

When I was done with that first day's lunch dishes, I swept and mopped the galley, tossed the garbage in the massive hydraulic trash compactor and fed the contents of the slop bucket to the Billy Goat—an industrial-sized disposal that ground up the organic trash and spat it into the Gulf.

Because the crew was so small, there wasn't much BR work for Cuz to do. So that afternoon, like every afternoon that followed, Cuz stopped by and we peeled the mountains of shrimp that were prepared for every meal.

When I asked why he was working as a galley hand, Cuz said that after three years in prison for drug trafficking, with no other job opportunities upon his release, it'd been his parole officer's suggestion. There were so many other parolee galley hands, Cuz said, it was widely assumed that parole officers received kickbacks for providing the company with fresh recruits. This new information answered my question about who braved the isolation and crummy pay to galley-hand on the Gulf. But at the same time, it raised a new question.

"What are you doing here?" I asked. "You should be out having fun, enjoying your freedom."

"Aw, it's no big thing," he said. "Besides, being out here keeps me outta trouble."

Naively, I assumed "trouble" meant returning to a life on the streets, running with a gang and selling drugs. I'd come to learn it really meant juggling six different girlfriends and fiancées, each of whom believed she was his one and only.

My seven a.m. to seven p.m. shift ended just as Cookie's began. When he appeared in the galley, I apologized for having disturbed his sleep earlier.

"This your first day on a rig?" he asked.

"Yeah," I said.

"Well, the first day is the worst and all the rest are just the same."

The next morning, during breakfast, some of the Cajun crew members teased Redneck by claiming *they* were rednecks, not him.

"*You* ain't fuckin' rednecks," he protested. "Y'all's just a buncha Cajun coon-asses!"

In the middle of all the bickering, Cuz stepped into the galley and listened for a minute. Then, in all sincerity, Cuz— a black man—asked Redneck, "What is a redneck anyway?"

Redneck exploded. "*I'm the only real fuckin' redneck on this whole motherfuckin' rig!!*"

Redneck was always moving and always talking. As he cooked, he paced frantically and babbled constantly. His nervous energy was attributed by everyone (himself included) to the seven years he said he spent as a CIA mercenary in Southeast Asia during the Vietnam War.

He grew especially agitated when he and I were alone in the galley and I stood staring out my porthole.

"Goddamn, Pardner, say fuckin' *something*!"

If I had nothing to say, I'd usually just curse for his amusement.

"Fuck it," I'd say.

"You got that right, Pardner—fuck it." He'd laugh. Then, after further contemplation, he might add, "*Mother*fuck it."

When Cuz was around, he and Redneck would discuss one of their favorite topics: ways to kill a man. Between Redneck's experiences in Southeast Asia and Cuz's experiences in street gangs and prison, they had no shortage of anecdotes and tips to exchange. Another of Redneck's favorite topics for discussion was sex with farm animals. Raised on a farm in the South, he was quite knowledgeable about the subject. And Redneck wasn't shy about sharing this information.

Sometimes, when I interrupted my daydreaming at the

window, it was hard to decipher exactly which of his favorite topics Redneck was discussing.

"You just sneak up behind 'im and get your arms around his fuckin' neck like that and that fucker's all yours. . . ."

For hours on end, I stood at the sinks and stared at the dozens of oil rigs scattered across the watery plain. I wondered if the galley hands on those platforms—no larger than a dot in the far distance—were staring out their portholes back at my rig, which, to them, was also nothing more than a dot in the distance.

A hundred feet below my porthole, the water sloshed up, down, back and forth as a parade of porpoises, fish, seaweed, stingrays, driftwood and jellyfish swam and floated by. Sea birds soared past on a fixed course to some unseen destination beyond the horizon.

My porthole was my salvation. When Woody Guthrie worked as a dishwasher on merchant marine ships transporting troops to Europe during World War II, he once wrote about his view from the ship at anchor off the coast of Sicily: "I get to see lots of pretty hills and scenery out of my porthole while I'm washing my dishes. The good part of it is that the ship keeps swinging around on its anchor chain and the mountains and hills and the beach and the shore line are always changing." Though my view never changed and offered nothing as exciting as hills or beaches, I cherished my view as much as Woody had his.

Whenever I felt anxious or considered leaving, I'd have Cuz tell me tales of rigs where he'd previously galley-handed. On some rigs, the crews numbered over a hundred roughnecks and roustabouts. That meant a twelve-hour shift in the galley was spent washing dishes for twelve straight hours.

Cuz never had a free moment to stare out any portholes or to sit around and chat. His horror stories served as the perfect pep talks to discourage quitting.

Another lifesaver was my evening stroll. Though I'd initially feared the three-platform colossus, the fact that the platforms were connected was a blessing. It gave me the opportunity to wander, something a single-platform rig couldn't provide. From the middle platform to the northern one, the bridge spanned precisely 320 paces, or about one-sixth of a mile. Every evening, like a caged rat, I paced several miles as the sun set over the Gulf.

Another source of entertainment was playing with the hot-tub-sized hydraulic trash compactor. I'd toss cans of soda or a bucket or whatever happened to be lying around into the compactor to be squished. I'd wait eagerly for the giant metal plunger to slowly rise to reveal a new mangled mosaic at the bottom.

Or I'd feed the Billy Goat, which, by chewing slop and spewing it into the water, was actually feeding the marine life in the Gulf. Some folks feed squirrels and pigeons in the park for kicks. Me, I fed ground-up chicken bones and half-eaten steaks to the fish in the Gulf of Mexico.

The Billy Goat got more than just slop-bucket leftovers. I also fed it plenty of edibles that hadn't yet been cooked or served. Every other day, the rig's crane plucked a big metal box of groceries off a supply boat and set it down on the platform beside the galley for me and Cuz to unload. Because the galley only had one tiny pantry, one freezer and two refrigerators, our challenge was to find room for all the incoming food. Redneck's solution was to have us feed the "old" food from a couple days before—Tater Tots, breakfast cereal and whatnot—to the Billy Goat and the happy fishies.

"Fuck it," he often said. "It's free."

This opinion wasn't shared by the Company Man. Whenever Redneck submitted his grocery list to the Company Man, the latter would randomly veto items he felt were nonessential. Redneck was then left frustrated when the expected food items never arrived.

To outfox the Company Man, one day Redneck ordered a half-gallon of all nineteen available flavors of ice cream. When the Company Man inspected the grocery order, Redneck reasoned the ice cream would work as a decoy. The Company Man would veto the ice cream and leave the rest of the order intact. I told Redneck his plan was brilliant.

But we gave the Company Man too much credit. When the groceries arrived the next day, all nineteen cartons of ice cream had survived the veto, but the three sacks of flour Cookie needed for baking hadn't. I, for one, was thrilled about the Company Man's screwup, but we didn't have the freezer space for all that ice cream.

"Aw, fuck it," Redneck said. "Throw all that shit away. It's free anyway."

Throw it away? Was he crazy?! Yeah, okay, he was crazy. But still there was no way *I* was throwing away perfectly good ice cream!

While Cuz handled the rest of the groceries, I raced to make freezer space for the ice cream before it could melt in the 95-degree heat. I shuffled stuff from the freezer to the fridges, stuff from the fridges to the pantry and yet more stuff from all three places to the Billy Goat. By the time I'd made room for all nineteen cartons, I had shoved so much food into the Billy Goat, the fishies were wiggling with glee.

My relief was short-lived. In two days, another shipment of groceries would arrive and force out the ice cream. Though I could put away a lot of the stuff, eating nineteen half-gallons of ice cream in two days was out of my league. So I spread the word by listing all available ice cream flavors to everyone who entered the galley. Redneck was pleased with my sudden improvement in "customer relations." And I was proud that, despite my affinity for the Billy Goat and the fishies, they never got a single drop of ice cream.

On the morning of the eleventh day, the Company Man stood by the sinks and watched me scrub the breakfast pots.

"I'm hot on washing dishes," he said to me, "as long as I have me some gloves."

A dishwasher afraid of water, I thought, is like a lifeguard afraid of water: useless. But I said nothing.

He turned around and watched Redneck bounce around the kitchen in his hyperjerky, talking-to-himself mode.

"You know why Redneck is goofy like that, don't you?" the Company Man asked me. "It's from killing all those Vietnamese."

"Cambodians," I corrected him.

"What?"

I turned to him and said, "Redneck says it was Cambodians he killed."

"Vietnamese . . . Cambodians . . . What's the difference?" the Company Man said. "They's all gooks, ain't they?"

The sea hadn't been gazed at in a good thirty seconds, so I turned back to my porthole and the pots.

"Hey, Redneck, I sure miss the old days," the Company Man said as he eyed me. "Ninety percent of these pussies on the rigs nowadays couldn't have hacked it twenty years ago."

Pretty macho talk for the ruffian who couldn't even dish without gloves. *Ha!*

The Company Man was the ruler of his own little sea kingdom. He relished his complete authority over everyone on the rig. The rigid pecking order of the rig's hierarchy made everyone strive toward someday being the bigwig who pushed everyone else around—to be the Company Man. When he entered the galley, guys scurried to make room for him at the counter, Redneck waited on him hand and foot and everyone else humored him.

But the second the Company Man stepped out of the galley, he was the butt of all the jokes.

"That pea-brained porker couldn't run a treadmill, let alone an oil rig!"

I failed to understand what was so enviable about having a position that a pack of phonies sucked up to. Dishwashing suited me because nice people were nice to me and assholes were assholes to me, yet no one ever sucked up to me. Usually, just as I liked it, I was ignored. Well, most of the time.

When I arrived in the galley one morning, I found everyone in a somber mood. As the rig hands ate breakfast in silence, Redneck told me that the drilling crew's night shift had screwed up and broken the drill bit in the well thousands of feet below the sea floor. When the Company Man arrived for breakfast, there was tension in the air. The crew sheepishly slipped out of the galley. The Company Man sat alone, ate alone and seethed. Even the ever-chatty Redneck was scared to utter a word to him.

An hour later, the Company Man erupted. On the southern platform, he chewed out the rig's number two man, the

Tool Pusher. News of this outburst had just reached the galley when in walked the Tool Pusher himself. Redneck's attempt to placate the guy by doting on him only backfired. The irritated Tool Pusher complained about the food and questioned Redneck's sanity.

"And your stupid fucking galley hands," he yelled. "Cuz and that bald-ass motherfucker—they're always tying up the fucking phone!"

After the Tool Pusher left, Redneck started in on me and Cuz. He claimed we were useless, and that we did nothing but sit around.

"And the two of you aren't allowed to use that fuckin' phone anymore!"

I looked out my porthole and chuckled. A multibillion-dollar, multinational corporation's multimillion-dollar oil rig was on the blink and the two who washed the dishes and scrubbed the toilets for minimum wage were bearing the brunt of the backlash.

I didn't take Redneck's scolding personally or even seriously. Useless? I kept the dishes clean. And the nonsense with the telephone? That was Cuz's department.

Several of his six girlfriends and fiancées had been hearing rumors of his having other one-and-onlys. To keep up his intricate charade, he'd been on the phone refuting accusations and professing faithfulness. He then began telling five of the women that he had only one day off the rig. When he was back in New Orleans, he'd spend a half or a full day with each of the five women. Then he'd take the sixth woman—the gal he liked the most, a prison guard he met while locked up—to Las Vegas and marry her. Afterwards, he'd rush back to Louisiana and the security of the oil rig—and all the women would be none the wiser.

Cuz thought his plan was foolproof. I thought otherwise.

Cookie thought the scheme was so harebrained, he forbade us from discussing it in his presence.

"You'll learn your lesson," Cookie told Cuz, "when one of those women sticks a knife in you."

Cuz and I were both so gung ho to go, we counted down the days together. Three days and a wake-up. Two days and a wake-up. One day and a wake-up. Finally, the last morning, we just had to wake up and jump on the helicopter.

But first, I had to retrieve my box of goodies from the pantry. For two weeks I'd been collecting a variety of Cajun and Creole bottled hot sauces, spices, mixes, canned foods, etc. to ship ahead to the fishing boat in Alaska. I slipped unnoticed from the galley with my box of illicit stash. But when I entered the bunkroom, there stood Redneck. A couple of awkward seconds passed as I wondered how to explain the box in my hands. Then I noticed all the food items and toiletries (even a roll of toilet paper) that Redneck was in the middle of stuffing into his bags.

"Fuck it," he said. "It's free."

He was the boss, so who was I to argue? I crammed my loot into my duffel bag. Failing the Clinton-clone's honesty exam hadn't been a fluke after all!

When I heard the helicopter approach, I grabbed my bag and ran across the platform, only to find a line of rig hands winding down the stairs from the landing pad. It was bad enough not making it onto that first of two flights, but worse was the news brought by the relief steward: he'd seen no relief galley hands at the heliport. If my relief was a no-show—which was highly probable, considering the high turnover rate—then I was expected to remain on the rig until a replacement arrived. That could take the dreaded "day or two."

I'd attempted to survive a two-week stint at sea—and I'd done so admirably. But my sanity had been budgeted to the last second. If I had to stay any longer than originally planned, I'd crack. I had to be on that last flight.

The wait for the helicopter's return was agonizing. Cuz paced in the galley while I, through the porthole, searched the heavens for any sign of the helicopter. Finally, a speck crossed the sky.

"Here comes the bird!" I yelled.

We ran outside and charged up the stairs. The wind kicked up and the roar grew louder as the helicopter landed. Cuz eyed each of the arriving crew as they passed us on the stairs.

"None of them's a galley hand," he moped. "Guess we should stay and wait for our replacements."

He turned to descend the stairs.

"Are you nuts?!" I shouted.

Though Cuz was taller and heavier than me, I managed to push him up the stairs. At the top, he finally stopped resisting. We dashed across the roof and boarded the helicopter.

Terrified that the relief steward would shoot up the stairs and try to prevent Cuz and me from leaving, I strapped myself in and repeated under my breath, "Let's go. Let's go. Let's go."

The copter revved up and we lifted off. Overcome with so much relief, I hadn't realized how tense I'd grown over those last few days until I was in the air. Over my shoulder, I watched our rig shrink until it was one among dozens of dots across the stretch of sea.

At the heliport, I let the others exit before me. Then I stepped out, knelt down and kissed the concrete. Cuz saw me and laughed.

"It's all right, dude," he said. "I know how it is."

Cuz gave me a lift back to New Orleans. When he dropped me off at Cheryl's house, I told him, "Good luck with all those ladies."

"It don't have nothin' to do with luck," he said and then drove off.

Since Cheryl's door was locked, I checked the mailbox for the key. Instead, I found my paycheck, paid in full.

I sat down on the steps. Despite being locked out, I felt pretty good. I'd made Louisiana #20, proved I could survive breaking the Fundamental Rule and now had enough money to reach Alaska. I felt *so* good that I even toyed with the idea of doing another stint on an oil rig. A few days later, the dispatchers began calling Cheryl's and Tanio's houses looking for me again. But by then, I'd already left town.

Months later, the company sent me a "safety check"—a $100 bonus—because no one died during my tenure on the rig. For the first time ever, I felt an employer truly appreciated my zeal in killing those damn germs.

20
Pearl Divers
Who Passed Before

The Alaskan fishing boat plan didn't pan out. Lara's fishing season ended prematurely when she suffered a hernia. So instead, we met in New York, where I had an apartment-sitting gig for a few weeks. Later, she went with me to Philadelphia, where I housesat for another few weeks. Then, in Pittsburgh, after I dropped my dish job in the cafeteria at a women's college (Pennsylvania: #21), she began inquiring about when I'd be leaving town and where I'd be going to.

I didn't know yet—and it frustrated her that I didn't know. Letters with offers of couches and floors had recently come in from Indiana, North Carolina and Maryland. And now that I'd successfully broken the Fundamental Rule, I was keen to dish on a riverboat or a cruise ship. I'd even picked up an application for a dish position with Amtrak.

Just as I never knew when the urge to quit a job would strike, I never knew when I'd wake up and think, I gotta leave this town pronto. Or when someone in town would say, "Hey, I'm driving to another state, you wanna tag along?" Or, better yet, when an invitation would come from far out of left field, like the one Lara herself had given me at the Seattle airport when she asked me to fly to Alaska with her.

So even if I gave Lara a date of departure or named a destination, there was no guarantee that the plan would be carried out. So every time she asked, I continued to answer, "I don't know yet."

Then one day, while she was washing our hosts' dishes, she happened to inquire one more time. Hearing my standard answer—yet again—made her furious. She took the soapy mason jar she was washing and chucked it at me. It whizzed past my head and shattered against the wall.

When she dumped me not long afterwards, I was glad to regain the freedom to whimsically make and change my plans. But I was still slow to understand why any woman wouldn't want to have a relationship with me.

My dad, on the other hand, had grown to become a Dishwasher Pete fan. He was now telling me tales of how, when asked at family functions about my whereabouts, he took pleasure in saying, "I don't know. He was in Kentucky or Georgia or somewhere." Then, turning to my mom, he'd ask, somewhat proudly, "Sally, where's Pete now?"

After all my hemming and hawing in Pittsburgh, I ended up next in Madison, Wisconsin. Not only was a couch waiting for me, but there was a job in that town at the very top of my To Do list. Of the thousands of letters I'd received from dish dogs writing to tell me about dish gigs past and present, there were more testimonials about a certain Madison dish-pit than about any other place. Though each of the letter-writing alumni had dished there at different periods, they all described the job similarly—a loose atmosphere (boom box blaring, beer drinking, pot smoking) and a tight camaraderie (an ad hoc labor union that the dishwashers were somehow involved with).

The famous dishroom was part of the immense student union on the University of Wisconsin campus. This pit had become, in my eyes, so mythical that I was surprised when I arrived at the building's personnel office. Not only were they hiring, but there were heaps of openings for dishwashers.

After I sat and filled out an application—which included signing up as a member of the renowned Memorial Union Labor Organization—I endured an obligatory interview.

"Why do you want to work here?" the personnel lady asked.

I wanted to reply that I wanted to work in America's most illustrious dishroom while adding Wisconsin (#22) to my scalps.

Instead, I played it cool and said, "'Cause I need a job."

"And what days can you work?"

"Any day is fine," I said.

"Fantastic," she said. "Because we can use you *every* day."

Three minutes later, I exited the building with my sched-ule in hand, still surprised, but delighted, to have so easily landed what I'd been led to believe was a choice job.

The next morning, I descended the stairs from the Lakeview Cafeteria into the basement of the Memorial Union. When I found the kitchen supervisor, she led me to the dishpit, where I expected to be greeted with open arms by my comrades.

Instead, when we stepped through the doorway, I was greeted only by a wretched stench.

"You'll have to excuse that smell," she said. "The food in some of these pans is starting to rot."

It reeked like a puddle of dumpster juice on a 100-degree day.

Parked throughout the vast dishroom were dozens of wheeled racks that, collectively, held hundreds of soiled hotel pans and sheet pans. Counters and sinks were overrun with dirty pots. Filthy plates were in abundance.

"Some of this stuff has been sitting here three days waiting to be washed," she said.

"*Wow!*" I let slip.

Though I'd seen my share of dishpit disasters in the past, this, by far, was the worst. As awestruck as I was to see the mess, even more awesome was knowing that it needed cleaning.

Then I noticed no comrades were in sight.

"Where is everyone?" I asked.

"A lot of people quit recently," she said.

I couldn't possibly be the only pearl diver responsible for this catastrophe. I looked all around the dishroom, but the only sign of human life was the back of the kitchen supervisor as she exited the pit.

On my own, with no clue of where to begin, I held my nose and toured the room. There was a long conveyor dishmachine, a pot-washing machine, a silverware-washing machine and various sinks. Much of the floor space was devoted to the dozens of racks which, upon closer inspection, showed that I wasn't the only visible living organism.

This was hardly the suds buster's Valhalla described in the letters I'd received.

Feeling like I'd been purposefully duped, I expected the

letter writers to jump out from behind the racks and yell, "Gotcha!"

A cook then wheeled in yet another rack of dirty serving pans.

"Here ya go," he said, and pushed it over to me.

A quick survey of this newest arrival revealed a hotel pan that was a quarter full with scrambled eggs and another that contained bacon dregs. Since no one had yet told me what to do, I washed a fork and helped myself to breakfast.

A minute later, a guy walked in and started loading the conveyor machine. I went over, introduced myself and asked, "So what should I do?"

"I don't know," he said and shrugged.

"Oh," I said. "I thought maybe there was some sorta system."

"I've only been here three days," he said, "and I don't know nothin' 'bout a system."

"Well, is there something that maybe needs to be done first?"

"Do whatever you want, man," he said. "It don't matter to me."

I walked over to one of the pot sinks and started draining the cold, grungy water. While I was arranging the dozens of pots, another guy entered. He introduced himself as Matt and said the other disher's name was Joe.

"Whew!" I said, waving my hand before my nose to state the obvious.

"Stinks, huh?"

"Yeah," I said. "I can't believe some of this stuff has been sitting here for three days."

"*Three days?!*" he scoffed. "I'd say it's more like a week."

"Is it always like this?" I asked.

"Nah, a buncha people just quit," he said. "And now they can't find anyone else to work down here."

Except for a sap like me, I thought, who'd traveled hundreds of miles for the job.

"Normally, seven or eight people work the breakfast shift," Matt said. "And there's what—three of us?"

Working the skeleton crew in a smelly dungeon was definitely not the reason why this place had topped my To Do list.

When the sink was full with hot, soapy water, I started attacking the pots. My heroic effort lasted less than half an hour before Matt came over and said, "Dude, mellow out."

He pointed out that even with a full staff, we'd just keep pace with what was coming in. So with only three people on the job, we were going to fall behind regardless of whether we worked hard or not.

"Besides," he said, "what are they gonna do? Fire us?"

This dishman made my kind of sense. I left the pots and helped myself to some more scrambled eggs.

Matt explained that, while we did wash the plates from the cafeteria upstairs, we were expected to also wash stuff generated from the adjoining kitchen. That's where most of this came from. Next door they cooked for cafeterias in dorms and buildings all over campus. After the food was trucked over to those places, all the dirty serving trays and hotel pans—complete with leftovers—were returned to our pit.

After my shift, in the afternoon, I tracked down the office of the Memorial Union Labor Organization (MULO)—the union I'd heard so much about and that now included me as a dues-paying member. The office turned out to be only a desk in the corner of the Teaching Assistants' Association office. No one from MULO was there, so I left a note saying I'd like to talk to someone about the organization's history. When I told one of the TAs in the room that I was interested in learning about MULO, he showed me decades' worth of MULO newsletters and welcomed me to borrow them.

For the next few days, I dished mornings and read the newsletters during the evenings. Despite the gigantic amount of cookware and dishes that needed to be cleaned, it may have been the least stressful job I'd ever had. Since no one expected us to clean everything, Matt and Joe and I could work as slowly as we wanted. And whenever another rack of hotel pans was rolled in, we'd break from whatever work we were slowly doing, grab our forks and pore over whatever still-warm breakfast items were on our menu. It was the best Bus Tub Buffet I'd ever attended.

Still, where was all the camaraderie I was reading about in the newsletters? In the 1980s, almost every president and vice president of the four hundred–strong labor organization came from among the dishroom workers despite the dishers' making up less than 5 percent of the total membership. In that decade, the dishwashers challenged groups of other workers to games of softball and soccer. They even walked off the job once to protest the asbestos-covered pipes right outside the pit.

Reading about the past made me nostalgic for the dish-pits of yore. I missed the glory days, even if I'd never experienced them in the first place.

Going back even further through the newsletters, I discovered that the dishwashers *had been* instrumental in the union's founding! In fact, the group's very first president came from the pit. And it was a key, radical act by a dozen or so dish dogs that galvanized support for the fledgling organization.

On Thursday, March 9, 1972, dishwasher/budding-labor-activist Elaine Koplow stopped by the dishpit and found the crew shorthanded. To help out, she clocked in, then dove in. When the kitchen supervisor, Rose Bass, entered and saw Koplow doing some unscheduled dishing, Bass accused the dishwoman of having purposefully clocked in in order to create a disturbance. Koplow denied this. The two then exchanged heated words.

The next morning, a suit entered the dishroom and asked Koplow, "Are you Elaine?"

"Yes," she answered.

"I've heard you're a damn good little worker," he said, "and we're going to take care of you."

"Then I knew I was fucked," Koplow later recalled.

He summoned her away from the dishes for a meeting upstairs with management. There, she was falsely accused of having been loud, profane and abusive to Bass. She was also told she lacked a positive attitude. Formally, Koplow was charged with "disrupting normal work activities" and suspended from her job for ten days.

After the meeting, Koplow returned to the basement pit and reported her sentence to her fellow workers. Their response to her was automatic: "If *you're* not working, *we're* not working!"

Before departing, they posted a sign on the dishroom door.

Afternoon Shift:
Elaine was suspended.
Go to Jerry & Arlette's house.

The afternoon shift followed the morning shift's lead; later, the evening shift did the same. Nobody punched in. Nobody worked.

The entire dish staff met that evening. They agreed to remain on strike until Koplow was reinstated to her job. The dishwashers had another agenda in mind as well: to kick-start the stalled negotiations for a labor contract between MULO and the university.

After picketing for a couple days in front of the Memorial Union—carrying signs like "Your Dishes Are Washed by Scabs!"—the pearl divers then called for a boycott. Students and faculty were asked to not patronize any of the building's units. On a campus that was a hotbed of the late 1960s/early 1970s student activism, a single glance at the picket line was all that was needed to send the sympathetic longhairs in the opposite direction.

For two days, the boycott showed signs of success. Business at the Memorial Union was visibly down. Finding willing subjects to cross the picket line to work as scabs in the dishroom proved so difficult that management personnel had to be pressed into dish duty. But the schmucks couldn't hack the work. Soon, the few meals that were still being served in the Lakeside Cafeteria were being eaten from *paper plates*! All the while, the university was losing scads of income as it continued to pay cooks and cashiers to prepare and serve food that went unpurchased and uneaten.

On Thursday night, MULO held a general meeting of its members to discuss the union's official position on the wildcat strike. An overwhelming majority voted in favor of a resolution that called for the reinstatement of the dishers without any disciplinary action. They also authorized a MULO-wide strike vote.

Less than a week after a lone dishwoman was wrongly disciplined for insubordination, the university now faced losing hundreds of student-workers to the strike—an event that would certainly shut down the entire Memorial Union.

Management—who'd all but fired the dishwashers—were now eager to negotiate.

On Friday night, dishroom shop steward Bob Liek met on the Memorial Union's fourth floor with personnel director Tom Cleary. According to Liek:

> *Right outside the student union is the library mall and that was the main gathering point for the demonstrations. The anti-war people would meet there before they marched. That particular night, there was a big demonstration scheduled. As we were negotiating, there was a build-up of students in the library mall. Looking out the window, you couldn't even see the ground from the student union. People were spilling into Langdon Street and up State Street—there were thousands of people there.*
>
> *I told Cleary, "Look, I can go outside right now and talk to the demonstrators out there and in ten minutes they can come and take this building down brick by brick."*
>
> *Now, that wasn't true at all. They were out there for a demonstration against the war in Vietnam and were definitely not thinking about dishroom workers at the student union or anything like that. But in the university's paranoid crazed state at that time, that was a critical threat to them. So Cleary hopped on the phone with Chancellor Young and came back and said, "Okay, we'll meet your demands."*

Koplow and the others were then reinstated to their jobs. The wildcat strike made such a big impression on the building's other student-workers that, a month later—with negotiations on the labor contract still stalled—more than four hundred MULO members staged a general strike of the Memorial Union. That strike ended with MULO signing its first contract with the university—a labor agreement that would remain in place for decades, right up to my own stint in the dishroom. And it all came together thanks to that walkout by those dozen-odd heroic dish dogs.

One morning, when Matt had the day off and Joe failed to show, I had the pit all to myself. I loaded plates in one end of the conveyor dishmachine and then plodded thirty feet to the other end to unload them. Then I'd plod back to the front to load it again.

Whenever a rack of hotel pans was rolled into the pit, I grabbed my fork and went to see what was for breakfast. After being disappointed by vacant hotel pans each time, I told the next cook who appeared, "I hope that one's got some grub in it."

"Nope," he said. "No more leftovers."

He explained that the kitchen supervisor had ordered all leftovers to be tossed out before they reached the dishroom. The rotting food was a health hazard.

After I resumed running the dishes through the conveyor machine, another guy walked in and started unloading the dishes from the far end. We worked like this for about ten minutes before he came over and said, "I hear you've been looking for me."

"I have?"

"Yep," he said. "You left a note on the MULO desk saying you wanted to talk to the president."

"Oh yeah," I said. "I did."

"Well, I'm Benjamin," he said. "MULO president."

Since the golden days of the dishpit had long passed, I

was pleasantly stunned to learn that MULO was still headed by a dishman.

He admitted that it was a low point for both the pit and MULO.

"When I first began working down here a few years ago, it was still a happening place," he said. "Now they can't convince students to wash dishes."

As we chatted, another rack rolled in. Benjamin instinctively turned to check it for available eats. I told him about the kitchen supervisor's edict.

"She can't do that!" he said. "It's in our contract. We have a right to those leftovers!"

As soon as he said that, I recalled having read in the old MULO newsletters that the dishroom's right to leftovers had been negotiated into that very first contract between the labor organization and the university in 1972.

"The dishwashers fought for that right a quarter century ago!" I echoed.

"Well, it's still in the current contract," he said.

Ben went straight to the kitchen supervisor's office. He threatened the kitchen supervisor with filing a grievance. She folded immediately, telling him she'd reverse her decision. Within minutes of her bowing to the pressures of the labor organization's president, leftovers reappeared in the pit. Benjamin and I continued our conversation while snacking on pancakes and sausages.

If I'd felt nostalgic about yesteryear's dishroom, now I felt proud. Though the dishpit and MULO were both down on their luck, I was eating free grub, thanks to my predecessors.

When I quit, I felt obligated to honor the memory of those

pearl divers who'd passed through that pit before me. So I taped a piece of paper to the front of the Memorial Union. On it, I'd written:

**On this spot in March 1972,
fifteen dishwashers fought for workers' rights
by staging a successful wildcat strike.
And I, for one, thank them.**

21
Sure You Can Wear Pants

People asked plenty of questions about my quest. Easily the most popular question was "What will you do when it's finished?"

Settle down? If I could only find a place that would cure my wanderlust, sure, settling wouldn't be so bad.

Dish abroad? Well, because my grandparents were born in Ireland, I was eligible to become an Irish citizen, which would enable me to legally live and work in any European Union nation. So, maybe.

Canadian readers wondered if I'd go on to tackle the provinces up north. Seeing more of our northern neighbor was absolutely tempting.

Washington, D.C., readers wondered if I'd ever hit their town. Dishing at the White House sounded interesting. But since I'd failed to gain a security clearance to work as a small-town meter maid years before, the chance seemed awfully slim that I could gain access to the White House dishpit.

And many mainlanders wanted to know if, after the States, I'd then knock out the American territories, like Puerto Rico or Guam. As islands, U.S. territories posed the same problem as Hawaii: no interstate bus service. And since no one ever just happened to say, "Hey, I'm driving out to Hawaii—you wanna tag along?" I always assumed the union's fiftieth state would end up being #50 on my mission.

I pictured going there and staying with any (or all) of the four *Dishwasher* fans who'd offered me their couches and land a job at some Waikiki beachfront hotel. Then, one day, mid-shift, when the very last notion struck, I'd give the dishmachine a hearty farewell smooch and yank off my apron. Chin up, I'd march out through the front door and post a handwritten flyer on the building's façade that would read:

**In this building's dishpit,
Dishwasher Pete completed his quest
to wash dishes in all fifty states.**

Reclining on the beach, I'd open a bottle of beer and bask in the pleasure of having finally achieved my goal.

In the meantime, without much chance of just passing through, say, Guam, I gave little thought to bagging the territories. But then an invite arrived for a dish job in the Virgin Islands. The letter described the crystal-blue waters, white-sand beaches and relaxed work environment. The beachside resort gig sounded so cushy and so easygoing that I decided to give the Virgin Islands a shot.

Traveling south to Miami—my departure point to the Caribbean—the farther south I got, the hotter and wetter the air became. By the time I reached New Orleans, the heat and humidity were miserable. The day after I arrived, I went out wandering. When I returned to Cheryl's house hours later, my T-shirt and pants were drenched in sweat, my neck and arms sunburned. As I whined to Cheryl about the weather, she said, "You think it's gonna be any cooler in the Caribbean?"

As always, she had a point. My goal suddenly changed—to wear pants all summer without getting drenched.

So the Virgin Islands were scrapped and I set off for Alaska. But first, Oregon, to earn money for the trek farther north.

A couple weeks later, I sat in on a friend's community radio show. To raise money for the station's pledge drive, I made his listeners an offer: for a mere $25 pledge, I'd dish in the pledge-maker's home. Four people took up that offer.

In turn, I *received* an offer. It was from a fellow Reading Frenzy volunteer whom I'd only recently met. Amy Joy called to pledge twenty bucks for a gift certificate donated by a diner—and then she asked me to help her go spend it.

Free food? Offer accepted!

Days later, I sat in a booth opposite Amy Joy. She wore eyeglasses and her dark hair short. With flowered vines tattooed on her forearms, she looked like an equally sweet *and* dangerous librarian. In the dark and dreary diner, she shone in a bright orange flowery vintage-store dress.

She was so suspiciously dolled up, I had to wonder, Is this a date? If it was a date with me she sought, then why hadn't she just pledged five bucks more and had me come dish at her home like the clean-cut yuppie guy the night before had done?

That home-dishwashing session had ended with the dishes clean and the pledge-giver saying, "So . . ."

"So . . . what?" I asked.

"So . . . you wanna spend the night?"

Through the years, I'd had a lot of guys invite me to spend the night on their couches or floors. But apparently that wasn't the kind of sleeping arrangement this pledge-giver had in mind. What he was suggesting wasn't covered by the $25 pledge.

So I decided that if Amy Joy had wanted a date, she would've gone for the home-dishwashing angle. Then I ordered a burger and a beer and an ice cream sundae.

When she ordered a soda with her meal, I asked, "You don't wanna beer?"

"Actually," she said, blushing somewhat, "I'm not twenty-one."

Cripes! When she then said she was only nineteen, it was *my* turn to blush. How could I have suspected that this was a date? No nineteen-year-old could possibly be interested in a bald thirty-year-old fart like me.

Freed from worrying about her motives, I spent the rest of the meal stuffing myself. When I was done, I thanked her for the eats and went on my way.

While I was getting ready to leave for Alaska, my friend Poppy contacted me from California.

"Hey, I'm driving out to Maine," she said. "You wanna tag along?"

I'd already dished in Maine. Then again, I'd already dished in Alaska. Both states offered good pants-wearing weather. It was a tough call. But Maine won the tie-breaker, if only because it was a newer plan. So I ditched Alaska and I set off for Maine via California.

Auburn, California: the foothills of the Sierra Nevada mountains. While I was waiting for Poppy to get ready for the trip, spring was turning to summer. As the temperature increased, the challenge to ramble around in sweat-free pants mounted. While waiting impatiently to depart, I got a call from my friend Jon. He was working at a summer camp higher up in the Sierra Nevadas. The camp's teen disher wasn't cutting it; Jon wanted to know if I wanted the job.

"What's the climate like up there?" I asked.

"The climate?" he said. "Oh, it's warm during the day. But at night it gets kinda chilly."

"*Chilly?*" My interest piqued. "So I can wear pants up there?"

"Sure you can wear pants," he said. "You can wear whatever you want."

It was a deal. Maine was history and I set off for the camp.

Echo Lake Camp sat perched on a pine-covered ridge, seventy-three hundred feet above sea level. Jon explained that the city of Berkeley had started the camp for its residents in 1922. Now, it was a place to send the city's eight- to twelve-year-olds, to get them off the streets during the summer. Jon led me to my tent-cabin—a wooden floor and frame covered by a canvas roof and walls. I threw my duffel bag and sleeping bag on a bunk. Seeing the cabin's four beds, I was glad to hear I had it all to myself. Even more thrilling was that the cabin sat nestled on a cliff. If a rock was thrown from the porch, it wouldn't have landed till it first dropped two hundred feet. And the view was incredible. The sparkling blue waters of Lake Tahoe shone twenty miles in the distance, a thousand feet below.

Jon showed me around. It was a pretty low-budget operation. Instead of horseback riding, there was a horseshoe pit. Instead of canoeing, there was a small swimming pool. But what the camp lacked in luxury, it made up for in natural beauty.

That first night, after downing my hot-dog-and-watermelon dinner, I got started with the dishes. After the others finished their meals and exited the dining hall, one of the teen employees lingered behind. As he watched me work, he introduced himself as Robert and asked, "So how many dishes can you wash in an hour?"

"In an hour?" I said. "I have no idea."

"Oh," he said. "I thought you were supposed to be really fast or something."

"I'm not very fast," I said, being more honest than modest. "But I think I'm a pretty good dishwasher."

Robert said nothing else and left the kitchen looking dejected. Later that night, I learned why. The week before, Dan—the camp director—had been browbeating Robert. If the teen didn't shape up, Dan threatened, he'd replace him with a "top-notch professional." However, Dan knew of no such dedicated dishman. It was supposed to be just a scare tactic. But after Robert failed to be spooked into working harder, via Jon's recommendation, Dan happened to hire me. What the camp director didn't know, though, was how well he'd made good on his threat. He actually *had* hired a dishwashing mercenary.

The first few days, this mercenary had to get used to life in the mountains. In the early evening, since the tent-cabins had no electricity, I had to write letters and read in bed by flashlight. In the late evening, with the flashlight off and the front tent-flaps open, I'd lie in bed and watch the meteorites and satellites cross the black sky. Sometimes in the middle of the night, the eerie silence was disrupted by an owl hooting or a coyote howling. And in the morning, the rising sun would peek over the opposite mountaintops and shine directly in my face to wake me up.

Washing dishes in the woods proved not so different from washing dishes in a city. Rats and mice running around the kitchen were replaced by chipmunks and squirrels. Cockroaches were replaced by mosquitoes. And rather than a homeless person picking through the trash out back, there was a black bear who'd get into the dumpster and strew garbage for yours truly to clean up the next morning.

The hardest adjustment for me was being cut off from tried-and-true sidewalks lined with change. According to my detailed records, in the twelve months prior—in nineteen states—I'd found 1,362 coins and 8 bills (1,089 pennies, 79 nickels, 151 dimes, 43 quarters, 6 ones and 2 fives). I'd even arrived at the camp in the midst of a record run. Through seven states, I'd found change *forty-seven days* straight!

But on my first full day in the mountains, despite all my eagle-eyed effort while wandering the dirt paths, I spied not a single coin—not one thin dime, not one red cent. I couldn't even find a quarter-resembling squashed bottle cap to give me false hope. With one record ended, another began: number of straight days *without* finding change.

•

Though it wasn't the Virgin Islands, it was certainly the cushy, easygoing summer job I'd desired. I had my own pad, had twenty-four-hour access to free food and the weather was so crisp I wore pants not only every day, but also as I slept through each of the even chillier nights.

For years, the camp had employed teen dishers like Robert who were working their first job. Away from home for the first time, they'd dilly-dally with the dishes as they goofed off or flirted with teenage counselors of the opposite sex. Sometimes they'd rush out of the dining hall, leaving a mess behind in the dishpit. Other times they didn't show up at all for their shifts.

As the camp's first "top-notch professional," it was easy to impress the camp director. Even while working half-assed by my standards, this thirty-year-old was cleaning the dishes better and faster than any whole-assed teenager. And by doing the little things without being asked to (like picking up the mess after a visit from a bear), I wowed Dan. This made my job even cushier and easier-going because then no one ever challenged me for leaving the dining hall mid-shift. I could slip back to my tent-cabin for a nap or follow the path along the mountainside to the general store to mail letters or treat myself to ice cream cones.

Actually, postage stamps and ice cream were the only things that required my cash. I didn't even have to pay for beer. My drinks were earned via the teen counselors. A couple times a week, they'd send over to my cabin a representative with a shopping list for booze and cigarettes. My fee was a straight six-pack of beer for each booze-and-cigarettes run.

Since I was spending almost no money, I hadn't thought much about my paycheck until payday arrived and there was no check with my name on it. Despite having worked for weeks, I'd never filled out an application and thus, wasn't yet officially on the payroll. So I marched straight to the camp office to become official. Among the usual paperwork to be filled out was a pledge I'd never seen before. Its lone paragraph read:

> I, _____, *do solemnly swear (or affirm) that I will support and defend the Constitution of the United States and the Constitution of the State of California against all enemies, foreign and domestic; that I will bear true faith and allegiance to the Constitution of the United States and the Constitution of the State of California; that I take this obligation freely, without any mental reservation or purpose of evasion; and that I will faithfully discharge the duties upon which I am to enter.*

"What is this?" I asked Dan, waving the sheet at him.

"Oh, that?" he said. "That's the loyalty oath."

A *loyalty oath*? From—of all places—the city of *Berkeley*? I'd thought loyalty oaths had died out with Joe McCarthy decades earlier.

What did supporting the U.S. Constitution have to do with busting suds? If I signed it and then a camper leapt onto a dining table shouting, "Fuck the U.S. Constitution!" how was I supposed to support and defend the Constitution against domestic enemies? By running from the sinks to go smack the kid? Or was I expected to support and defend his constitutional right to free speech by protecting him from getting smacked?

It sounded like much more responsibility than I was willing to take on for a cushy, easygoing gig. Even Sidney Poitier—the actor with a storied dishwashing past—had once proclaimed, "I would far rather wash dishes . . . than sign a loyalty oath I considered repugnant." I considered this oath repugnant and—like Poitier—preferred to wash dishes than sign it. Then again, in order to wash dishes, I was *expected* to sign it.

"I'm not signing this," I told Dan.

"Why not?" he asked.

"I have a rule about signing loyalty oaths."

A minute before, I didn't. Now I did.

"What happens now?" I asked. "Am I fired?"

"I don't know," he said. "You're the first person in my eight years here who's ever refused to sign it."

Dan sent my unsigned oath and the rest of my paperwork down to Berkeley. In the meantime, I was left to hope that my lack of sworn loyalty wouldn't work against me. The goal remained: get hired officially, get a paycheck for all the weeks I'd worked, keep wearing pants.

Meanwhile, I spent a lot of time reading on my cabin porch. From there, I could just make out the casinos across the border in Stateline, Nevada. So close, yet so far away, dishes awaited in the many buffets and restaurants that littered those buildings in a state where I'd never worked before. To top it off, I could only sit and daydream about all the loose change that drunk gamblers dropped on the floors around the slot machines. (And dream I did. One night's sleeping fantasy: finding three dimes, two pennies and a nickel.) If the camp's higher-ups deemed me too un-American or too un-Californian to be officially hired, then I'd allow myself to be drawn down to the bright lights of the casinos instead.

The teenage counselors did their best to hasten my departure in the way they punished the delinquent campers. They dragged every pain-in-the-ass troublemaker into the kitchen and made them wash the dishes. The counselors assumed I'd appreciate the forced labor. I didn't. Playing detention monitor wasn't my thing. Plus, the camp hooligans only created bigger messes than they cleaned. And since the only one punished by their punishment was the dolt merely trying to do his cakewalk job, the notion to leave stirred.

Then one day I received a package containing several weeks of my post-office-box mail. Among the dozens of letters was one from Kevin in Michigan, who complained that on the first day of his latest dishwashing job—at a swanky waterfront restaurant—he was forced to work nine hours straight without a single break. Susan in Missouri wrote to update me on her latest dish gig, where a surveillance camera in the kitchen was part of an inconsistently enforced two-dollar fine policy on consuming *any* food—even the garbage off the dirty plates. And Allen wrote from a state prison in Arizona, where recently he'd been happy with having scored a dish job in the kitchen. But after he'd spent only two days in the suds, the authorities recalled that he had an attempted escape on his record. So they considered him a flight risk in the kitchen—and he was fired.

Working without breaks? Fined for Bus Tub Buffeting? And *fired in prison*?! Man, if my worst gripe was that I didn't care for the quality of the help sent my way, then I really was spoiled with a cinchy job.

So I stopped bellyaching about the delinquents. For a few days, at least. But they remained underfoot. They continued to splash water everywhere. And I still had to rewash the dishes they'd "cleaned."

Finally, I cracked. I told Dan that it was the delinquents or me. He could have one or the other in the dishpit, but not both. Not wanting to lose his hotshot, Dan relented. The kids were pulled off dish duty and I resumed dishing solo.

Apparently, my loyalty to the dishes impressed the city of Berkeley more than my disloyalty to the American and Californian Constitutions. The evidence of this came in the form of a paycheck with my name on it. Jon drove me down to a casino on the state line to cash it. My intrigue with casino dishing grew when I learned that the joints not only willingly cashed paychecks, but garnished each cashed paycheck with a *free drink*!

Now that I was getting paid, any notion to quit remained at bay and I was able to enjoy my stay. The best part of the job were the days in between sessions when the camp was free of campers. There was less work to be done. The placid setting became even more placid. And with no kids present, the facilities were for the exclusive enjoyment of the employees.

So when Dan asked me to stay on into the autumn to break down the camp and prepare it for the twenty to thirty feet of winter snow, the proposition was alluring. Not only would the campers be gone, so would everyone else. Jon and Dan and all the other employees would be back at their "real" jobs or back at college—and the whole place would be *mine*.

When that last day of camp finally arrived and everyone was leaving, no one was more excited than I was. To see them off, I took a front-row seat on a picnic table and watched with satisfaction as the kids boarded the school buses.

But as the buses drove away, I started feeling kind of funny. And, as the procession of cars full of counselors drove past, the feeling sharpened.

"Good-bye, Pete!" the counselors yelled out.

Even though I'd rarely talked to the counselors (and had trouble telling them apart from the campers), watching them depart, I grew melancholy. For some reason, I missed them already.

Sitting there, I realized that throughout my life, if leaving was to be done, then it was always *I* who did the leaving. If good-byes were to be made at a bus station, then it was always *I* who was getting on that bus. If farewells were made at a job site, then it was always *I* who was walking out that door. But now, I was the one being left behind—and I didn't like it.

Within twenty-four hours, the population of the camp plunged from one hundred to one. I had the solitude I'd desired but didn't know what to do with it.

Aimlessly, I tramped around the camp's grounds. I roamed the empty dining hall, across the empty basketball court, past the empty swimming pool to the empty cabins. I examined the interior of each cabin as if to assure myself that I really was alone. Halfway through my inspection of the forty-odd cabins, I saw a quarter and some pennies on the floor.

Ooh! It'd been so long, I almost didn't recognize the li'l fellers.

As I bent down to pick them up, I was grateful they hadn't fallen through the half-inch gaps between the floorboards. Then again, who was to say coins *hadn't* fallen through the floorboards?

I rushed outside and peered under the cabin. A dime lay on the ground. I wormed my way into the eighteen-inch-high crawl space and grabbed it. Through the cobwebs and the dirt, I found more change. Coins had been falling through these floorboards for years—decades even—without anyone ever retrieving them. There was no telling how much fake-silver and copper lay beneath the cabins.

As I eagerly plundered below one cabin after another, the feeling of melancholy slowly dissipated. An hour later, I finished quarrying, covered in dirt and cobwebs. I raced back to my cabin, spilled my bonanza across my sleeping bag and counted: 38 quarters, 49 dimes, 26 nickels and 91 pennies. In total: $16.61!

I slept well that night. But the euphoria proved temporary. Over the next few days, as I removed the canvas coverings from the cabins and broke down the bunk beds, I realized that living alone up in the mountains wasn't for me. Wandering around through the woods amidst wildflowers and wildlife was an interesting change, but I was still homesick for wandering through city streets filled with crowds of people. And with it now autumn, it was safe again to descend from the hills and wear pants anywhere in the country.

When Dan stopped by that next weekend, I proved my disloyalty—or better yet—proved my *plongeur* morality. I left him in the lurch by bailing on the camp and rambling onward.

I hitchhiked down to Reno to get myself a casino job, but flush with almost a thousand bucks I'd saved while at the camp, I had second thoughts on working just yet. Casinos were put off for the time being. The cash held me over through the fall of 1997 while I hung out in Colorado, Kansas and Wisconsin. Come winter, when the money finally did run out, I holed up at a ski resort in Vermont (#23). The spring of 1998 saw more nationwide moseying and then—amazingly—I was invited back to the camp. After another summer stint at the camp, I bused it up to Portland and slept on the floor of the Reading Frenzy office as I put together *Dishwasher* #15.

●

One day while I was in town, Amy Joy asked me to stop by Reading Frenzy at five o'clock. She said she had a present to give me for my thirty-second birthday. When I arrived, I was late. It was six o'clock—and she was sullen.

"Forget it," she grumbled.

"What? Can't you just hand me the present?" I asked.

"No," she said. "We have to go somewhere for it—and *now* it's too late."

"Nah," I said, trying to cheer *her* up about *my* birthday. "C'mon, let's go!"

After further coaxing, she relented. She blindfolded me, sat me in her car and told me I'd never guess where we were going. But with my keen mental map of the city, each time we turned, I pictured our location. Even when she circled a block or two in an apparent attempt to throw me off, I knew right where we were.

When Amy Joy finally parked, she said, "Guess where we are!"

"Mount Tabor Park!" I blurted out and lifted the eye mask.

My correct answer had apparently spoiled the surprise. She looked disappointed.

We got out of the car. Amy Joy spread a sheet on the grass and opened a bottle of red wine.

"I made these myself," she said as she handed me a large Ziploc bag of chocolate-chip cookies.

Watching her sit down on the sheet, I wondered, Is there something more to this than just a birthday present?

She patted the spot beside her and invited me to sit down.

"I thought we could sit and watch the sun set over the city," she said, pointing to the skyline before us. The view was magnificent, except that, in the distance, the last sliver of sun was now disappearing behind the West Hills.

I didn't even get a chance to sit down before a park ranger drove up.

"You have to leave," he said. The park closed at sunset.

We packed up and left. Back downtown, Amy Joy dropped me off on Oak Street. She handed me the bag of cookies and then drove off in such a hurry that I didn't get a chance to thank her for them.

But the cookies *were* delicious.

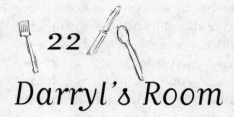

22

Darryl's Room

A week later, the call of the casino became too strong to resist. I made it to Reno, Nevada (#24), and promptly got hired at Harrah's—the large downtown casino and hotel.

When I arrived at the personnel office for my first day, a guy in a navy-blue jumpsuit walked up and asked, "You Pete?"

"Yeah," I said.

"My name's Lima," he said. "Follow me."

He led me upstairs to the employee-only cafeteria, where I sat and waited for Tony, the dishroom steward. As "If you like pina coladas" played over the cafeteria's speakers, I looked around at the dozens of other workers on their breaks. Everyone was dressed in some sort of costume, er, uniform—from the boobs-spilling-out-of-their-tops cocktail waitresses to the card dealers and housekeepers and bartenders. Their garish outfits looked as if a partially digested box of crayons had been barfed all over them.

Then I watched two dozen workers file past Tony's table. Though they represented a mix of ages, ethnicities and genders, they were all clad in the same navy-blue short-sleeve jumpsuits. Half of them were day-shift dishers signing out; the other half swing-shift dishers signing in. Maybe my aversion to uniforms actually stemmed from never having seen one that suited me. Because now, I was having second thoughts about my company-duds rule. In contrast with the other employees, the pearl divers looked so damn sharp in their outfits, I instantly thought, *I want one!*

When the crowd of dishers thinned out, Tony told Lima, "Take Pete to wardrobe and get him suited up."

Lima led me up to the wardrobe department, where I was assigned a locker and issued my very own size "large/long" dishman's jumpsuit.

That night I worked in the buffet dishroom with Lima and three others. When the buffet closed for the night, we still had a couple hours before our shift ended. While the other three drifted off to the casino's other dishpits, Lima and I were the last ones out of the buffet.

"Follow me," he said.

I followed Lima down some stairs, first to the basement and then farther down to the sub-basement. This was exciting. Before I'd even been hired, friends had told me of the mysterious tunnels beneath all the old downtown buildings. Bootleggers had used the tunnels to shuttle illicit booze to the casinos during Prohibition.

Through the dark, dank passages, we walked until we

came to a wooden door. Hand-written on it were the words: "Darryl's Room".

"This is Darryl's Room," Lima said. He opened the door. Inside the small storage room, stacks of dust-covered dishes sat on shelves.

"Who's Darryl?" I asked.

Darryl, Lima explained, was a dishwasher from years before. He often snuck away from work to nap in this storage room. One day, he failed to awaken from his nap; it was days before his lifeless body was discovered. In his honor, someone had since written on the door "Darryl's Room."

"What happened to him?" I asked.

"I don't know," Lima said.

"What, he just *napped* himself to death?"

Lima shrugged his shoulders. "No one knows."

For a few weeks, I bounced from pit to pit. Some nights I worked in the buffet, other nights in the Italian restaurant; some nights in the steakhouse, other nights in the banquet kitchen or the room-service kitchen.

No matter where I worked, I usually ended up hanging out with Lima, who, prior to his six years at Harrah's, had worked as a carpenter in his native Honduras. His annual routine was to dish in Reno for eight months and then take his savings down to Honduras to live with the wife and kids for four months.

Lima even invited me to go to Honduras with him, where, he said, with my dishwasher's earnings, I could live like a king and easily find a wife.

"Yeah, but she'd probably want me to speak Spanish."

"No, I can translate for you!" he said.

"But isn't it hot down there?"

"*Yes!*" he said. "Not like here—it's *always* hot."

Too hot, I thought.

Like me, Lima liked to wander. The rule of thumb among the swing-shift dish crew was that it was okay to disappear for a spell, as long as no one was stuck shouldering too much of a load. While most of the others used the opportunity to socialize in the other dishrooms, Lima preferred to explore the never-ending labyrinth of passageways throughout the complex. For fun, he'd lead me around until I was thoroughly confused and then ask me to guess where we were. After I'd guess, he'd reveal how wrong I was.

Other times we'd cut across the casino's large gambling floor. When we did, I'd pretend we weren't dishwashers heading from one dishroom to another. Rather, we were like the casino's Groucho Marx or Charlie Chaplin impersonators who mingled about entertaining the gamblers. Except, as two random jumpsuited guys passing in the background, we were entertainers on a subtler level—not headliners, but the necessary extras who set the scene.

On the casino floor—whether in character or not—my eyes were locked in on finding change. That a gazillion coins were in the building was made abundantly clear by the constant clattering as slot machines pissed out endless streams of coinage into the metal urinals beneath them. From those metal basins, or from the gamblers' plastic carrying cups, coins had surely fallen to the floor. But where were they? It turned out, the casino already had men on the case. Elderly Filipinos shuffled about with brooms and long-armed dustpans sweeping up stray gum wrappers, cigarette butts—and coins. What a job! They were essentially employed to find—*and pocket*—the change! But try as I might, I couldn't envy them—not in the insufferable rainbow-colored vests they had to wear.

•

One night, looking to emulate the napping martyr, I slipped out of the banquet dishpit with a couple of clean rags. Down in the sub-basement room, I arranged my rag pillow on the cold concrete floor, turned out the light and lay down on my back. From the hall, light seeped in under the door. Machinery hummed in the distance. I closed my eyes.

As I tried to get comfortable, my thoughts drifted to Darryl. How had he died? By natural causes? Had one of these shelves of dishes toppled on him? A gas leak?

My eyes were open and staring at the ceiling. Okay, I told myself, let's get serious. I rolled onto my left side and closed my eyes again and exhaled. Aah . . .

How long had he been there? Who'd found him? Where'd he been lying?

I was looking around.

On my back again; eyes closed. *Concentrate,* I commanded.

How'd Darryl managed to relax on a surface so icy? Had he constructed some sort of rag mattress? Was he able to get *any* shut-eye?

Now on my right side, I wondered if there'd *even been* a Darryl. Maybe he was merely a legend created by management to discourage dish dog napping—a morality tale to counter *plongeur* morality. If that was the case, the scare tactic worked; I couldn't sleep. But it wasn't because I was overly concerned with my own demise—but rather, because I was so preoccupied with Darryl's.

On my first payday, I was more than happy to redeem my paycheck at the casino's cashier window and receive my free drink token. Liquored up and with a pocketful of cash, I was essentially being challenged by Harrah's to get past all the slot machines and card tables without leaving behind some of my pay—if not all of it—in the casino. But it'd take more than free booze to get this cheapskate to part with any of his cash. If I gave a single nickel back to my employer, it'd essentially mean taking a cut in pay—and I'd be forced to kick my own self in the ass for being so stupid.

Instead I took my pay and skipped up the street to another casino. There, I stood by the dime slots. When a cocktail waitress would walk by, I'd drop a dime in the machine and—as a rightful gambler—give her my order for a complimentary beer. I'd keep a tight grip on my dimes until she returned with my beer. Then I'd drop another dime and immediately ask for another round.

After having worked a couple nights straight in the steakhouse pit—a solo gig that hampered my ability to wander—I was stoked to be assigned to the employee cafeteria dishroom. Not only was it the one dishpit of the casino's six that I'd yet to work in, but working with a crew of four others, I'd be able to roam around once again.

When I arrived in the cafeteria dishroom, Charlie walked up to me and said, "C'mon, I'll show you what to do."

I'd seen Charlie around but had never worked with him because he only worked this one pit.

Charlie led me over to the conveyor belt that carried the trays of dirty dishes back from the dining area. He scraped some dishes and loaded them in the dish racks.

"See how I'm doing it?"

"Yeah," I mumbled.

"*See?*" he repeated.

"Yeah," I said. "I got it."

He stepped aside. "Now *you* try."

As I scraped the dishes and loaded them in the racks, Charlie stood uncomfortably close. He continued to watch.

"*Dude*," I said, "I can handle it."

Charlie moved back a few feet. Yet he kept eyeing me.

For about thirty seconds, I scraped until Charlie said, "No, no, you can't do that."

He pointed at some chicken bones and napkins on the floor. Not all of my scrapings had found their way into the garbage can.

"It's okay," I told him. "I'll clean it up later."

"It's *not* okay," he said. "You've gotta clean that up *now!*"

In the weeks I'd been there, I'd had no problems with any of the fifteen or so other swing-shift dishers. And none of them had ever voiced any problems about me. But now, within sixty seconds of working with this sourpuss, he was breaking my balls.

But I ignored him and kept on scraping.

Charlie didn't leave.

"Listen, I'm the *head dishwasher* here," he said. "And you have to clean that up."

I stopped scraping.

Head dishwasher? Was he for real? The authoritative scowl on his face said yes.

I knew there was no way I could endure another seven hours and fifty-nine minutes working with some delusional jerk who wanted to hang a title like that on himself.

Normally, I would've then dramatically pulled off my apron and stomped away in a huff. But I wore no apron. And while pulling off my jumpsuit would've made a dramatic statement, standing there in my drawers wouldn't exactly convey the statement I was looking to make.

So instead I just said, "Fuck you."

Then I stomped away in a huff up to the wardrobe department and changed back into my street clothes.

A week later, those same street clothes became work clothes again at a Main Street café in Newton, Kansas. I was supposed to dish in a café there and stay in the apartment above with the café owner. But when the owner's boyfriend discovered that some passing-through-town dishman was to stay with his girlfriend, he raised a ruckus and nixed the plan. So instead I took up an even tastier position: dishing in Wichita, Kansas (#25), at a mom-and-pop malt shop. There, I wore my street clothes, answered to no head dishwashers and served as a willing test subject for all the soda jerk's experimental concoctions.

After I moved on from Kansas, I found two-thirds of a penny in the Oklahoma City bus station and was quite pleased with myself when, twenty minutes later, I was able to pass it along when purchasing a 49-cent Fudgsicle. Then, while house- and dog-sitting in New Orleans, I got a call from Amy Joy. She was being driven down from Missouri and the next morning would be catching a flight from New Orleans back to Portland.

"Do you think I could spend the night with you?" she asked.

"Sure," I said.

When she arrived that evening, she asked, "Can you recommend a good restaurant in the area?"

Not ever having eaten in a restaurant in New Orleans, I had to tell her, "No."

"Aw," she said. "But I wanted to go out to dinner with you."

Eat out? That afternoon I'd just spent 34 cents on a newly designed box of Schwegmann brand macaroni and cheese. My stomach was set on eating it and my heart was set on cutting out the box cover to add it, as #211, to my collection.

"I was just about to whip up some mac-n-cheese," I told her. "But we can split it if you want."

"No," she said. "I was really hoping to treat *you* to dinner—for letting me stay here."

"Oh," I said. "In that case, there's some restaurant around the corner."

We walked around the corner. It was a pizza place. Well, not really. A pizza place is somewhere where you can walk up to the counter and say, "Gimme a slice" and one gets handed to you on a paper plate. Though this place *did* sell pizzas, its toppings menu included crap like shrimp and roasted eggplant. Sitting and looking at the other diners' puny individual pizzas and seeing the listed prices, I thought, *Thirteen bucks* for one of those itsy-bitsy things?

But Amy Joy thought otherwise.

"Those look delicious," she said.

I felt bad for her spending so much money for me to eat such a paltry amount of food. So I just ordered a simple cheese pizza—hold the weirdo toppings.

Amy Joy ordered us a bottle of red wine. It was another first: I'd never before drank wine in a restaurant—at least not as a customer.

While she told me about her trip to visit her family in Mississippi and Missouri and I told her about my trials and tribulations of playing dog walker to a dog too old to even stand, I guzzled the wine like it was beer. I felt bad again when Amy Joy had to order another bottle, but not so bad that I didn't refrain from guzzling after the new bottle arrived.

When the place closed, we walked back around the corner

to the house. Amy Joy sat down on the couch and said, "Thanks again for letting me stay here."

"No problem," I said. "And thank *you* for feeding me."

The hour was late and I was tipsy. It was time for bed so I went to the bedroom. A second later, I returned to the living room, steadied my gaze on Amy Joy and said, "Sleep tight."

Then I tossed her a pillow and a blanket.

The next morning, she left for the airport. For lunch, I finally broke into my box of Schwegmann.

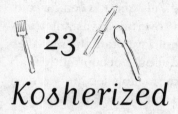

23
Kosherized

After bouncing around the South, the Midwest and the East Coast in the spring of 1999, I went to Portland to publish *Dishwasher* #16—the cafeteria issue. It was about cafeterias I'd worked in and contained news clippings about cafeteria dishers, book excerpts, some dishwashing comics and letters to the editor from fellow dish dogs about *their* cafeteria gigs.

While putting together the zine, I noticed in the want ads that a Jewish nursing home was in need of a dishman. *Aha!* Another chance to cross something off my To Do list.

The year before, I'd received a letter from a dishman who was working in a Chinese joint in Boston. He referred vaguely to special Jewish dishwashing rules and asked if I'd ever "dished kosher." Sadly, I hadn't. I was embarrassed to admit in my reply that I didn't even know what kosher dishing entailed. Even more so, I was jealous that, when it came to ancient dishwashing rites, this cat had been initiated and I—the Dish Master—*hadn't*!

The dishwashing traditions *I* was following—laziness, drunkenness and ditching jobs without even a minute's notice—were public knowledge and only about a century old. So the idea of being entrusted with covert dishwashing traditions that were *thousands* of years old was tantalizing. After reading the want ad, I broke my rule about not commuting farther than a comfortable walk or bike ride to a job and jumped on a bus out to the nursing home in southwest Portland.

I filled out the paperwork—which mentioned nothing about upholding traditions—and was sent to the kitchen to talk to Riki, the kitchen manager. While waiting for her in her office, I wondered if she'd ask me if I was Jewish or what I knew about kosher dishing. If she did ask, I'd be at a loss. I kicked myself for having hurried to the place without first stopping by the library.

When Riki arrived, she glanced at my application and said, "So Pete, tell me—what recent accomplishment have you made that you're proud of?"

"Um . . . ," I said, caught off guard by yet another idiotic question that boss-types learn in boss school. Of course, I thought it was a major accomplishment to be on the cusp of washing dishes in holy water with candles and incense and whatever other Catholic imagery from my altar boy days I could attach to my vision of kosher dishing. But maybe that'd scare her off.

"Um, I'm kinda proud that I've shaved almost every day this week," I said.

"*Terrific!*" she said. "Can you start right now?"

Without any questions about my faith, without being asked to pledge to uphold thousands of years of dishwashing tradition and without even being sworn to silence about the ancient secrets that I'd be entrusted with—I was apparently hired.

Riki handed me an apron and led me over to the dishroom. There, she introduced me to Martin, who was busy washing the lunch dishes.

"Martin, Pete's going to be working with you," she said. Then to me, she added, "Okay, Pete, Martin will show you what to do."

As Riki left, I threw on the apron and stood ready to be initiated into the world of magical dishwashing. My new mentor, though, was in no hurry to reveal any secrets. Since Martin was silently rinsing the dishes and loading them into the machine, I took my cue and started stacking the clean plates coming out of the Hobart.

For five minutes, we worked without saying a word to each other. Then Martin came over to me.

"Hey, Pete," he said. "You like *Star Trek*?"

He was wearing a *Star Trek* baseball cap and—visible behind his apron—a *Star Trek* T-shirt.

"Sorry," I said, "I never watched that show."

"Oh, okay," he said.

He was obviously disappointed, so I asked, "Do *you* like *Star Trek*?"

"Oh, *yeah*." He lit up. "I like *all* kinds of science fiction— *all* genres."

"Yeah?" I said. "Who's your favorite *Star Trek* character?"

As a big fan, I figured, he'd have a strong opinion on the matter. But Martin didn't respond. He stood there, frozen, and gave no indication of what was going on in his head.

Had I said something wrong? Had I mishandled the kosher dishes or something? After waiting for his answer for about thirty seconds, I assumed our conversation was over, so I resumed stacking the dishes.

After two full minutes of standing silently, Martin finally spoke.

"Pete, I'm sorry. I don't think I can answer your question," he said. "I just love *all* the characters so much."

I didn't want to cause him any anguish.

"Don't worry about it. It doesn't matter," I told him. Then I admitted, "This is my first time working in a Jewish place."

"Really? Well, let me show you around," he said. "This is the dairy dishroom, where we wash the dairy dishes—the breakfast and lunch dishes."

He held up an orange-rimmed plate.

"These are a different color than the blue dinner plates, so never mix them up."

From the dairy dishroom, he led me through a pantry and into a dishroom that was—amazingly—the mirror image of the first one.

"We wash the meat dishes—the dinner dishes—in here."

Identical dishpits? *Nice!*

Back in the pantry, Martin picked a pot off a shelf and pointed to a marking crudely scratched into its side.

"What's that say?" he asked.

I studied the marking for a moment, then answered, "I don't know."

"It's an M!" Martin said. "Can't you see the M?"

"Oh yeah, I see it now."

"And you know what that means?"

"No, what's it mean?"

"*Meat,*" he said, a bit exasperated. "Get it? M for *meat*?"

"Okay, yeah," I said. "I got it—M for meat."

Martin then led me over to the other side of the pantry, grabbed another pot and handed it to me.

"What's that one say?"

I found the etching and said, "D?"

"And what's D stand for?"

"Dairy?"

"Right," he said. "On that side of the room are all the meat pots and pans. On this side, the dairy ones. And you have to make sure that they never get mixed up."

"Why?" I asked.

"Because it's a sin or something if the Jews eat meat and dairy together," he said. "Watch out, 'cause sometimes the cooks put dirty pots in the wrong dishroom. So always check before you wash a pot and then double-check it before you put it away. It's really important you don't mix them up."

"But isn't there a rabbi around that takes care of that?"

"No," Martin said. "It's *our* job."

"There's no rabbi that blesses the dishes with holy water or says some prayers or anything?"

"Not that I've ever seen."

Back in the dairy dishroom, we worked on the lunch dishes. Martin pushed the dishes into the machine while I pulled them out and put them away. We worked in silence for a couple hours until Martin asked, "Pete, are you single?"

"Yep," I replied.

"Oh good. Then you'll be interested in this group I belong to."

He held out a leaflet to me.

"We meet every Tuesday night and one Saturday night a month."

I took the leaflet.

"It's a really neat group of people. Pastor John and his wife lead the meetings. We go roller skating and have birthday parties."

As he boasted about the wonderfulness of his group, I

stared down at the leaflet—titled "Christian Singles"—and dreaded where all this was heading.

Mercifully, a big bearded guy in his forties then walked in.

"Oh hey, Zlatko," Martin said to him. "This is Pete—new dishwasher."

Then to me, Martin added, "Zlatko washes dishes, too. He's from Bosnia—doesn't really speak English."

As Zlatko left to get cracking on the accumulating dinner pots in the meat dishroom, I fled to the break room before Martin could resume his sales pitch. When I returned fifteen minutes later, Martin said not a word about Christian Singles or even about *Star Trek*. In silence, the two of us finished the lunch dishes.

After Martin left, Zlatko and I worked the dinner dishes in the meat dishpit. Though I riddled Zlatko with questions about kosher dishing, he provided no answers in English—or in Bosnian.

The next morning, before work, I stopped by the library to better understand kosher dishing. In the Torah—the Old Testament—it was stated: "Thou shall not boil a kid in his mother's milk." In other words, don't eat meat and dairy together, so cheeseburgers were off the menu. Furthermore, any dishes or cookware or flatware that came into contact with meat or dairy took on the "kosher" status of being either meat or dairy. Thus, a bowl used to serve chicken soup was considered tainted with meat and therefore should never be used for serving ice cream until it was first neutralized by being burned in fire or boiled in water. To be on the safe side, though, it was best to prevent cross-contamination by only using dishes or cookware or flatware exclusively for either meat or dairy.

During my bus ride out to the nursing home, I filled out the rest of the story: After more than a thousand years of keeping their meat and dairy separated, along came Jesus who apparently told the Jews it wasn't a big deal after all. He told anyone who'd listen that boiling a young goat in his mother's milk wasn't really a commandment from above, rather just a helpful culinary tip like "Don't oversalt" or "Thaw before eating."

Such sermons were welcomed heartily by those Jews who were sick of having to stick their chopped liver plate in the fire before they could eat their cheesecake dessert off it. They flocked to Jesus in droves and the whole affair was capped with the famous ham-'n-cheese-sandwich Last Supper. Then—ta da!—Christianity was born.

In the meantime, Orthodox Jews continued to keep their dishes separated. But fine, if the Jews had stuck to special dishwashing rules for more than three thousand years, then I was glad to lend my services to enable their obsessive-compulsiveness.

Toward the end of that second afternoon, Martin and I cleaned up the dairy dishroom and shut it down for the day. Then we headed over to the meat dishroom, where Zlatko had already started washing the dinner dishes.

"You—" Zlatko said, pointing to Martin. "*You* wash."

"*Me* wash?" Martin said. "No, I'm going home. *You're* washing."

Zlatko insisted, "*You* wash."

As Zlatko tried in vain to explain himself in his native tongue, the head cook happened by. He took one look at Zlatko and asked, "What's wrong with him?"

"I don't know," Martin replied. "He wants me to stay and wash the dishes."

"He doesn't look good," the cook commented.

After the cook retrieved a chair from the dining room, Zlatko flopped down and started moaning.

More cooks crowded into the pit to take a gander at Zlatko and to listen to his foreign mutterings. His wife—a cook—usually acted as his translator, but she'd already left for the day.

So the nurse on duty was sent for. When she arrived, she inspected Zlatko for a second and then yelled, "Somebody call an ambulance! I think he's having a heart attack!"

The ambulance arrived and the paramedics carted Zlatko away.

Martin wasn't happy. The Bosnian's departure meant he was stuck working overtime.

The next morning, I was back at eight o'clock. The schedule had me working the morning shift with Zlatko, but he was a no-show. His wife stopped by the dairy dishpit later to apologize for his absence.

"He have heart attack," she said. "Still in hospital."

Fortunately, breakfast wasn't very busy. When Martin arrived at noon, we worked the lunch dishes in silence for a half hour. Then he walked over and asked, "Pete, do you have to work Tuesday night?"

I knew the answer was no, but didn't trust where Martin was going with his questioning.

"I think I am," I said.

"No you're not," Martin said. "I already checked the schedule."

"Oh, okay," I said. "Then I guess I'm not."

"Great!" he said. "Then you can come to the singles meeting, right?"

Wrong, I thought.

"Martin, what I said about being single wasn't entirely true," I lied. "Actually, I do have a girlfriend."

"That's okay," Martin said, without missing a beat. "Your girlfriend's welcome to come, too. We've got a few couples in the group."

He wasn't letting me off the hook so easily.

"Well, there's another thing," I said. "I'm not Christian either."

"No problem!" he said. "We aren't prejudiced against non-Christians."

Wait a minute.

"You don't have to be Christian *or* single to be part of your Christian Singles group?"

"That's right," he said, cheerily. "We welcome *every*body."

I had the sinking feeling that if I told him I was a Satan-worshiping free-lover, he would've replied, "See you Tuesday night!"

My attention returned to the plates I'd been loading into a rack.

"I already phoned some other group members this morning and told them about you," he said. "They're *all* excited to meet you!"

"Look Martin, I appreciate you inviting me to your get-together and all—" I began, then looked up. Martin—with sad, puppy-dog eyes—waited for me to finish my sentence.

I had to tell him flat out.

"—but I'll never go to one of your meetings."

Martin said nothing, turned around and went back to the other side of the dishroom. I watched him for a moment, then I continued loading the machine.

Martin began to pace back and forth and started mumbling. Then his grumbling grew louder.

"I don't know what it is with people," he said to himself. "You try to be friends with people but nobody wants to be friends anymore."

Then he marched up to me.

"You know, when you started working here, I thought I had a new friend," he said.

I didn't look up from the dishes. He resumed his pacing.

"I thought I was being nice by inviting you to join our group. All I wanted was to be friends."

I figured the tantrum would blow over. Instead, he kept ranting about how he'd been wronged until I snapped.

"Dude, we just met! You hardly even know me!" I said. "How'd you like it if I asked you to join some group that you didn't wanna join?"

"If you asked me to join your group, I would," he said.

"What if it was for people who hated *Star Trek*?"

"Wouldn't matter," he replied. "I'd join because I considered you my friend."

"Well, that's a stupid reason," I said.

Muttering to himself, Martin turned and left the room.

I spent the rest of the afternoon finishing the lunch dishes and shutting down the dairy pit for the day. My shift ended and I clocked out while Martin was in the meat pit, starting on the dinner dishes.

The next morning I arrived a tad late. Martin was already busy with the breakfast dishes when I walked into the dairy dish-room.

"Hey," I said. "Good morning."

Martin glanced over at me but said nothing. As long as he didn't want to rant about what an awful friend I was, I didn't mind if he sulked.

As he pushed, I pulled. I reshelved the clean dairy plates and pots. It was while I was putting away a dairy sheet pan that I noticed the M scratched into the sheet pan I was about to let it touch. How'd that get there? Were the meat pan and the dairy one beneath it now tainted?

I took the suspect pans into the dairy dishroom and said, "Hey, Martin."

He didn't react.

I walked up beside him.

"Hey, Martin," I said. "This meat pan was lying on top of this dairy one."

Martin turned and looked at the pans in my hand but said nothing.

"What are we supposed to do with them?" I asked.

Finally, he spoke.

"Oh, you don't want to be my friend but you want me to tell you what to do?"

Sensing drama, I dropped the tainted dairy sheet pan in the sink and carried the meat sheet pan over to the other pit. I scrubbed the already spotless pan but didn't know if that was enough to rekosherize it. Did I need to burn it or boil it as well? I scrubbed it again and then stood it diagonally in the dishmachine and ran it through two full cycles.

Hoping the meat sheet pan was now rid of all the dairy cooties, I brought it to the pantry. Before shelving it with the other meat sheet pans, I checked the top few to make sure no dairy ones had infiltrated the stack. As I was doing so, Martin walked over with a soup pot in his hand. He tapped the pot against some of the meat pots sitting on the shelves. Then he ran the soup pot along the edges of the stacked meat sheet pans. Finally, he set it down atop the meat pan I'd just—hopefully—kosherized.

Then Martin stood there with a smug grin on his face.

I picked up the soup pot. Sure enough, etched into it was a D. He'd just defiled dozens of M pots and pans.

I wanted to backhand Martin with the soup pot. But instead, I walked off with it to the dairy dishroom.

While scrubbing the soup pot, I was concerned about the other newly infected pots and pans. Even if I raced to rekosherize them all, there was nothing to prevent Martin from spitefully pulling his little stunt again. Why should *I* have to clean those pots and pans? It was Martin who'd infected them. But if I didn't tend to them, and the meat ware remained teeming with dairy toxins, in effect, a kid would be boiled in his mother's milk.

Some of the elderly residents may have strictly followed kosher dietary laws their whole lives—exactly as their parents and grandparents and generations of ancestors had done before them. Now these folks were nearing the front of the line to the entrance of their god's eternal nightclub. But before He'd let them past the velvet rope, first they had to have led good kosher lives. And who was responsible for ensuring they had? *Me!*

Ugh. I stood at the sinks wondering what to do. Upholding more than three millennia of Orthodox Jewish dishing traditions was supposed to be a thrilling adventure. Instead, busting kosher suds was now riddling me with anxiety. Maybe that's what did Zlatko in—he'd cracked under the pressure. I sure didn't want to end up like him.

A few minutes later, while still confounded, Riki entered.

"Zlatko obviously won't be in tonight," she said. "So Pete, we're gonna need you to stay and work dinner as well."

Breakfast, lunch *and* dinner? That was *twelve* hours of dishing!

"Why me?" I asked. "Why not Martin?"

"Martin stayed past his shift the night Zlatko went to the hospital," she said.

Behind Riki, Martin's smug look grew smugger. The urge to backhand him resurfaced.

I left the dairy dishroom, went to the break room and brooded. Now I *really* didn't want to rewash those pans. But then again, it was Martin who'd caused the damage. Any bad mojo was on him, not me.

So, not wanting to work overtime, not wanting the stress of kosher dishing and not wanting to keep fighting the urge to backhand Martin, I walked over to the meat dishpit and gave the dishmachine a kiss. Then I walked to the dairy dishpit and—in front of Martin—kissed the dairy dishmachine.

"What are you doing?" Martin asked.

"Carrying out my own traditions," I said.

My timing for quitting this job couldn't have been more perfect. After pulling off my apron and clocking out, I reached the bus stop the same time the bus did.

24

We Never Forget

Leaving the kosher kitchen job meant a setback in fund-raising to publish *Dishwasher* #16. By now, I was producing ten thousand copies of each issue. On the sly, I'd xerox a couple hundred or a couple thousand pages at a time wherever copy shop friends worked, in whatever town I was in. But all that slinking out of copy shops with my duffel bag or some boxes full of illicit photocopies (that I'd then spend hours collating, folding and stapling) had left me burnt out. Even though I shied away from publicity and turned down requests from distributors, I couldn't keep Reading Frenzy or Quimby's—or any of the couple dozen other bookstores and newsstands—stocked with *Dishwasher*. So this time I planned to pay to produce ten thousand zines all at once. But in order to do so, I needed cash. So I asked my brother to lend me $2,000. He lent it and straightaway I spent a few hundred bucks to have ten thousand covers of #16 printed while I finished laying out the inside pages.

With all that dough in my pocket, I started fantasizing about the other things I could do with it. I could go without working for months. Or I could buy a plane ticket to anywhere in the country. Or I could even buy a van.

Not long before, I'd completed a grueling weeklong bus trip that had mentally broken me. The hundreds of hours and tens of thousands of miles I'd logged on Greyhound had finally taken their toll. Now I was left unable to face spending another mile, let alone another hour, cooped up on the 'Hound. Besides, I wanted to go places the bus couldn't get me to.

When I saw a listing for a 1973 Dodge Tradesman van, I went and looked at it. The owners—a lesbian guitar/flute duo—had customized the vehicle for their tours. It had a loft bed in the back—and it ran. What more could I ask for? I immediately forked over the $1,400 asking price. That afternoon, I affixed a brass nameplate from a circa 1910 dishwashing machine to the dashboard. It was from the company founded by Josephine Cochrane—dishmachine inventor—and read: "Crescent Washing Machine Co." The van was thus dubbed Crescent.

With the cash for the printing now blown, I set *Dishwasher* #16 aside, put the ten thousand covers in a friend's attic and hit the road. I crossed along the northern edge of the country. From Minot, North Dakota, I called my parents. My dad was now so into my travels that whenever I'd call, he'd pull out his road atlas and pinpoint my location. Then he'd see what geographical landmarks were in my vicinity.

"Can you see the Souris River?" he asked on this occasion.

"Not from this phone booth," I said.

"There's a big lake just south of you—Lake Sakakawea," he said. "You should drive down there and see what it's like."

After heading down to Lake Sakakawea and looking at the water for a minute—just to be able to report to my dad that I'd done so—I poked about Minneapolis and Milwaukee. Then, in Grand Rapids, Michigan, I tracked down the location of where a diner had been in the 1930s. On the outside of the building—which now housed an office—I posted sheets of paper that read:

Gerald Ford
washed dishes here
1929–31

Though it felt somewhat odd to pay tribute to such a scumbag—he'd pardoned Richard Nixon, former *busboy*—Ford *had* washed dishes on that spot during his last two years of high school. And not content with just the one experience, in the couple years that followed, Ford went on to dish in Ann Arbor for his board at his University of Michigan fraternity house.

Remarkably, while a teenage Ford was scrubbing in Michigan, at the very same time, only a couple hundred miles away, another future president and fellow scumbag was also in the suds. At Eureka College in Eureka, Illinois, slumped over the sinks through his first two years of college was Ronald Reagan.

But maybe it's unkind to call these two dishpit alumni scumbags. After all, Ford had once complied with my mailed request to inscribe a photo of himself—while president—as he loaded a dishwashing machine. He'd written, "To Pete, another fine dishwasher, Gerald Ford." And besides, these two characters actually busted suds, unlike that malarkey-spewing president/scumbag Lyndon Johnson.

When not busy warmongering, LBJ often regaled anyone who'd listen (friends, diplomats, biographers) with tales of how, after graduating high school in 1924, he left Texas and set out for California in search of adventure. One LBJ biography quotes him as saying, "When we got there, I had several jobs but didn't hold any of them for long."

In another biography, he says, "Nothing to eat was the principal item on my food chart. That was the first time I went on a diet. Up and down the coast I tramped, washing dishes . . . always growing thinner."

Though LBJ did drive out to California with four buddies, that's as far as the truth goes in the story. Oft-repeated "facts" of the tale simply weren't true. Johnson was not in California for two years; he was there for a little over a year. He did not tramp up and down the coast; he remained in San Bernardino. He did not sleep outdoors or in rooming houses; he lived in his cousin's four-bedroom ranch house. He did not go hungry; he ate rather well. He did not hitchhike back to Texas; his cousin Clarence Martin drove him back in a Buick.

Most important, Johnson did not "scrub dishes in hash houses" (as one biographer put it). He spent his time in his cousin Tony Martin's law firm—as a *clerk*! The story apparently wouldn't have been nearly as captivating had Johnson tried to regale visiting foreign dignitaries with tales of a rebellious youth spent "tramping up and down the coast, clerking in law firms."

After Michigan, at a cemetery outside Chicago, I sought to pay tribute to a notable figure from dishwashing history who was certainly no scumbag.

On previous stops through Chicago, while reading through old newspapers, I'd learned about Thomas F. W. Scanlon. In 1903, he was a leader of the Miscellaneous Workers Local 513, representing the "unskilled" workers—including dishwashers—in the Hotel Employees and Restaurant Employees International Union, the craft union that was largely anti–unskilled labor. When hotel and restaurant workers staged a massive strike throughout the city, Scanlon spoke before the delegates of the Chicago Federation of Labor in order to win the support of the city's other labor organizations. In that speech, he said:

> *I represent a union that has grievances of the most pronounced order. These humble people work in watches from 6 a.m. until 2 p.m. Then they get a rest until 5 p.m. and work from that hour until midnight. They are given a small room to sleep in—ten or more in one room—and they are given stuff to eat that is rejected by the customers. What do they get for all of this toil? The munificent sum of $20 a month.*

His speech was key in convincing the CFL board to endorse the strike. But during the hectic peak of the labor action, when strikers and picketers were facing off in the streets daily, Scanlon suffered a heart attack and died at the age of thirty-one. His death was widely attributed to the strenuous work he did on behalf of those he represented.

For several days after his death, Scanlon's body lay in state in the union's headquarters on South La Salle Street. The room was filled with bouquets, floral pieces and stray blossoms that were purchased with the small contributions of the porters, chambermaids, scrubwomen and dishwashers he'd represented. Two pearl divers in their pressed kitchen whites stood at attention at the head of the coffin. More than four thousand mourners filed through to pay their respects. After the funeral service at the union hall, hundreds of mourners followed the funeral cortege through the streets to the train station. From there, the coffin was taken to the suburb of Hillside for burial.

One of Scanlon's contemporaries, so moved by his death, wrote, "We have lost our brightest star and his name shall be emblazoned on the scroll of organized labor's history that babes unborn shall sing his praises, and time shall never be able to efface it."

I was one of those unborn babes seeking to sing Scanlon's praises.

In Hillside, at the cemetery's office, I learned the row and plot number of Scanlon's gravesite. But in that part of the cemetery, I soon discovered, most of the headstones had disintegrated. On the spot estimated to be Scanlon's grave, I laid flowers. On a small piece of stone that'd crumbled off a nearby headstone, I wrote in marker an inscription. The front of it read:

> **Thomas F. W. Scanlon**
> **d. August 28, 1903**
> **aged 31 years**

The back:

> **We Never Forget**

25

Utopian Dishwashery

In northeast Missouri, I pulled up to the farmhouse feeling apprehensive. For a couple of years, I'd been receiving invitations from Lindsey, one of the farm's residents. The most recent one was a postcard that read: "This is your annual notice that a Missouri dishwashing opportunity is upon you. End of Sept thru Oct is our sorghum harvest. 20–30 folks = lots of dishes. Your services are needed. Room, board, no boss, peace & quiet, fresh air—who could ask for more?"

I was intrigued. Obviously—after Michigan (#26) and Iowa (#27)—it'd make Missouri #28. But it'd also give me the chance to experience farm life and see if it was for me. Furthermore, the farm was a commune. What exactly that entailed, I wasn't sure. But I was interested in checking out a democratic, nonhierarchical live/work situation for its possibility as a place to settle. At the same time, though, I was unnerved by visions of touchy-feely, patchouli-soaked hippies spinning in circles to the tired groans of the Grateful Dead.

I'd just have to keep an open mind.

At the farmhouse, I was greeted by Lindsey. After admiring Crescent, she said, "There's a guest bedroom available if you want—or you can stay in your van."

The thought of a bedroom for a month was tempting. But I wasn't so sure I wanted to get too committed just yet. Having to gather up my stuff and hastily explain in a hallway why I was bailing could complicate things if I had to split in a hurry.

"I think I'll just stay in the van," I told her.

"You sure?" she asked. "There'll be more volunteers arriving tomorrow, so if you don't take the room now, it's gone for good."

The need for a quick getaway was too valuable.

"The van's fine," I said. "Where can I park it?"

"Somewhere out of the way," she said. "How 'bout down by the pond?"

She got in the van and directed me off the dirt road and through the tall grass. With all the bumps and dips, we couldn't go faster than three miles an hour. But we found a nice spot beside the pond, out of view from both the road and the main farmhouse. If nothing else, the seclusion would be nice.

Then it was time for dinner. Standing in a circle around a central serving table, the twelve of us held hands. The others fell silent. To feel less awkward, I closed my eyes. The woman to my left squeezed my hand. Keep an open mind, I reminded myself. Five seconds later, she squeezed my hand a bit harder. I knew I was fresh meat on the scene but hadn't expected the female communards to be quite so forward.

A couple seconds later, she really wrenched my hand.

Then the woman to my right squeezed my other hand. What, her too?

When I looked up, all eyes were on me. The cook then held up the hand of the guy to her right. He held up the woman's hand to *his* right. She held up my hand. I finally understood. I held up the hand of the woman to my right. When the chain reaction returned to the cook again, she said, "All right, let's eat."

The meal of millet burgers and Indian dal was actually quite tasty. Lindsey explained that all the ingredients from the salad were from the farm's huge vegetable garden. The muffins—baked the day before—were smothered in butter made from milk from the farm's own cow. Even the beer I was drinking was brewed on-site. It was pretty cool to feel—for the first time—so connected to the source of a meal.

I finished my eats before the others and was raring to get started with what brought me there. At the kitchen sink, I found a note taped to the window above it that read: "Pete, welcome to our funky farm sink!"

I donned my custom-made Dish Master apron and got to it. An hour later, when I was nearly done with the dishes, one of the women announced that it was time for the sing-along.

"Pete, are you gonna join us?" she asked.

"Uh . . . " I said. An open mind, I thought. Keep an open mind. "Uh, I need to finish the dishes first."

"Okay," she said. "Come join us when you're done."

The group of communards gathered in a circle in the

front room—in view of the kitchen sink—and began singing a Joan Baez song. My mind began to close.

After a few songs, the chorus leader called out, "Are you done yet, Pete?"

"Not yet," I replied, which was true only because I'd been dragging out the dish work. But a few minutes later, when all the dishes were put up and the sink sparkled, the singing was still in progress. It looked like there was no avoiding it. But then I noticed the bucket I'd been tossing the food scraps into. Aha! I grabbed it and announced, "I gotta dump the compost!"

Out the back door, I emptied the bucket's contents onto the compost pile. Then I fumbled my way through the dark to Crescent. Once inside, I wondered what I'd gotten myself into. I wasn't cut out for a dish job that entailed group hand-holding and sing-alongs. I wanted to rev up and tear out of there. But my plan to be readied for a quick getaway had backfired. In the dark, I doubted I could successfully navigate through all the bumps and tree stumps to get back to the dirt road.

So instead, I crawled into bed and went to sleep.

In the morning, I ate breakfast with Lindsey.

"I heard you ducked out on the singing last night," she said.

"Yeah, but . . . " I said, starting to defend myself before realizing I had no alibi.

"Don't worry about it; I skipped it too," she said. "Group singing doesn't happen that often."

"And the hand-holding at dinner?"

"That's just something we do," she said. "It's harmless."

I took her word for it.

Though I was there for the dishing, I didn't mind helping out with the harvesting as well. So after breakfast, Lindsey walked me out to the fields. There, she taught me how to use a machete to first strip a sorghum stalk of its leaves and then cut it down. The stalks were then loaded on a flatbed trailer, which a tractor hauled to the farm's mill. There, the juice was squeezed from them, boiled and reduced down to a syrup that was jarred and used like molasses.

Just before lunch, I returned to the farmhouse and got started on cleaning the mess that the cook-of-the-day had already made.

A daily routine soon developed for me: a couple hours of field work in the morning, then lunch and the lunch dishes. A couple hours of field work in the afternoon, then dinner and the dinner dishes.

The view out the kitchen window above the sink might have been the best view I'd ever had at a job. It beat the oil rig porthole's view of the Gulf of Mexico. And it even beat the summer camp tent-cabin's view of the Tahoe Basin. Most of the time, the view was of just part of the organic garden. But then at lunchtime, it often livened up when female communards in their twenties came in from the fields—topless.

One day, after lunch, one of the women approached me at the sink.

"You seem to have a real bond—a deep connection—with dishwashing," she said. "Is it spiritual for you?"

"No," I said. "Just something I do."

"But don't you find washing dishes to be zen?"

"Not really," I said. "Seems like if it were zen, it wouldn't hurt my back and arms so much."

●

I had to keep on my toes to not stick out too much. It wasn't always easy, like when I'd forget myself and ask, "Has the mailman been by yet today?"

"Mial-*co*," I was corrected more than once about using the gender neutral term.

Or the time I broke out a box of Little Debbie brownies. When I offered them around, they were received as if I was trying to hand out used diapers. From then on, I kept my store-bought snacks hidden in the van.

Or the time when I found myself engaged in a conversation with a woman about her beliefs in goddesses and faeries. It took me too long to realize she wasn't putting me on.

Despite all that, it wasn't quite the hippie-fest that I'd feared. Male hair was short, most everyone was lucid and intelligent and I didn't hear a lick of jam-band music the whole time.

After a few weeks, I found myself asking everyone—both the commune's residents and the farm's other visitors—about the rationale and philosophy behind intentional communities. For historical background, someone suggested reading the behaviorist B. F. Skinner's 1948 novel *Walden Two*. A tale of a fictional utopian intentional community, it was the influential book that directly—or indirectly—inspired the founding of many communes in the 1960s and '70s.

While reading the farmhouse's copy of the book by flashlight one night in the van, I came close to dozing off. But my eyes popped wide open when the author introduced the tricky subject of shit work. In any discussion of utopian societies, it's the thorniest of issues: Who will pick up the trash?

Who will dig the ditches? And, most important, who will wash the dishes?

In Skinner's egalitarian world, the dish work was a responsibility shared by all of the thousand-odd residents. This is exemplified when the reader is introduced—in one of Walden Two's cafeterias—to the dishpit (or, as Skinner termed it, the "dishwashery"). It's staffed not by some wino or an immigrant but by "a very pretty girl" and "a distinguished man with a full beard."

Skinner makes requisite dishing less arduous through his innovations and "cultural engineering." Foremost among these are trays with little beveled compartments for the main course, side dishes, dessert, etc. By modifying the residents' behavior to accept eating their meals off such a contraption, Skinner boasts that the sheer number of plates and bowls dirtied would be reduced. Moreover, the trays would be made of transparent glass. This would enable the dishwasher to see whether or not the bottom side was clean without first having to flip it over. The result: wrists would be taxed less; time would be saved.

I begged to differ.

Granted, decreasing the total number of dishes *would* help alleviate the dishwasher's lament of "too many dishes." That's a given. Even a hundred years before the publication of Skinner's book, Henry David Thoreau—a dude who apparently hated unnecessary dishing—had advocated in the original *Walden*, "Simplify, simplify. Instead of three meals a day, if it be necessary eat but one; instead of a hundred dishes, five; and reduce other things in proportion."

But *glass* trays as a solution? They sounded more like a nightmare!

If Skinner's very pretty girl were to spot some splotch on a tray, I imagined, she'd start scrubbing at it. But if it didn't disappear, she'd think, Crap, all that scrubbing for nothing.

She'd then have to flip it and scrub all over again. Yet if she had opaque dishware, she'd know good and well what side any splotch was on. Thus, in Walden Two's innovative dishwashery, her wrists wouldn't be doing less twisting; they'd be doing *more*!

Besides, who really cares if a bottom side is cruddy? In the heat of battle, even a Dish Master doesn't have time to go chasing after every splotch in every corner of every piece of dishware. And as long as there are no outbreaks of salmonella or hepatitis A, no one's ever the wiser. But a disher can't get away with laxness like that with clear glass. A diner who sees crud through the plate won't just ignore it. Customers— who never bother to commend a disher for sparkling clean silverware—won't miss the opportunity to scream bloody murder at the sight of some harmless crust on the bottom of their glass plate.

Skinner was full of it. For all his highfalutin ideas, the guy had obviously never busted a single sud. He'd probably dreamt up all this as he sat back with his feet propped up on his desk, dictating the tale to his secretary. Surely even she'd rolled her eyes when he let out, "I've got it! *Glass trays!*"

If I couldn't gulp his idea for utopian dishing, how was I to swallow his plans for an entire paradise?

The next morning in the kitchen, while complaining to Lindsey about the glass tray conundrum, I flipped my breakfast plate over and over to illustrate my point.

"*See?*" I asked. "See what I mean?"

"Well, I don't know anything about that," she answered. "It's been a long time since I read that book."

Later, out in the sorghum field, I continued to press my case.

"And what about Skinner's idea to have the dirty trays first rinsed with *milk*?!" I asked one woman. The resulting milky slop would then be given to the hogs. "Why milk? *Water* isn't good enough for rinsing? Sounds like a waste of resources to me!"

"I've never read the book," she sighed and then retreated to work a different row of sorghum stalks.

By the time I cornered Tess—a woman from a different intentional community who was here to help out during the harvest—I was onto the pot issue. Skinner says that Walden Two is largely self-sufficient; its food is mostly produced on its own land or comes from nearby farms. Preparing all that food from scratch—and not taking it out of a can or box—would dirty more than the average number of pots, pans and cooking utensils.

"Who's washing all those pots?" I demanded of Tess. "Skinner thinks his pretty girl and his distinguished man are just gonna putz around with glass trays? *Somebody's* gotta knock out all those pots!"

"Man, if you like washing dishes so much," Tess replied, "then you really should come to *my* community. We got *lotsa* dishes and *nobody* who likes to wash 'em."

As opposed to this small farm commune, where washing the dishes was a mere pastime, she said, at her place—with eighty inhabitants—dishwashing was an actual job.

"Come there and you'll be loved for going anywhere near the dishes," she said.

An appreciated, full-time disher at a large commune? It sounded tempting.

Life on the sorghum farm—hippies or no hippies—wasn't really for me. While milking a cow the first time was a novelty, the second time it was a chore. And though riding my bike three miles on dirt and gravel back roads to reach town to mail letters or pick up an ice cream bar was a pleasant change, it didn't top riding a bike through city streets. And for miles around, there was no public transit to joyride.

But the main reason why I'd never be able to hack it at the small-time farm was because it counted only seven or eight full-time residents. Living year-round in such close quarters with so few people out in the countryside didn't seem idyllic; it'd drive me crazy. Though the commune where Tess lived was also not in an urban setting, its population was ten times greater, maybe it wouldn't feel so isolated.

A couple weeks later, I arrived at Tess's community. She promptly gave me a tour of the settlement. It straddled a creek on a thousand acres of mostly forested land in southern Missouri's Ozark Mountains. While strolling through the main part of the compound—past the sandal-making trailer, the nut-butter processing plant and various residential buildings—we encountered some of her fellow communards.

"*You're* the dishwasher?!" one woman asked. "You sure came to the right place!"

I was taken aback by her fervor. Word of my arrival had apparently spread fast; others greeted me with equal enthusiasm.

On the tour, Tess showed me the communal clothing room next to the bathhouse. After a shower, one could grab whatever clothes they chose to wear from the thousands of articles available. Having such a huge stack of shared things to wear could mean never having to endure clothes-shopping again—a comforting thought.

The one-room library looked like it had enough books to keep a reader busy for years. But it held no books by Philip

Roth. So I retrieved nine of his paperbacks from Crescent and donated them to the cause.

At the facility that produced nut butter—the community's main income source—Tess jumped in and helped jar some organic peanut butter while I washed the same product from a number of five-gallon buckets. It might sound like a hellacious task but actually just some warm water and a sturdy scrub brush was enough to chase the peanut butter out of the buckets in a hurry.

Tess explained that according to the commune's labor arrangement, everyone was free to choose how they'd fulfill the weekly forty-hour work requirement. Some toiled in the fields; others did child care. Some worked in the office; others gave massages. Some made sandals, others produced nut butter. People gravitated to what they preferred to do. Positions—even outhouse cleaning—tended to be filled without problem. There was one exception: dishwashing. Here, my calling was classified as HTA: hard to assign. And since no one *chose* to do it, everyone was *required* to do it—just as Skinner had envisioned. Thus, because I wanted to *only* wash dishes, I'd been received like a savior.

That night, after dinner in the main dining hall, Tess and I stuck around while the others slowly drifted out. In return for the hospitality I was receiving, I hoped to donate my skills. But not wanting to step on anyone's toes, I sat and waited for the arrival of the three people who were signed up for that night's dish duty so I could ask to join in.

After a fruitless hour of sitting, I got impatient and went to check out the facilities. I was shocked by the sight. While this community was following Skinner's call for egalitarian dish shifts, it utterly failed to live up to his—and Thoreau's—

call for simplification through less dishware. Countless dishes were strewn across the counters. The sinks were filled with the pots that were so conveniently absent at Walden Two. The pit was so disorganized and everything was so squalid, I couldn't distinguish between what was *waiting* to be washed and what already *had been* washed!

Reading the astonishment in my face, Tess said, "I *told* you people here don't like washing dishes."

Thankfully no transparent glass trays were in sight. Unmissable, though, were the country cockroaches. From wee young'uns to fat grannies, they strutted back and forth along the counters and walls. They must've been spared harm by the commune's back-to-the-woods pacifists because the pests roamed the dishwashery with the same impunity that allowed sacred cows to roam the streets of Calcutta.

Now, of course, I'd toiled alongside roaches in grubby pits plenty of times. But those were all places where the diners *weren't* privy to the secrets of the kitchen. On the other hand, here—owing to the HTA rule—*all* diners knew firsthand exactly the sad state of the dishwashery. Judging by the fact that they could willingly consume food produced in a kitchen so obscene, the eighty residents must not have cared about the conditions in the dishwashery.

Since so much work needed to be done, I decided to give that night's crew a head start. I began by tackling the pots. Tess took the initiative to run some dishes through the machine.

As I scrubbed, I considered the prospects of settling there.

What was needed was someone to take charge—not a *head* dishwasher, mind you, but a *stable* disher to coordinate the operation and organize the pit. I immediately saw the advantages of taking on such a position myself. It'd provide me with a place to live, clothes and books. I could set my own hours. I could be boss-free.

While a cook may go on to own his own restaurant one day, there isn't an equivalent for a dishwasher who wants to be *his* own boss. Quite possibly this was one of the only—if not *the* only—positions in the country where a dishwasher *could* be his own boss.

After I'd spent an hour in the pit, a messenger arrived. He informed Tess that the scheduled dishers wouldn't be filling their shifts. They'd heard a celebrity Dish Master was on the scene so they were using the occasion to chill in the sandal-making trailer and get blitzed.

The next day, I hiked through the woods and along the river. Then, that night I returned to the dishroom. Again, the night's scheduled dish-duty communards were no-shows.

As I dished solo, I envisioned possible changes. Having only ever passed through dishpits, I'd never had a chance to personalize any of them. But if I remained in this one, I could make some cosmetic alterations. A fresh coat of paint could go on the walls. And they could be adorned with some of my artifacts, like the vintage 1950s "Dishwasher Wanted" signs or the dozens of sketches and paintings and photos of dishes and dishers that readers had sent me over the years. Better yet, I could use the wall space for a permanent exhibition of the mac-n-cheese box collection.

Despite working by myself, I enjoyed envisioning the utopian dishwashery.

The third night, I dished alone again. This time, though, one of the no-shows actually showed up.

"Thanks, bro," the dreadlocked white boy said as he stood beside me at the sinks.

After the previous nights of absent dishers, I was grateful for the gratitude.

"Dude, you're one brave amigo," he said. "I *hate* washing dishes."

From my hunched position, I looked over at him. He smiled back at me and said, "Thanks again for covering my shift."

As I watched White-Boy Dreads turn and leave, my blood began to boil. I'd only wanted to help out, to be an extra hand. I'd never intended to cover his—or any goldbricker's—assigned shifts. Nor had I even offered!

If this was what it was like as a short-term guest, then what could I expect if I were to settle down as the commune's resident Dish Master? My presence would enable work-shy residents to shirk their dish duty. In fact, as dishroom coordinator, I'd probably be stuck working far more than forty hours a week in order to cover all the laggards' shifts. And I wouldn't be appreciated for doing it; I'd be *expected* to do it.

The communards would abuse my position.

Hell, I realized, standing there alone in the dishwashery, the fucking hippies are *already* taking advantage of me!

I pulled my arms from the suds and let be the rest of the pots and dishes. I didn't know who was responsible for them. I just knew it wasn't me. Then I kissed the machine, wiped my lips with my sleeve and dropped out.

26
Dude Wants His Free Meal

After realizing communal life wouldn't suit me, I skipped around the state and raked in some cash dishing at a café in Columbia, Missouri. Then I gravitated to Branson—the self-proclaimed "Live Music Show Capital of the World" in the Missouri Ozarks. With dozens of dinner theaters devoted to acts like Dolly Parton, the Osmonds and Andy Williams, the town was crowded with restaurants to service the busloads of music aficionados that flocked there from throughout the South and the Midwest. And where all those folks went, a great deal of dirty dishes were left behind.

With so many dish gigs packed into an area so small, it sounded like an ideal place for a postquest settled dishman. If I lived there, the notion to quit could run wild. I could discard jobs left and right yet always have plenty of other jobs at my disposal. In fact, I could even sample the dozens of dinner theaters and then settle into whichever one was the best in town.

Arriving in Branson, I found in the local newspaper evidence to prove my theory. In a town of only about five thousand inhabitants, the classifieds listed a dozen "Dishwasher Wanted" ads. I felt even more wanted than at that last commune.

Also in the newspaper, I noticed a listing for a $200-a-month room for rent. Two hundred bucks was far more expensive than it cost to live in the van or at a job site or on a friend's couch. But heck—with $373 in my pocket, I felt rich enough to do something self-indulgent like rent my own room.

At the rental's address, I found a country gift shop that sold porcelain angel figurines, wooden duck cut-outs and the like. Each crafty product was covered in ribbons and lace. When I stepped inside, the place smelled like someone had shat out a dozen scented candles.

"I think I've got the wrong address," I told the woman behind the counter. "I was looking for a room to rent."

She told me I had the right place, and that the building was an old house converted into a shop.

"The rent is two hundred and the deposit is another hundred," she said as she led me through the store and up the stairs.

Filled with more lacy and ribbony crap, the room appeared almost to be an extension of the sales floor. Fake dried flowers hung from the red felt wallpaper. Above the bed hung a painting of two swans facing each other (their necks forming a heart shape). And strands of red shag carpeting hung over the tops of my shoes.

While I was trying to think of how to jokingly ask if the

place had ever been a bordello, she gave the top of the bed a nudge. In response, the dozen crimson pillows bobbed up and down like buoys.

"Room comes with a waterbed." She smiled.

I hadn't reckoned renting a room would be *this* decadent. Did my dough really need to be blown on luxuries so vulgar?

Well, since she asked for no credit references or personal references or even for any evidence of income, I told her I'd take the place . . . mostly just because I could.

I handed her three hundred bucks.

Now that I had a place to crash, there was the matter of a job. After throwing my duffel bag on the waterbed, I reviewed the twelve dish ads. The one for the Remember When Theater stood out because it sounded like a dinner theater. If I was going to work in a town devoted to live entertainment, then dinner-theater dishing needed to be on the agenda.

On my way there, I passed a marquee sign whose foot-high letters shouted:

DISHWASHER WANTED

I pulled over.

This place—Golden Corral—wasn't even one of the twelve ads listed in the newspaper. It was an all-you-can-eat chain restaurant, and chain restaurants weren't really my thing. They lacked local character and soul. They required donning the ubiquitous company clothing. And they had too much hierarchy: assistant managers, store managers, district managers, general managers, etc. It was bad enough having one boss without having to answer to a whole nationwide string of command.

Still, the enormous sign beckoned me.

I stepped out of the van, went in and filled out an application.

"Dishwashing, huh?" the manager said when he glanced at my completed application. "Can you start right now?"

The lunch rush was in full swing. The dishes were piling up.

"Sure." I shrugged.

I threw on an apron and was led to the pit, where another guy was too busy scrubbing to properly welcome me to the fold. So I sorted silverware for a while.

"*And?*" my new coworker finally said a couple minutes later. "How you like the job?"

I looked down at the silverware and said, "It's not bad."

"Yeah, it ain't bad, is it?"

Actually, with all the openings in town, odds were that there was a better place to work.

"You think this is the best dish job in town?" I asked.

He answered with only a nervous laugh. Was that a good sign or a bad sign? I had no idea.

Over the next couple hours both my coworker and the manager eagerly asked for my opinion of the job. It seemed to give them the sought-after reassurances when I'd provide them with rather neutral answers like "It's all right" or "I've worked in worse places."

At four o'clock, the afternoon lull set in. Action in the dishroom died down. The boss told me to take a couple hours off but to be back at six o'clock for the dinner rush.

With time to kill, I drove over to my original destination—the Remember When Theater. It was between the Shoji Tabuchi Theater (featuring a Japanese country music star) and the

Country Tonight Theater (featuring, apparently, a night of country music). On the Remember When's marquee, the lettering for the star of the show—Jimmie Rodgers—was smaller than the names of his hit songs from decades prior— "Honeycomb" and "Kisses Sweeter Than Wine."

While making quick work of the application, I paused to reread the part that stated that if I didn't provide two weeks' notice before quitting, my pay would be docked. I'd never before heard of that rule. And it worried me. The notion to quit never provided *me* with two weeks' notice, so how was *I* supposed to know when to give notice?

I'd just have to take my chances.

When I handed the application to the boss-guy, he asked, "When can you start?"

"Well—" I began. There was the petty matter of already being employed.

"Start now?" he asked.

I wasn't due back at Golden Corral for another hour.

"Aw right," I said.

I'd give Jimmie Rodgers' a one-hour audition. If the place seemed like a better deal, I'd stay. If not, I'd split and head back to Golden Corral.

The boss-guy led me down to the dishpit. From the four guys in their twenties standing there—all with backwards baseball caps, Metallica/Pantera T-shirts, ponytails and goatees—the boss singled out one in particular to show me around. Since he—Jason—appeared to be the dishroom's most senior employee, I asked him how long he'd been working there.

"Shit, man," he said as he did the calculations in his head.

"Um . . . almost two months. *Man,* I can't believe I've been here so long!"

First, Jason showed me around the dishroom and kitchen. Then he led me out back, past a loading dock where a couple other suds busters were lounging. Finally, we rounded a corner to the backside of a dumpster.

"This is where you go when you wanna hide," he said.

Jason pinched his thumb and forefinger together, put them to his lips and inhaled. His eyebrows wiggled up and down.

"Know what I mean?" he asked.

Back in the dishpit, I asked Jason where else he'd dished in town.

"Just before I came here, I was over at Grand Country Buffet with Dom and Phil," he said, pointing at the two guys at the pot sinks. Then he added, "I came over here first and those fruits couldn't stay away from me."

He asked about me. I told him I'd been hired over at Golden Corral and was due back at six o'clock.

"*You're splitting?!*" he asked. Heads turned in my direction. Upon hearing that I was already on the verge of becoming their ex-coworker, concern filled the room.

"There's supposed to be seven dishwashers here," Jason said. "With you, this was gonna be the first night since I've been here that we'd have a full crew."

"Well, I don't *have* to go back," I said.

One of the other dishers—Heath—said he used to work at Golden Corral.

"You went there 'cause of that sign out front?" he asked.

"Yeah."

"Man, that sign's there *all* the time," he said. "Don't that tell you something?"

"So you think this is a better place to work?" I asked.

"Hell yeah!" he said. "Here you even get a free meal."

Heath convinced me. This *was* a better gig. In fact, maybe it was the best gig in town.

I stayed.

"How many buses there gonna be tonight?"

That was the question on everybody's lips in the dishpit. Instead of pondering the number of expected *diners,* the talk was about how many *busloads* of tourists would be rolling in. A waitress finally provided us with the number: forty-one.

"Forty-one," Phil said. "Shit, that's like eight hundred people. We're gonna be busy."

"Don't worry," Jason told him. "We've got a full crew now."

That night, I spent the shift as the dishpit's "runner"—running the clean dishes back to the kitchen, which left my hands dry. I did get wet, though, when a tussle broke out between Dom and Heath. They were arguing over who'd be "sprayer"—the guy who sprayed down the racks of dishes before they were shoved in the machine. As the two wrestled with the spray hose, enough water shot around the room to soak us all.

Later, when I asked Jason about my free meal, he led me into the kitchen.

"Dude wants his free meal," Jason said to a cook as he jabbed his thumb in my direction. For a couple seconds, the cook sized me up as if to assess my worthiness to eat. Then he put together a plate of fried chicken, sweet-potato fries and cornbread.

I took my grub out back to the loading dock and sat among the lounging pearl divers. Was this the best place in town that any of them had dished? They all responded with resounding "Yeahs."

But when I then asked which other dinner theaters they'd dished in, they all answered that this was the only one. Because most of their previous employment had been at chain restaurants—Golden Corral, Western Sizzler, Cracker Barrel, Denny's—I decided to hold off on awarding the Town's Best Dish Gig title to Jimmie Rodgers' just yet.

At the end of the shift, Jason and two other dish dudes all commented to me about how smoothly the dishroom had run that night.

Jason's exact words to me: "*You* made the difference."

After work, on my way back to my room, I again saw The Sign at Golden Corral. This time the familiar words took on a very different meaning: they read as if an all-points-bulletin had been posted for me.

"Be on the lookout for an at-large, disheveled dishwasher. He was last seen promising to return for an evening shift. Suspect considered lazy and harmless."

As Crescent and I passed The Sign, we sped up.

That night, I climbed in bed feeling gratified with my experience as a resort-town disher. In the span of fourteen hours, I'd found a place to live, worked two jobs and moved up the dish-gig ladder. Maybe it was just a taste of what life in a place like this could be like on a permanent basis.

But though the day's events had been fulfilling, they weren't enough to get me to sleep soundly on my new bed.

I'd slept on a slew of floors, couches and chairs; on buses, ferries and backseats of cars; and even under bridges and in doorways, all without problems, fuss or complaints (well, with maybe the exception of the floor in Darryl's Room). But this waterbed: each time I moved, it moved. The swells left me woozy. So I abandoned ship and slept comfortably on the shag carpeting.

The next few nights, I remained the dishpit's runner (or, more accurately, the *walker*). With thirty to forty busloads of customers each night, we stayed busy in the dishroom.

Each day, I put off eating until my free dinner at work. Then I'd take a break, go to the kitchen and fill a plate high with chicken pot pie, mashed potatoes, fried chicken, chili and chicken fingers.

On my fourth night, a cook asked, "What do you think you're doing?"

"Getting my dinner," I said.

He yanked the plate from my hand and growled, "You already *had* your free meal!"

As he glowered at me, I thought, He can't be serious. I expected him to smile and say, "I'm only foolin'."

But he didn't. Instead he said, "You waitin' for something?"

I left the kitchen empty-handed. Out back, I related the incident to the pot-smoking dishers behind the dumpster.

"Didn't you already get your free meal?" Jason asked.

"Not tonight," I said.

"But on your first night you did."

"Well, yeah," I said. "I've been getting my dinner *every* night."

My comrades laughed.

"Dude, you just get *one* free meal," Jason said. "Just one. *That's it!*"

This couldn't possibly be true.

"Hey, man, I was working here two weeks before any of these fags told me I had a free meal coming," Dom said. "So consider yourself lucky."

But I didn't consider myself lucky. I considered myself hungry.

After the others finished their joint and filed back inside, I remained hidden behind the dumpster. Any place that didn't feed its dish dogs couldn't possibly be the best gig in town. Since the notion to quit had now struck, there was no way I could work another two weeks without eating on the job— even if leaving meant taking a pay cut.

I made a beeline straight from the dumpster out to my van.

On the way back to my room, I stopped by a convenience store and picked up a newspaper, a pint of cookie dough ice cream for dinner and a Creamsicle for dessert. Lying on the waterbed, I devoured my meal while reading the dish classifieds. Of the nine ads, one stood out: the Lawrence Welk Resort.

The next morning, I applied to dish for Welk. Though the accordion-playing bandleader was dead, the legacy of his "champagne music" was doing swell judging by the immense size of the complex.

"Oh great," the receptionist said. "We've been looking for dishwashers."

"Well, you just found one," I told her.

Unlike Golden Corral or Jimmie Rodgers', Welk's wasn't so needy for dish help that they asked me to start on the spot. Instead, I was asked to hold off for a few hours and then start a shift at three p.m.

When I returned, I was met by the kitchen manager, who immediately ushered me over to the head chef. Who immediately ushered me over to the apparently ranking dishwasher. Who immediately ushered me over to another disher. I'd only been there three minutes and had already been passed around among four people.

Mike—the dishman now stuck with showing me around—was busy running some clean pots to the kitchen. Thirty seconds into this training session, he had trouble figuring out where to put a certain 80-quart stock pot.

"Sorry, I don't really know where this stuff goes," he said. "This is only my second day here."

Mike called over Rocky—the guy I'd assumed was the ranking disher. As Rocky approached us, he joked, "Do I have to do *everything* for you guys?"

"Oh, like *you* know everything?" said a female cook who'd overheard him. "You've been here, what, a week?"

"*No,*" our ranking dishman told her. "I'm in the middle of my *second* week."

Rocky showed me around the dishroom and the vast—but empty—dining area.

"They can cram a thousand old geezers in here," he said. "Tonight I heard we've got about thirty-eight, thirty-nine buses coming—about eight hundred people."

As we walked past the buffet setup, he said, "When the restaurant closes at eight o'clock, we take a break and can eat whatever we want from the buffet."

"For free?" I asked.

"Of course, for free," he said.

I'd yet to touch a dish, but compared with Jimmie Rodgers', this was already clearly a better gig—another step up.

Though the food was as bland as Welk's music and mushy

enough for the elderly patrons to gum it down, I appreciated its free-ness.

●

Since I needed a decent paycheck to pay the rent in a few weeks, I stayed put at Welk's. Usually we had anywhere between thirty and fifty busloads of his fans—the entire parking lot was essentially one massive handicapped zone. Back in my room, I learned to sleep on the edge of the waterbed, hanging an arm and leg over the side railing to anchor myself. I still bobbed up and down anytime I moved, but remained anchored enough to not get seasick.

One afternoon, I picked up my paycheck, took it to the bank it was drawn from and cashed it. Then, on my way to work, the notion struck. Why return to Lawrence Welk's? Now financially independent, I had the opportunity to leave that gig and find an even better one at any of the other dozens of dinner theaters in town.

But which one would be better than Welk's? The Osmonds'? The Oak Ridge Boys'? Dolly Parton's? Whose dishpit topped them all?

In a town packed with cheesy acts, I figured my best bet was to head straight to the cheesiest of them all: Wayne Newton's.

It was still early afternoon when I pulled into Newton's nearly empty parking lot. At the ticket counter, I asked the saleslady for an application for a dishwashing job.

"We don't have dishwashers here," she said.

"You mean, you don't have any openings?"

"No," she said. "We don't have *dishwashers*."

"Who washes the dishes then?"

"We don't *have* dishes," she said. "Just the concession stand."

Since I refused to believe her, she invited me to have a look in the lobby.

Sure enough, in the lobby there was a concession stand. A peek inside the theater itself revealed rows of theater seating. I'd held an image of a dinner theater where people sat at tables around the stage as they ate steak and drank martinis while Newton performed his lounge act. Instead, the audience sat in theater seats as they popped popcorn and slurped sodas as if Newton were a circus act.

When I expressed my surprise to the ticket lady, she told me that almost none of Branson's theaters were *dinner* theaters.

I couldn't believe it. How could I work my way through the town's dinner-theater dishpit circuit when one didn't even exist? If I were to leave Welk's and stay in town, my options would be limited to the loathsome chain joints.

Back in the van, I started driving. But when I reached the entrance to Welk's, I kept going. The notion had already struck. There could be no going back. Besides, no matter how many more places I worked at in Missouri, the state would always remain #28.

At the country gift shop, I told the landlady I was moving out.

"You didn't give me much notice," she said.

I replied, "I didn't know myself that I'd be leaving so soon."

On my way out of town, I again passed Golden Corral's "Dishwasher Wanted" marquee. I hit the gas.

Part III

Quitting Time

27

Just Wandering

After a few weeks of rambling, I landed in Boise to finally hit Idaho some six years after the state had first been targeted unsuccessfully during my Northwest Tour. Within twenty-four hours of my rolling into town, Idaho clocked in as state #29: a gig was landed in the cafeteria at Hewlett-Packard's corporate campus.

At 3:30 p.m. on my first day, the soon-to-be-former pot-scrubber who was training me said it was time to go.

"What about the rest of this stuff?" I asked, pointing to the stacks of awaiting baking sheets and pots.

"Just leave it for tomorrow," he said.

On my way out, the kitchen manager caught my attention by looking at me and stroking her jawbone.

"Don't forget," she said.

Earlier that day, at the daily kitchen staff safety meeting

(the morning's topic: Be careful—knives are sharp), she'd introduced me to the fifty-odd cooks, bakers, cashiers and dishwashers. Then she remarked that if I didn't shave the scruff from my face by the following day, I'd be working in a beard net.

Movie stars don't shave for a couple days and they look chic. I don't shave for a couple days and I look jobless—even when I *have* a job!

Though I didn't have a rule about not working in a beard net, it was only because it'd never occurred to me to establish one. Normally, something like a beard-net requirement would've provoked me to leave a sterile fluorescent-flooded kitchen and go snatch up a dish job someplace where I could be as whiskered as I wanted. But those places didn't have what HP had: full-time pot scrubbing. With the opportunity to move "pot-scrubber" from my To Do list to do to my Done list, I had to suck it up and break the not-yet-established beard-net rule by not walking out.

It was midwinter and my nights were spent parked in a dirt lot behind an apartment complex. Lying under my sleeping bag and seven thrift-store blankets, by flashlight I would read through the latest batch of mail, then write replies until falling asleep. At 6:30 a.m., I'd get up and smash the half-inch-thick layer of ice in my plastic water jug so I could shave—in the dark—with the frigid water and get to work by seven o'clock. Each morning, I'd trudge past a maze of office cubicles that covered an area the size of a football field (I'd walked off the measurements) on my way to my own cubicle—the pot cubicle—where I'd be greeted by the pots and pans I hadn't finished the previous afternoon.

Then I'd scrub all day, trying to finish the burnt pots and

pans by the end of my shift. But come 3:30, when I'd finally drain the sinks, a stack of dirties would be left to await my cleaning the following day. I'd exit past the cubicle maze. Peering over the dividers, I'd see people sitting at their desks but had no idea what they were doing. In contrast, anyone who'd see me in action at work would automatically know I was a pot-scrubber. But they just sat at their desks—like professional desk-sitters.

After work, it was back to hanging out by myself since I knew no one in Boise. Even HP's dishwasher crew was anonymous to me because their cubicle was on the other side of the cafeteria from mine. So I tried to look up some of the locals from the thousands of names in my address book. At the first two addresses, the search resulted in awkward encounters, with me asking for people who no longer lived there. On the phone, though, I managed to reach a guy who'd regularly corresponded with me years before.

"This is Pete," I told him. "Dishwasher Pete."

"Dishwasher *what*?"

"Dishwasher *Pete*," I repeated. "I write that *Dishwasher* zine."

There was a long pause, then a slow, suspicious, *"Yeah?"*

"Yeah, I'm in Boise, scrubbing pots out at the Hewlett-Packard plant."

"And?"

"And I was calling to see if you wanted to go get some ice cream or something."

Another pause. "No, I don't think so."

"Oh, okay," I said. "I just thought, you know, maybe you would."

"No," he said.

"Aw right," I said. "See ya."

After I hung up, I felt pathetic. Years before, this guy had probably gotten a kick out of corresponding with an itinerant dishman. But since then, he'd probably thrown out his zines, got married, bought a house, had kids. . . . When he hung up the phone, his wife probably asked, "Who was that?"

"Nobody," he'd have said to her. "Just some weirdo wanting me to eat ice cream with him."

People changed, I guessed. But somehow, I didn't. I was still just wandering around, washing dishes as usual.

I put away my address book and didn't bother contacting anyone else.

That night, in Crescent, I opened a letter from a Los Angeles filmmaker who'd written to ask if she could capture my quest on film. The request was hardly unique; it was the fourth query from a documentary filmmaker.

Having a camera in my face held no appeal. But then, who knew? Maybe this woman would dig gallivanting around with me. After all, her letter was so enthusiastic, it boarded on being flirty. As we traveled together in Crescent from state to state, maybe she'd fall for both my lifestyle *and* me. Maybe—*just maybe*—it could work between us as she turned my life into a movie.

I could see it already on the big screen: scenes of camping out under a tent of blankets, shaving with ice water in the dark in the back of a customized 1973 van, calling up strangers looking for ice cream dates in the middle of winter. . . .

Wait a sec. What woman would want to stick around for that? This filmmaker lady would surely get sick of the bumming around. She'd bolt back to L.A. before she could say, "Cut!" And experience already showed that a mailbox full of postcards and letters from me wouldn't be enough to tide her over until the next time I passed through town. In fact, every relationship I'd had always ended, in part, because of my foolish belief that I could keep traveling while still maintaining the romance.

Certain it wouldn't work out with the filmmaker, I wrote her one of my usual "thanks, but no thanks" replies.

The next afternoon, I used my phone gizmo to call Jess and told him what a downer Boise was.

"Yeah, but just think—you're the world's most famous dishwasher!" he said, trying to cheer me up.

Jess had enjoyed saying this ever since he had a cush dish job handed to him in San Francisco merely because the restaurant owner was trying to get him to introduce me to her.

"No I'm not," I told him.

"Well, if *you're* not," he said, "then *who is?*"

Maybe he had a point. I couldn't think of any other rightful claimants. Until the day an exceptional dish dog went straight from the sinks to either become president or assassinate one, I was probably stuck with the title. But little good that did me. I couldn't even find someone to eat ice cream with me in Boise.

So then, one Thursday night, I went by myself to an ice cream parlor. It was February 10, 2000, a date that seemed like it shouldn't go unnoted. So I spoiled myself by ordering a banana split.

It was supposed to be a celebratory dessert. On February 10, 1990—exactly ten years earlier—I'd proclaimed my fifty-state goal. But as I shoved the scoops down my throat, I wondered, What am I celebrating? Ten years of clean dishes? Ten years of roaming? Or ten years of cultivating carpal tunnel syndrome, tendonitis and a stiff back?

Embarking on the quest had enabled me to satisfy my curiosity about what lay beyond San Francisco's borders. During those years, not only had I seen so many corners of the nation, I was also able to window-shop the country for a place to live once all fifty states had been dished. But the more I traveled, the harder it became to stay put. And now I was on a course toward total rootlessness.

By the time I'd scraped the last of the cold hot fudge out of the bottom of the dish, I determined that if I'd learned just one thing from a full decade of travels, jobs and ailments, it was this: I didn't want to settle down in a van in Boise.

As miserable as I was, I couldn't afford to leave town for another couple weeks, not until the next payday. So I slaved onward. Day by day, I gained ground on the pots, leaving fewer and fewer of them to soak overnight. Finally—after striving for twenty-two straight shifts—one afternoon, I managed to clean every single pot, pan and cooking utensil. At the end of that shift, I was able to stand for a minute and take in, for the first time, the sight of a vacant, sparkling pot cubicle.

The following day was payday. The weeks of struggling to keep pace with the pots were over. Come 3:30, I left behind in the cubicle dozens of sheet pans coated with burnt bacon grease—an offering to whoever would replace me. At 3:45, I cashed my check. At 5:58, Crescent and I said good riddance to Idaho and crossed the state line.

I reached Portland, Oregon, and within two days was dishing again at two of my old haunts: Paradox and La Cruda. Though the gigs were in state #15—a state I'd conquered many times over—they were at places where I could be as slovenly as I wanted about shaving, where I got paid in cash after each shift and where I was able to wash both the pots *and* the dishes.

•

While it was good to be back in a town where I had no shortage of pals to eat ice cream with, I was sad to find that so many of my colleagues had gotten out of the dishwashing racket. Hawthorne had left Genoa and was now in advertising. At La Cruda, Lauren was now a cook. Yanul ditched Montage to become a full-time musician. It was all part of a larger trend. Letters were frequently arriving from long-time pearl divers who apologetically confessed to me—the Dish Master—that they'd hung up their aprons and found other, less worthy employment. While I soldiered on, others were dropping left and right.

The worst was when, not long before, I'd slipped through the back door of a café in Arcata and found Jeff chopping vegetables. When my dish guru noticed me, he looked as guilty as if I'd caught him chopping up a baby. He averted eye contact and said, "It pays twenty-five cents an hour more."

In Portland, I was volunteering again at Reading Frenzy while crashing at the house of the shop's owner, Chloe, and its lone paid employee—Amy Joy. It'd been three years since Amy Joy had taken me to lunch at the diner, two years since she'd gifted me the sunset picnic and a year since she'd treated me to dinner in New Orleans. As cheap as I was, it was painfully obvious that it was now *my* turn to feed *her*.

During a pizza-slice dinner, I told Amy Joy about my miserable time in Boise. And about how constantly bouncing around the country like a pinball was wearing me down. And about how I only ever had affairs with places—and dumped each for the prettier one just down the road.

Later that night, while treating her to drinks at a bar, I said, "I just wanna have some little place of my own."

I wanted to experience the change of seasons year-round in the same spot, to stick around long enough to join a bowling league, to cultivate a garden.

"At the very least," I said, "I wanna own a plant."

I was telling Amy Joy that I wanted to buy a house somewhere—a home base for the last years of my quest until I finally settled down for good. Amy Joy said she wanted to join me.

This time I finally got the hint.

On the surface, it appeared that I'd finally discovered the answer to the question: "What woman chooses to live with a dishwasher?" To be honest, though, I didn't believe it could work between us. I figured I'd take off for the dishes, go roaming around while thinking everything was hunky-dory. And in the meantime, she'd dump me.

Amy Joy assured me she wouldn't.

Yet how did I respond? By unconsciously trying to shake her off my trail.

But whenever I'd suggest we go for ice cream in stormy weather, Amy Joy never daintily demurred. She was always ready to ride her bike with me in the rain to the ice cream shop.

And when—during a trip up to Washington—I'd suggest we ride another ferry, Amy Joy was always game. In a single day, we rode six different Puget Sound ferries.

And whenever I mentioned that I didn't know where I wanted to buy a house, Amy Joy was never bothered. It didn't matter to her, as long as we were together.

For once, I couldn't shake a woman—no matter how hard I tried.

Amy Joy was definately a keeper. Only problem: *where* to keep her.

28
Cheap Houses,
Cheap Dishman

So ... where to live? That'd always been the kicked-about hypothetical question while I traveled. Now, though, it really needed to be answered.

From all my years of bouncing around I knew settling down in the mountains or in the country or even in just a small town like Colby, Kansas, was out of the question. I'd go stir-crazy and quickly become restless if I lived somewhere where there weren't plenty of old neighborhoods to explore by bike or foot. That also ruled out the nation's many sprawling suburbs. A city like New Orleans would've fit the bill if it weren't for its relentless humidity. For that matter, the climate canceled out the entire South. Southern California was easily ruled out because it was a nightmare for cycling or walking. At the same time, cities that were landlocked, like Phoenix or

Denver, were especially suspect and to be avoided since they didn't feel like they should even have a reason for existing.

Cities like New York, Boston and San Francisco were alluring candidates because they had plenty of old interesting neighborhoods suitable for exploring. They fit almost all of my criteria, in fact, except that a dishman simply couldn't afford to live in them. According to a survey of wages by the Bureau of Labor Statistics, of 505 occupations, dishwashing came in 505th—dead last—with only a $13,000 annual average. To be able to settle into my own home in my own hometown of San Francisco, I'd have to work at least five or six full-time dish jobs at the same time. With my occupation's crap wages, even a town like Portland—the place I'd drifted back to so many times—was out of my league.

After much contemplation, I finally determined the ideal place for me to establish a base. It was a good-size city and had numerous old and interesting neighborhoods. Though it was still somewhat decaying since its industrial glory days had ended, it *was* tree-filled, river-lined and hilly. The people I knew there were all nice. And it seemed like a place I'd remain excited about each time I woke up and slowly realized where I was. Most important, it had heaps of cheap houses that even a cheap dishman could afford.

It was back in state #21—Pittsburgh, Pennsylvania.

When I told Amy Joy it was my destination, she eagerly packed up her stuff and threw it in Crescent. She left behind her life in Portland to move two thousand miles away to a town she'd never even seen before. I grabbed about seven thousand of the ten thousand *Dishwasher* #16 covers, figuring I'd finally get around to publishing that issue since, by now, I had thousands of orders for it. Then we left.

My plan to find a cheap home was to scour the hillsides for a vacant house that could only be reached by one of the city's many municipal stairwells. In an age when everyone needed to be able to drive their car right up (or even into) their house, the demand for homes that were inaccessible by car and could be reached only by climbing/descending hundreds of stairs couldn't be that great. And in a town of cheap houses, a hundred-year-old house in that kind of a location would be the cheapest, especially if it sat empty.

After a few days of climbing and descending thousands of hillside stairs, I finally found a good prospect for my future base of operations: a rinky-dink house on the South Side Slopes, a hillside overlooking the Monongahela River. It sat a hundred steps below the street above and two hundred above the street below. Through the county assessor's office, I tracked down its owner, who showed me the house the next day. Modest, secluded and vacant for several years—it fit the bill perfectly. After the owner led me around the old place that his late parents had called home for decades, he asked me how much I was willing to pay for it.

"I don't know," I said honestly. "Fifteen thousand?"

"*Really?*" he said, raising his eyebrows.

I didn't know if this meant my figure was too high or too low.

He then added, "I was thinking more like . . . *thirty* thousand."

There was a pause on my part before I realized we were now negotiating.

"Uh, okay," I said. "How 'bout—seventeen thousand?"

"Twenty-five," he shot back.

"Nineteen."

He thought for a second, then said, "I really can't go lower than twenty-five."

Geez, I thought, *twenty-five thousand dollars!* Even though he would've been asking twenty to thirty times the price if the house were back in San Francisco, twenty-five thousand meant washing a shitload of dishes. The biggest purchase I'd ever made up till then was the $1,400 I'd blown on Crescent.

To stall for time before making such a decision, I told the owner I'd have to get a second opinion.

When I returned the next day with my friend George, he immediately pointed out something I'd overlooked. The building sat on a foundation made up of loose rocks the size of pizza delivery boxes, one corner of which had already given way to a minor landslide.

"That's bad?" I asked George.

"Not if you don't mind your house sliding down the hill," he said.

George warned me not to buy the place. And it was just as well he had. I barely had twenty-five *dollars* to my name let alone twenty-five *grand*. George and others told me that I needed to get approved for this thing called a mortgage, where a bank would buy the house and then I'd pay the bank back over the years. It was something I'd never even considered years before in Kansas, when I'd wanted to buy a $15,000 house in one lump payment. The reason that plan had failed was because I'd never saved up the $15,000. So this mortgage thing sounded like the way to go to make the Pittsburgh project work.

The mortgage application I picked up from a bank asked me to list stuff like my assets and credit history and job history. Assets? I still had my duffel bag and my sleeping bag and my three-speed bike after all those years. Crescent was good for a few hundred bucks. What else? Stocks? Nope. Trust funds? No. Bank accounts? I'd closed my last bank account twenty years earlier when I'd quit my paper route. With little to report, I skipped the asset section.

Next: credit history. Well, there was that student loan I'd taken out when I first went off to college at seventeen. Actually, maybe it was best I didn't mention that loan since I'd defaulted on it before eventually paying it back. Besides, I had other credit history to boast about. Of the umpteen times I'd bummed money from family and friends, I'd paid back every loan each time I was employed again. But the application didn't provide space to explain all this. There was space, though, to list my credit cards. I'd never had a credit card, so I moved on.

Next: employment. Now we're talking, I thought. If I had *too little* information for those other sections, I had oodles of info to fill this section, what with all the jobs I'd held. But then I realized, it wasn't the *quantity* of my past jobs the bank was looking for, but rather the *quality* and *security* of my current one. The bank wanted to ensure I wasn't just some shiftless habitual job-quitter who couldn't make monthly payments.

I left the mortgage application blank.

Before I could even think about buying a house, I had to liven up my mortgage-worthiness. I needed to open bank accounts and round up credit cards. More important, I needed to find a steady dish job and hang on to it for months or even—gasp—*years*.

29

The Blue-Rimmed Plate

My dream of a house temporarily deferred, Amy Joy found us an apartment to rent and I heard that the deli at a Pittsburgh co-op food market needed a dishman. Seven years earlier, I'd dished at a similar food co-op in Boston. I'd appreciated that the fruits of my labor went toward the good of the store and its members rather than toward lining a restaurant owner's pockets with profits. So this Pittsburgh co-op sounded like a promising workplace for trying to hold down a steady job.

Getting hired was a snap. The tough part was—for the first time ever—to try to do what most people did routinely. It was what my dad had always done: go to the same job . . . work it every day . . . *indefinitely*.

At every stop along my fifty-state quest, an end to each job always remained comfortably within sight. Whether it was a couple weeks or—at the very most—a few months, the fact I knew there'd be a day not far off when I'd no longer have to come to the job helped me to ever go to the job in the first place.

Breaking the Fundamental Rule on the oil rig had been an easier challenge than this one; on the oil rig, I knew from the start I only had to survive two weeks, tops. Here, there was no telling how long I'd have to stick around in order to convince a banker that I wasn't a habitual quitter.

So any morning I was scheduled to dish, I couldn't roll over and go back to sleep. When I was riding my bike to work, I couldn't flake out and keep on pedaling. And if a cook burnt a pan or my back acted up, I couldn't pull off the apron and walk out. Every urge to succumb to the notion had to be suppressed.

That I actually didn't completely hate the job helped the suppression. The young deli manager seemed scared of me and gave me a lot of leeway. The other deli employees were all interesting and entertaining. I ate well on the clock and was even able to take home tons of leftovers to Amy Joy. Best of all, after three months, I'd have health insurance for the only time in my adult life aside from when I dished in Alaska.

As the weeks passed and the impulses were quelled, little by little, I transformed into Mr. Reliable. I was never late, always arrived clean-shaven and kicked ass with the dishes. Not only did I never blow off work, I became the guy the deli manager called when the *other* disher was too hung over to work.

Life as Mr. Reliable was good for a couple months, until I started to notice the blue-rimmed plate. The deli used only plain white plates, so the sudden appearance of the oddball blue-rimmed plate was a mystery. Had a coworker brought in a plate of homemade cookies and forgotten to take the plate home again? Had a customer somehow slipped it in? I asked my coworkers, but no one knew where it'd come from.

Each time I washed him, Blue-Rimmed caught my attention. As soon as he was returned to the clean stacks, up he'd pop again in my sinks. It seemed like I was washing him constantly. Then, on a busy Saturday in the deli, I counted how many times Blue-Rimmed passed through my hands. *Twenty-seven times!* I couldn't believe it.

Up until then, I'd always considered dishwashing a progressive pursuit: I'd start a shift with dirty dishes, finish it with clean ones, then move on to the next town, the next job, always moving forward. But, as Blue-Rimmed went round and round, he pointed out that I had it all wrong. Really I was just moving in circles: washing things that only got dirty again within minutes. The next town, the next job, the story would always be the same: the dishes would never remain clean.

Over and over, Blue-Rimmed seemed to ridicule me, saying, "Dishwashing is pointless."

I tried to silence Blue-Rimmed by hiding him on the bottom of the clean stacks or by leaving him on the bottom of the sink while I washed the anonymous white dishes in his place. But no matter what I did, Blue-Rimmed always worked his way back into my hands, where I was subjected to his taunts yet again.

Finally, I had enough of him. And with great satisfaction, I threw him at the floor and watched him smash into blue-rimmed shards.

But the satisfaction was short-lived. Though the messenger was dead, his message lived on. Despite the shattered corpse on the floor, dishwashing still remained pointless. Even worse, my nemesis had the last laugh. Instead of just kicking the shards under the counter as the Dishwasher Pete of old would've done, Mr. Reliable dutifully swept up the remains and deposited them in the trash.

A couple of nights later, I took a tumble of my own. While exploring a new route home from work, my bike hit a speed bump in the dark. I flew over the handlebars and landed on my face. When I awoke, my very first thought was: That's odd—the street's wet, but it isn't raining.

I lay there with a damp face until I heard a car approaching and then scrambled to sit up. The car slowed as I stared directly into its red headlights. *Red* headlights? I looked down. The little puddle my face had been lying in was blood.

I looked up at the car's driver and he looked back at me aghast.

"It's bad, huh?" I asked.

"No, no, no," he stammered while looking visibly ill at the sight of me. This wasn't a good sign. It seemed like he should've been able to handle it. After all, he was a cop.

The driver and his partner stepped out of their patrol car and helped me to my feet. They wiped some blood off my face and wrapped my head in a bandage. They had no fasteners, so they affixed the bandage by simply tucking it into itself.

"You sure you don't want us to call an ambulance?" one of them asked.

"No," I said. "Can't afford it."

My health insurance from work was still a couple weeks away from kicking in. And an ambulance ride was nothing but a thousand-dollar taxi ride and—for someone too cheap to even take a regular taxi—out of the question.

The cops then got a call over their radio and had to go.

Slumped over the handlebars, as I pushed myself home on my bike, the bloody bandage began to unravel and trail in the wind behind my bloody face. Judging from the leeway motorists gave me at intersections, it must've made for a gruesome sight,

Once home, I didn't first inspect my injuries or even lie down. Instead, I did something that would've made the old Dishwasher Pete puke: Mr. Reliable called work.

"Hey," I told the baker, "I won't be in tomorrow."

"What's wrong?" she asked.

"I'm not sure," I said. "I fell off my bike and don't feel so good."

Amy Joy wasn't home, so a friend picked me up and drove me to the emergency room.

As a doctor stood over me and tweezed the gravel out of my head and sewed up the gash, I lay there in a daze. With the lamp shining in my face, I admired his work. It must be nice to be skilled, I thought. If someone had come to me with a nasty head wound and asked me to help him, I'd be confounded. If he'd bloodied his dishes in the process, then I could wash those. Otherwise, he'd be shit out of luck.

During my hours in the emergency room, I admired the work of all the nurses and doctors that treated me. Maybe it was the concussion, maybe it was the Percocet, but I couldn't stop thinking about how these people were using their skills to do valuable work. They were actually making a difference in the world. Meanwhile, what was I doing with my life? Over and over, I was just washing the same dishes (blue-rimmed or not) that only ended up dirty again within minutes.

I'd always joked that there was no hurry for me to complete my mission because I wouldn't know what to do with myself afterwards. Now, I wanted to know.

With a broken arm, two sprained wrists and a mangled knee, there wasn't much else I could do but lounge around the apartment to convalesce. I lay in bed and thought about the speed bump I'd hit. Whoever had designed it or installed it doubtlessly had done so without cyclists in mind. The angle of the bump was so severe, it could've been deadly for someone on a bike. But that wasn't surprising. There seemed to be a lot of road infrastructure intended for cyclists in Pittsburgh that didn't make sense—as if they'd been designed by someone who didn't ride a bike on a regular basis. There were too many civil servants who only drove their cars yet were responsible for dealing with the way cyclists, pedestrians and public transit users navigated their ways through cities. There needed to be more people in such jobs who viewed transportation from a nonmotorist's perspective. As I lay around, I realized that one of those someones should be me.

After all the cycling and walking and public transit riding I'd done throughout the nation, it seemed like I could put my knowledge to use to help produce better means of travel. It'd sure beat producing temporarily clean dishes. In order to get the skills to attain some sort of desk-sitting job in that field, I wanted to return to college and finally pursue a degree in something I was interested in: urban planning.

After mulling it over the whole week after my tumble, I told Amy Joy about my idea of returning to college. I'd first pursue a degree and then a desk-sitting job as some sort of transportation planner for a municipal agency or a nonprofit advocacy group.

She liked the idea.

First though: my mission.

When Jess had told Letterman that he (meaning: *I*) didn't want to finish the states before he/I was thirty-five, I was only twenty-eight. Now, on my next birthday, I'd turn thirty-five. And *before* that date hit, I wanted my apron to be hung up for good; the quest achieved once and for all.

To do so would mean racing to tackle the remaining twenty-one states while crossing off lingering items from my To Do list: dude-ranch dishing in Wyoming; working in Shelbyville, Illinois, where Josephine Cochrane had invented the motorized dishwashing machine; visiting my pals at the Champion dishmachine company in Winston-Salem, North Carolina, to work as an official test disher on their new models; and pearl diving in Pierre, South Dakota—one of only two state capitals I'd never been to.

In addition, I still wanted to dish on a riverboat and at a state fair and on a train and in a restaurant atop a skyscraper and in a catering firm's mobile dishwashing trailer.

And, of course, it would all culminate in Honolulu—the other state capital I'd never been to—where I'd finally enact the whole final dishmachine smooch and beer-on-the-beach Hawaiian grand finale.

To accomplish all this, a thorough, comprehensive push was required. It would call for an unprecedented Herculean effort. Thus, the Farewell to Dishwashing Tour was born.

With the buying-a-house-in-Pittsburgh project now dead, Amy Joy returned to Portland. I stored three thousand of the remaining seven thousand *Dishwasher* #16 covers in a friend's attic in Pittsburgh and loaded the rest in the van. Since orders were still coming in for the issue, I figured somewhere along the way, I'd finally get around to publishing it.

Then I set out on the Farewell Tour.

30
Hell Train

The Tour's first stop: Rhode Island.

I'd always wanted to bust suds on a moving train like Malcolm X had when he worked on the New York, New Haven and Hartford Railroad in the 1940s. In his autobiography, he recalled making the run between Boston and Washington, D.C.: "Against the sound of the train clacking along, the waiters were jabbering the customers' orders, the cooks operated like machines, and five hundred miles of dirty pots and dishes and silverware rattled back to me." Aah, traveling while dishing. Or was it dishing while traveling? Either way, I wanted to do it too.

The Amtrak application I'd toted around was now worthless to me. While I was busy being too lazy to send it in, Amtrak had gone and replaced its dishes with disposables. The few pots that needed scrubbing were done by the train's lowest-ranking cooks. The dishwashing crew was laid off.

After spending a couple years thinking I'd blown my chance, I rejoiced when I read a newspaper article about a Rhode Island dinner train. Maybe I had a shot, after all. So I called the outfit's owner and told him I wanted to dish on his train.

"I've already got a dishwasher," he replied.

Normally, as a job applicant, I remained extremely low-key, never wanting to present myself as a hotshot pearl diver—a Dish Master—lest anyone ever expect me to actually work like one. However, this was now not only the Farewell Tour but, very likely, my only chance to ever dish on a train.

I took a deep breath and then poured it on.

"I'm trying to wash dishes in all fifty states," I admitted. "And for Rhode Island, I wanna work on your train."

There was a long pause on his end of the line before he asked, "You writing about this or something?"

I didn't know what answer he wanted to hear. Would my owning up to dishwashing journalism scare him off or would it win him over? The odds seemed fifty-fifty.

"Yeah," I answered cautiously. "Yeah, I am."

"Great!" he said. "We'll get you all set up!"

Wow, I thought. Who knew that being honest when applying for a job could actually be beneficial?

A few days later, on a Saturday morning, I boarded the train in Portsmouth, Rhode Island (#30). In the cook car, John—the head cook—introduced himself to me. As the train started rolling, John explained our itinerary. In Newport, we'd pick up 125 passengers and feed them lunch while we traveled up the coast and back down again. Then, a couple hours later, we'd drop off the group and retrace our route with another 100 passengers.

John showed me the dishpit in the middle of the car. It had a sink, a sprayer and a Hobart machine. Aside from the railings that lined the counters to prevent the dishes from sliding onto the floor, it wasn't unlike dozens of dishpits I'd toiled in. Well, there was *one* major difference, which was made obvious as the train picked up speed. This was a pit on the move. It could take a dish dog places.

Since we wouldn't pick up passengers for another hour, there wasn't yet much for me to do, so John welcomed me to look around. The cook car was sandwiched between the first-class dining car in front of us and the coach dining car behind us. While the two cooks prepared meals, waitresses set the tables.

I stepped out onto the platform behind the cook car and took in the view of the passing Narragansett Bay.

A waitress stepped outside smoking a cigarette and said to me, "Welcome to the Hell Train."

"Hell Train?" I asked. "You mean we're bound for hell?"

"No," she said. "I mean we're *in* hell."

Hell? We were restaurant workers riding the rails with the wind in our hair and without a care in the world!

"I always thought working on a train would be fun," I said.

"Yeah, right," she snorted, then flicked her cigarette off the train and stepped back inside.

An hour after I boarded, we rolled into the Newport train depot. As our senior citizen passengers boarded, a very jittery older guy in a suit rushed up to me. He introduced himself as Bob—the owner of the train—and shook my hand frantically.

"Pete, we're glad to have you aboard," he said.

Then, just as suddenly, he hurried away.

When we were rolling again, the cooks dashed back and forth as they served up the food. The waitresses squeezed past me at my dishpit as they ran the salads and drinks out to the passengers.

Minutes later, the first wave of dirty dishes reached the dishpit and started sliding across the counter. I had to swiftly adapt to high-speed dishing. The trembling, wavering stacks of dishes had to be steadied lest they topple onto the floor. When the train hit curves, I had to brace myself by hooking my toes under the counter. The greatest challenge was carrying stacks of plates though the car's narrow passageway while dodging cooks and waitresses as the fun-house floor bounced and swayed beneath me. Having admitted I was a hotshot, I now had to back up the claim by not dropping any dishes under these adverse conditions.

After I ran a few racks of salad plates through the dish-machine, the water pressure in the sink's sprayer suddenly died. Without the sprayer, I couldn't rinse off the plates. In turn, loads of food scraps from the plates ended up in the Hobart and quickly turned its water dark and grungy. So I drained the water, cleaned the inside of the machine, then hit the Fill button.

After the machine had filled for a few minutes, I peeked inside and saw only a trace of water across its bottom. I hit the Fill button again.

As Bob scurried by, I asked him, "Is there a trick to filling this machine?"

He saw the Fill button was on and said, "It's filling."

"But there's no water."

"No, listen."

Together we paused and—over the rumbling of the train—listened to the machine's pathetic gurgling.

"See," he said. "It's filling."

Bob ran off again. He had a calamity to tend to. On this 90-degree day, the air-conditioner in Coach had gone down.

"Whoever knows CPR better get in Coach!" a waitress shouted. "These old farts are gonna start droppin' like flies!"

"This is horrible!" Bob exclaimed. "Free drinks for Coach! Everyone hear that? Coach gets free drinks!"

While still waiting for the dishmachine to fill, I tried to wash the dishes by hand. But without water pressure in my taps, I didn't get far. So I grabbed a bucket, stuck it in the sink at the bar and turned on the hot-water tap. Out dribbled cold water the color of iced tea.

I asked the "Hell Train" waitress, "Does the water always look like this?"

She looked in the bucket. Then she looked up at me, chuckled and walked away. If this really was part of some attempt to test the Dish Master, I was impressed.

I told John that the taps were providing only a trickle of cold brown water.

"Yeah, I think the engineer fucked up and forgot to fill the water tank," he said. "The brown is probably sediment from the bottom of the tank."

His suggestion was to boil the water and then add it to the machine. He took my bucket of water, poured it in a pot and set the pot on the stove. In the meantime, as the dirty dishes piled higher and the train rocked side to side, I spent my time steadying the teetering stacks to prevent them from crashing to the floor.

After ten minutes on the stove, the pot of water only managed to reach a tepid temperature. I couldn't wait any longer for it to boil so I dumped the lukewarm brown liquid in the machine and then sent the dishes through. There was no fresh water for the machine's rinse cycle. The same food-laden lukewarm brown water was splashing around inside. Thus, the dishes were soon coming out nastier than when they went in.

When Bob again asked how it was going, as the hotshot dishman, I reluctantly showed him the "clean" plates. Still, he didn't flinch.

"Yeah, okay," he said. "That's great."

The dishwashing fiasco was overshadowed by yet another, more pressing, calamity.

Because more people had ordered fish entrées than were available, some emergency chicken breast had been pulled out of the freezer and pressed into service as the non-red-meat entrée. Now these same chicken breasts were being sent back from the dining cars, their insides still frozen.

Bob was frantic.

"I'm gonna have to refund everyone in Coach," he said. "This is terrible. A disaster!"

Since, in a half hour, the dishes would be needed to feed another hundred people, I had little choice but to continue "washing" them regardless of how filthy they remained. This wasn't exactly how I'd fantasized train dishing. Surely Malcolm X—despite whatever primitive conditions he'd dished under a half century earlier—had, at the very least, running water.

I managed to finish the first group's dishes by the time the second group boarded. The second time around ran much smoother. By then, I was sending the used glasses back to the bar without making them suffer their fate in the Hobart. As for the plates, I was wiping them clean with a towel as best as I could do.

Bob walked by again.

"How's it going, Pete?" he asked. "Is the water running again?"

"No," I replied.

"Aw right," he said, still unconcerned. "You're doing a *fantastic* job!"

When we pulled into Newport for the third time, right before disembarking with the rest of the passengers, Bob stopped by the dishpit one last time.

"Sorry about all the problems," he said. "It's not usually like this."

"Well, thanks for letting me work on your train."

He then handed me a wad of cash and said, "I hope you write a good story about us."

After he stepped off the train, I locked myself in the bathroom and counted my take: $110! For less than seven hours' work, he'd paid me nearly sixteen bucks an hour. Was this a bribe? Hush money to keep me quiet? If so, instead of being offended, I was impressed to discover that dishwashing journalism could literally pay off.

When I finished the dishes fifteen minutes before we were due to arrive back in Portsmouth—the train's final destination— the head cook handed me a beer.

"Man, you're the best dishwasher I've seen in my four years here!" he said. "Usually guys don't finish until twenty minutes *after* we arrive."

"That was nothing," I said. "You should see me when I've got some running water."

I did feel smug, though. Even if the dishes weren't really

all that clean, I'd survived all the train's rocking and bucking without letting a single dish hit the floor.

Just before I stepped off the Hell Train, though it needed a whole lot more affection than I could provide, I kissed the poor dishmachine farewell.

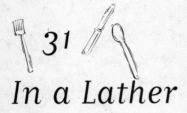

31

In a Lather

After Rhode Island, I hit a seafood place on a dock along the coast of Connecticut (#31), which finished off the last of the northeastern states. The Farewell Tour then turned south to the remaining southern states. In Gainesville, Florida (#32), for a few weeks I filled in for a dish dog buddy at his job at an Italian place while he took a vacation.

In Gulf Shores, Alabama (#33), I plied my trade at another coastal seafood place. One evening, after work, I was driving along looking for a place to park for the night when a truck pulled even with me. Its driver signaled for me to pull over. It was Cheryl's boyfriend, Jake.

On the side of the road, Jake explained he was driving from Florida back to New Orleans. He was amazed that we'd run into each other at night on a road in Alabama. Wasn't I amazed too?

"I guess so," I said, so frazzled from a long day of work, I wasn't sure. Then, while admiring Crescent, Jake said that if I ever wanted to sell it, he'd consider buying it. But for now, I had to put this amazing van's bed to use, so I said so long to Jake and was parked and sleeping within ten minutes.

A couple days later, while passing back through Georgia—state #5 from some ten years earlier—I stopped in Decatur to fulfill another long-standing goal: to work at the same bus station diner where, in the 1950s, Little Richard had dished. According to the singer, the boss would say to him, "When are you going to wash those dishes, boy?"

Little Richard would reply, "A wop-bop-a-loo-mop, a lop-bam-boom!"

His way of cussing out the boss without getting axed became the basis for the song he wrote while dishing—"Tutti Frutti."

But the bus station on Broadway where Little Richard had worked was gone. A few blocks away, the closest thing the new bus station had to a diner was a candy vending machine. The site of the old bus station was now but a tiny grassy square overshadowed by a large parking garage. Since I was unable to pay proper homage by dishing on the very same spot, I did the next best thing: I commemorated the site sacred not only to dishwashing history, but to rock 'n' roll history as well. Christening the square "Little Richard's Dishwashing Days Memorial Park," on sheets of paper that I posted around the square, I wrote the new name of the park along with a quote from the man himself:

I was the most beautiful dishwasher in the world!

•

Next stop: South Carolina. Nothing stirred this itinerant dish-man's heart like the allure of a resort town and its countless dish jobs. Myrtle Beach in the summer, I envisioned, would be the height of harvest season with plenty of plum dish jobs ripe for the picking. In fact, according to the Bureau of Labor Statistics, Myrtle Beach ranked second (behind only Atlantic City, New Jersey) among metropolitan areas with the highest concentrations of employed dishwashers. Nation-ally, there was one dish job for every 600 people. In Myrtle Beach, it was one dish job for every 170.

Yet, despite the existence of a reported twelve hundred dishwashing positions in Myrtle Beach, there was little evi-dence of them upon my arrival. Unlike my warm reception in Branson, Missouri, when I pulled into *this* resort town, no restaurant marquees begged for dishwashers, no newspaper want ads listed desperate pleas.

I drove up and down along the thirty-five-mile coastline past all the dozens of restaurants and hotels—and came up with nothing.

I popped into numerous eateries to ask for work—and popped out of each one of them still jobless.

For several mornings, I even paced the waiting room at the seedy day-labor office, biding my time till a call came in for a dishwasher. No call ever came.

This boomtown was a bust.

Then one afternoon, to search for a job online, I went to the town library. While I sat and waited for an available com-puter, I noticed most of the others in line were talking funny.

"You from Ireland?" I asked the teenage girl next to me.

"Yeah, we all are," she said, indicating the other dozen teens in the waiting area.

"You're here on vacation?"

"No, we're working here."

She explained that, like lots of other Irish teens, they were spending their summer breaks from school by working in Myrtle Beach as hotel housekeepers and waitresses.

"And dishwashers?" I asked.

"Yeah, dishwashing too."

Unbelievable! My own people had crossed an ocean just to snap up all the dish jobs in town! Weren't there any dishes to be washed back in Ireland?

I left the library with no leads and diminishing hope. A major reason why I'd taken on dishwashing in the first place was because dish jobs were so easy to land and I hated looking for work. I'd come to South Carolina to spend my time working. Instead, my time was being spent *looking* for work—by auto, no less, and not by foot.

A full week after arriving, I crawled out of the van and picked up the morning newspaper. Finally, a new ad appeared. Cracker Barrel—the restaurant chain of homogenized "home cookin'" popular across the South—needed me!

I jumped back in Crescent and raced ten miles straight to Cracker Barrel. With the van parked, I ran inside, pumped up to beat the Irish hordes to the job. At the hostess counter, my enthusiasm was rewarded only by being told it was Myrtle Beach's *other* Cracker Barrel that was hiring. So I hopped back in Crescent, raced through fifteen miles of traffic back in the direction I'd just come, parked the van and ran across the parking lot. Here it was—*at last*—my chance to finally wash South Carolinian dishes and make the state #34!

As I pulled open the front door, my gateway to employment was hindered. Through the doorway, a family of fatties slowly waddled out. I tapped my foot to try to hurry them along. After papa, mama and their two dumplings finally passed, I made a step to enter.

My entry, though, was blocked again. This time, I played doorman to an even heavier family waddling *into* the restaurant. Watching the second fatty clan squeeze past one by one, I was struck by a harrowing image: me, clad in some company-issue polyester knit shirt, bent far over the sinks, scouring the troughs after these pigs had finished gorging their countrified slop. . . .

This was my dream? *My life's goal?!*

For a guy who hated working, could I have been any more masochistic than by pursuing a goal devoted to prolific amounts of work? A decade before, why hadn't I chosen to be the guy who rode ferries in all fifty states? (If so, I'd have been much closer to being finished—just thirteen states to go.) Or to have been the guy who collected mac-n-cheese boxes from all fifty states? (Only five states to go.) Or had found change in all fifty states? (Just Hawaii left.)

No, it had to be dishwashing.

After the last lard-ass disappeared into the restaurant, I continued holding the door open. A dish job awaited me inside. Yet my feet wouldn't budge.

George Orwell wrote that dishwashing "was a thoroughly odious job—not hard, but boring and silly beyond words. It is dreadful to think that some people spend whole decades at such occupations."

Indeed it was dreadful to know that I'd spent over a decade at it. Worse, I faced months more of it.

How'd this happen? I'd hoped to settle down. But here I was roaming around again.

I'd wanted to quit dishing. But now here I was in a

lather to wash the blue-rimmed plates of these Cracker Barrel pigs.

And I'd finally answered Bukowski's question, "What woman chooses to live with a dishwasher?" But where was she? Three thousand miles away!

I'd dished at more than eighty places in thirty-three states. Hell, thirty-three states, fifty states—what was the difference? It didn't matter to Amy Joy if I'd dished in five hundred states. All she wanted was for us to be together in one of them. But for how much longer could I expect her to feel that way while I said my extended farewell to the dishes?

I let go of the restaurant's front door and watched it close before me. Then I crossed the Cracker Barrel parking lot to a street-side pay phone and used my gizmo to call Jake.

"You still wanna buy the van?" I asked.

His truck had been stolen the night before. He was game.

When I hung up the phone, that was that. It was officially over. The quest had ended.

I drove Crescent straight from the Cracker Barrel parking lot seven hundred miles to New Orleans. In a shed behind Cheryl's house, I stored the remaining four thousand *Dishwasher* #16 covers. Most of the five hundred bucks from the sale of the van was spent on a plane ticket.

When I flew to Portland a few days later, I was met at the airport by Amy Joy. She stood in her green-and-black flowery thrift-store dress. Her arms stretched open; her face beamed.

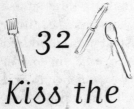

32

Kiss the Dishmachine Good-Bye

The next few days were spent looking up former colleagues to announce the news.

"I'm retired," I told them. "The quest is dead."

"I can't believe it," Jess responded when he heard. He'd already given up the dishwashing business and was now working in a Portland video store. For ten years, he'd only known me as a pearl diver. In fact, to almost everyone who knew me, I was "that dishwashing guy." Now all that was over—and what a relief that it was. But the feeling wouldn't last long.

"What are you gonna do now?" Jess asked.

"Good question," I said.

I was broke and, worse still, just as clueless about finding nondishwashing work as I'd been before the quest began.

And so, like a punch-drunk boxer who didn't know better than to remain retired, I slunk back into the Paradox.

"Dishwasher Pete, I heard you retired!" Caitlin exclaimed. "Too bad, 'cause we could really use you right now."

The café's current disher—an art student—was a dud in the suds. Meekly I admitted I could use the cash and decided to take one last job. The kid was promptly canned that night and I started the next morning.

For the next six weeks, I dished. In the meantime, I made arrangements to begin school at the state university in San Francisco and to rent a room in my sister's apartment.

Finally, one Sunday I was working what I vowed would be my final shift in a too-long dishwashing career. On that afternoon, as usual, my shirt was drenched in sweat and my back ached, but I was completely caught up. Every dish was washed and put up. The counters and dishmachine were wiped down. The garbage was taken out. I'd even scrubbed the mold out of the bus tubs, something that hadn't been done in ages—if ever.

I took a seat on a stool at the counter and Caitlin opened a beer for me.

"Your last day, huh?"

"Yeah," I said.

"We'll miss you around here," she said. "You're the best dishwasher I've ever seen."

This was hardly the Waikiki Beach grand finale I'd often fantasized about—well, except for the part about the beer.

There was little to celebrate. Though I was relieved to be done for real this time, I had regrets. All those years, all those jobs, all that work—and still, I hadn't dished in all fifty states.

Caitlin walked away to take an order. When I finished my beer, I got up to leave.

"You're not leaving already, are you?" she asked.

The clock read 5:00. My shift was officially over.

"C'mon, it's your last day!"

She opened me another beer.

Again she went off to deal with a customer. While still standing, I downed the beer, then headed for the door.

"See ya later," I called out to Caitlin and the cooks.

No one heard me.

As I rode off on my bike, the afternoon sun dried the sweat from my shirt. I was five blocks away when I realized I'd forgotten to kiss the dishmachine good-bye. But I rode onward. It wasn't worth turning back for.

Epilogue

T hree days later, I was eight hundred miles away, back in school and sitting in the front row of the classroom. A year later, Amy Joy and I were married aboard a ferryboat crossing the San Francisco Bay.

Then, while I was studying for a semester in Amsterdam, we were enchanted by that city's many bikes and ferries and progressive attitudes. In all my years of trying to find a place to settle in the United States, it'd never dawned on me that what I was looking for lay beyond its borders. We decided to stay forever.

Gaining my Irish citizenship made it legal for me—as a European Union citizen—to remain indefinitely. But now my education was rather useless. Any employer who needed a transportation planner or cyclist/pedestrian/transit-rider advocate would obviously hire someone who spoke fluent Dutch before they'd hire me. Simply put, getting a desk-sitting job in Amsterdam was out of the question.

Amy Joy was living in the country and supporting us (as a

nanny) illegally. In order for her to gain a residency permit and to be able to get legal employment (all via my Irish citizenship), I had to have an income. So I signed up as a job seeker at the government-run employment office.

Reading the descriptions of the hundreds of available jobs was even worse than when I was sixteen years old reading the "Help Wanted" classifieds in the newspaper. I still had no experience and no skills for any of the listed positions. Worse, my Dutch didn't exactly wow people. No jobs were to be had.

The situation became desperate. We couldn't last much longer on Amy Joy's under-the-table wage. If I didn't find a job soon, our European adventure would be over and we'd be back in the United States, where I'd not only still face the job-finding quandary, but I'd also be racked with the old predicament of where to live.

Going to the employment office and coming away empty-handed every day was a mess of stress. It got harder and harder to walk into the apartment and report to Amy Joy that I was still unemployed. My new role as breadwinner wasn't going well. I cursed myself for never having learned a trade when I was younger. Well, that wasn't entirely true. After all, I *had been* a Dish Master.

Dishing, I thought. There was always dishwashing.

I made up a batch of flyers that touted my qualifications and handed them out in restaurants around town. Many boss-types told me they had no openings. Others said they'd hang on to the flyer. One remarked that the flyer was "cute." Whatever the case, no one showed the slightest interest in hiring me.

Then, after several days—and dozens of restaurants—without any luck, someone finally set me straight.

In an Australian-themed restaurant, the kitchen manager

told me that even if he *had* a dishwasher opening, he wouldn't hire me.

"Why?" I asked.

"Because even if you *are* the world's greatest dishwasher—as your little note claims—I simply can't afford you."

"I'm not asking for much," I protested.

"Look," he said, "it's safe to say you're older than twenty-three, right?"

"Yeah," I said, "and then some."

"Then according to Dutch law, I'd have to pay you the full minimum wage. But if I hire a sixteen-year-old to wash the dishes, I pay him a minimum wage that's half yours."

I nodded while he explained the "graduated minimum wage," how it increased with an employee's age until topping out at twenty-three.

"All I need is my dishes washed and—no offense—I don't really need the world's greatest to do it when I can get any teenager to do it for cheaper."

My nodding slowed as I absorbed what he was saying.

"And you'll hear the same story from every restaurant owner in this city."

So it'd come to this. Not only was I not qualified to do anything else, but the one thing I *could* do, I was now over-qualified for.

In the city where many Americans go to indulge in their vices like pot-smoking and legalized prostitution, I found myself cut off from my own vice, cold turkey.

Author's Note

If you were one of the thousands of people who ordered—
and never received—a copy of *Dishwasher* #16 (among other
things), sorry about that. Please get in touch and I'll make
good on your order.

Write to: wheresmystuff@dishwasherpete.com.

Acknowledgments

My bumbling through life—the result of which is this book—couldn't have happened without the great many people who lent a hand along the way. Therefore, my deepest gratitude goes out to my mom, Sally Jordan, my siblings—Cathie, Johnny, Joe, Sheila—and to Aaron Walburg, Alex Hestoft, Alexis Buss, Alisa Dix, Andy Upright, Ann Cavness, Ann Sterzinger, Bob Helms, Bob Liek, Brian Bagdonas, Caitlin Troutman, Chris "Brutus" Christman, Colleen McNeilly, Craig Piper, Dameon Waggoner, Dan Benavidez, Dave Hernandez, David Naylor, Don Godwin, Doug Biggert, Doug Rogers, Ducky DooLittle, Edith and Rob Abeyta, Elaine Riegler, Elaine Koplow, Emily Elders, Eric Bagdonas, Fred Allen, Gina Amann, Grant Grober, Greg Davis, Greg Pierce, Hawthorne Hunt, Hector Welch, Ira Glass, Jake Springfield, Janelle Hessig, Jeanne M., Jeff Grimes, Jeff Kelly, Jeff Shelton, Jen Dolan, Jennifer Phistry, Jeni Matson, Jess Hilliard, Jim Thompson, John Gerken, Jon Sadler, Josh Baker, Julie Shapiro, Julie Snyder, Karl Jayne, Kathleen "Beanie" Keller,

Kathy Jensen, Kathy Molloy, Kerry McCrackin, Lara Mulvaney, Larry Naylor, Leroy Miles, Lucas Bennett, Miss Lindsey, Marianne Combs, Megan Kelso, Melanie Brown, Melody Jordan, Michelle Bergstrom, Ned Simonson, Nell Zink, Paul Curran, Paul Tough, Pete Menchetti, Phil Snyder, Sammy Travis, Sara Sandberg, Sarah Boonstoppel, Satchel Raye, Scott Eggert, Scott Gregory, Scott Huffines, Sean Tejaratchi, Shelley Brannan, Stephen Duncombe, Steven Svymbersky, Suzy O'Brien, Sven Holmberg, Tanio Klyce, Tess, Tony Peterson, Tony Slad, the entire Tuepker family, and, of course, especially Amy Joy and Ferris.

Special thanks to Erin Yanke and Rebecca Gilbert for their many years of forwarding my mail and to Cheryl Wagner and Chloe Eudaly for their many years of support and encouragement. And thanks to the four people in particular who made this book happen: my writing mentor Lisa Friedman, my agent David McCormick and my editors Jill Schwartzman and Amy Baker.

My gratitude goes out to everyone else who ever provided me with a couch or a floor to sleep on, let me bum a ride from them, corresponded with me, printed or photocopied (licitly or illicitly) issues of the *Dishwasher* zine and, in general, endorsed my quest. Without you, I would've been just another dope trying to dish in all fifty states.

About the author

About the book

Insights,
Interviews
& More...

Read on

Meet Pete Jordan

Self-portrait

PETE JORDAN lives in Amsterdam with his wife and son. He is a columnist for *OEK*—the magazine published by Amsterdam's chapter of the Dutch cyclists' advocacy group Fietsersbond—and is at work on a book about life as an American cyclist in the bike-mad Dutch capital. Occasionally Jordan gives cycling tours of his adopted city to American urban planners and architects. These days he washes dishes on a strictly non-professional basis. (Pete Jordan wrote this in the third person to make it sound like he's important enough that someone would bother to write a bio about him!)

Pete Jordan: Life at a Glance

Also known as:
Dishwasher Pete

Born:
1966, San Francisco

Present occupation:
Unemployed

Home:
Amsterdam 〰

> " [Jordan] is at work on a book about life as an American cyclist in the bike-mad Dutch capital. "

Beer, Books and Cake
A Dish Man Dallies with Publishers

AS NOTED IN THE BOOK, there was a point when I grew tired of pesky media-types approaching with requests to interview me or write about my fifty-state dish quest. Several of these encounters were so annoying, I found it best to just avoid them. So I took to throwing away—unopened—all envelopes with return addresses on official letterhead ▶

Cover of *Dishwasher* #13

66 I took to throwing away— unopened—all envelopes with return addresses on official letterhead from New York or Los Angeles. 99

Beer, Books and Cake *(continued)*

from New York or Los Angeles. After about a year of that, I realized most of those unopened envelopes probably contained cash—a dollar bill or two for a copy of my zine *Dishwasher*. There wasn't much point in throwing away the money. So I reversed my policy and resumed opening *all* mail, even pieces from members of the media.

Soon thereafter, a letter arrived from an editor at a New York publishing house.

"Whenever you're next in town," part of her note read, "I'd like to take you to lunch to discuss the possibility of publishing a *Dishwasher* book."

A month later, I happened to be passing through New York. Never one to offend anyone's generosity when it came to offers of free food, I called the editor and we arranged to meet. That next day, we met outside her office building and she walked me around the corner to a little café. As we entered, we passed the desserts displayed in a refrigerated case. Among the items on show was a chocolate cake with chocolate frosting and a thick layer of chocolate filling. A single slice looked dense and rich enough to be a meal in itself. I rarely encountered such cake on the job while scrounging through leftovers. And, at seven dollars a slice, it was an extravagance I could never afford for myself.

After we sat down, a quick glance through the menu revealed choices that I didn't want to make—arugula this

Cover of *Dishwasher* #2

and sun-dried that. Meanwhile, I couldn't shake that cake from my thoughts.

"I already know what I want," the editor said. "You know what you want?"

"Actually," I said, "that cake I saw in the window looked pretty good."

"*Cake?*" she asked. Her eyebrows rose and I worried she'd say that my expecting her to shell out seven bucks for a lousy slice of cake was an absolute deal breaker.

"Okay," she said instead. "And something to drink?"

I read through the list of beers and pointed to a Germanic sounding one. I wasn't familiar with the name, but it *was* the menu's most expensive beer.

Cover of *Dishwasher* #14

After we ordered, she asked about my travels, where I'd been recently and where I'd be off to next. When the food arrived, she told me about the book projects she was working on. Then the editor held up the copy of the zine I'd sent her and said, "You should publish this."

"Well, it *is* published," I said, pointing to the evidence in her hand.

"No," she said, "I mean, *really* publish it—in a book."

"It seems kinda complicated," I told her.

"Not at all," she said. "And I can help you. It'll be easy."

To comfort me, the editor walked me through the steps ▶

5

Beer, Books and Cake *(continued)*

necessary to publish a book. The terms she used—"agent," "contract," "deadline"—probably would've sounded commonplace to a writer. But I was a dishwasher, and, to a commitment-shy guy like me who couldn't even bother to give notice before quitting a job, everything the editor said reeked of obligations.

When my plate had been licked clean and my glass stood empty, she asked, "Is that all? You don't want another round?"

Well, if the cake had been my meal, then it *was* time for dessert!

"Sure!" I answered.

After the second round of cake and beer, we went up to the publishing house, where she led me to the book room and lavished upon me more than a dozen of the publisher's recent titles. Then, she introduced me around to her colleagues: other editors, associate editors, head editors, etc. Finally, we retired to her office. Again she stated her case for a *Dishwasher* book.

But I just couldn't see it. I didn't even know where I was sleeping from one week to the next. How could I be settled enough to write a book? Besides, writing a book about my quest before it was even finished was pure folly.

So I made it clear: While I agreed a *Dishwasher* book sounded nice, such a project would have to wait until I actually finished the dish mission.

"When will that be?" she asked.

Inside cover of *Dishwasher* #15
by Tony Slad

"Don't know," I said. "I'm in no hurry."

I said goodbye and departed with an armful of books. Outside, standing on the sidewalk, I leafed through my goodies. A few I could see reading; a couple others would make perfect gifts for friends. Then I walked down to the Strand bookstore and sold the rest.

A lunch, some books, a few bucks: *Not* signing

a book contract seemed to pay off almost as nicely as signing one! All without the obligations or stress!

Over the next year or two, I strictly adhered to my policy of not declining free meals by accepting requests to meet with editors from other publishing houses. The routine became familiar: a free lunch, an armful of free books, the rap about no *Dishwasher* book until it was all over. . . .

After one such lunch, when we returned to the editor's office, she called her publisher and told her that she was sitting with the *Dishwasher* guy. A few minutes later, the publisher walked in. The editor introduced us.

"So," the publisher said with a hesitance, "you wash dishes?"

Being the crummiest of salesmen—especially when the product is essentially myself—I said only, "Yeah."

An awkward pause followed. She seemed to struggle in what was possibly her first ever encounter with a dish man.

Finally, she asked, "Where are you working now?"

"In Brooklyn," I said.

Another awkward moment passed as the editor sat waiting for the publisher and me to click. But the publisher didn't know what else to say and, as usual, I was comfortable saying nothing.

Then a thought seemed to pop into the publisher's head, and immediately it popped out of her mouth.

"Aren't you worried about AIDS?" she asked.

AIDS?! She'd lost me.

"What d'ya mean?" I asked.

"From a glass used by someone with AIDS," she said. "If it breaks and cuts you. Or if it's in the dirty dishwater."

For a moment, I said nothing. I was no longer just being silent; I was speechless! It was the mid-1990s, AIDS had been around for more than a decade. Yet this apparently sophisticated, educated woman believed one could be infected with AIDS from—of all things—*dirty dishes!*

How could I respond? Was it really up to me to inform her how blood-borne diseases were transmitted?

"No," I finally said with an answer that probably left her thinking I was cavalier about the life-threatening perils of dishing. "I'm not afraid."

The editor—sensing doom—thanked the publisher for stopping ▶

Beer, Books and Cake *(continued)*

by. When we were alone again, the editor said, "We need to have her read some of your writing to get her on board."

I wasn't sure if I *wanted* her on board!

It didn't matter anyway because, in the end, I gave my usual speech. Then I quickly set off to the Strand with my new books.

When the quest did end—unfinished—outside that Cracker Barrel in South Carolina, so too ended any plan of writing a book about my dish days. I just couldn't fathom a book about a guy who *hadn't* washed dishes in all fifty states. So, aside from my wife's occasional playful threats that if I didn't write a *Dishwasher* book, she'd ghostwrite one, I simply put the book idea out of my head.

When thoughts of a book finally did come to mind, it had nothing to do with busting suds. Instead, I began work on a project about the bike culture of my new hometown of Amsterdam. When anyone asked about it, I'd tell them, "It's sorta like *Dishwasher* except that instead of it being about a guy washing dishes all over the United States, it's about a guy riding his bike all over Amsterdam."

To my friends and acquaintances in Holland, the *Dishwasher* reference meant little. Since most of them knew almost nothing about my pearl-diving past or about my old zine, they reacted with blank stares. So I had to explain the quest to them. They grew more curious and asked more questions. In turn, I told more stories and lent them copies of the zine. After suddenly talking so much about the quest, for the first time in years I began seriously thinking about a *Dishwasher* book. Eventually, I realized a book about a guy's unfinished quest just might work after all. And now that I was settled, I could actually picture writing it.

The only problem was, would publishers still be interested? Would any of them hold a grudge if they had thought I'd led them on in the past?

I put the bike book on hold, pulled out all of my old *Dishwasher* material and went looking for a publisher. Fortunately, a publisher *was* interested. Unfortunately, with an ocean now separating me from the freebies of New York, when I entered the world of book writing, it was without the luxury of being taken to lunch—without even a trip to the book room! Hey, Harper Perennial, where's my lunch?! ❧

Hearing from Fans and Fellow Suds Busters

Following is a sampling of the letters Pete Jordan received while maintaining his zine.

Dear Dishwasher Pete,
Recently you sent me *Dishwasher* #14. I was immediately put on guard when I read the "Common Dishwasher Q & A" ("Keep washing even if it means perishing in greasy flames!"). My suspicions were confirmed when I finished the zine—"Dishwasher Pete" is an imaginary character invented by restaurant corporations to keep the common pearl diver down!

Like Joe Camel and Rosie the Riveter before him, "Pete" popularizes the pride in serving capitalist interests! Already I have seen "his" skillfully engineered publicity stunts having their harmful effects upon the proletariat. "Pete" has made Gen-Xers and counter-culture folks alike think it's "cool" to wash dishes in capitalist institutions, to waste forty hours a week up to their elbows in a greasy mixture of soapy water and meat-juice, to perpetuate the sick system of food distribution and its effects: hunger, sexism, consumption of animals, disregard for human health, tourism, oppression of the working class, tedious lifestyles, destruction of the environment, etc.

There's nothing wrong with having pride in a job well done. And indeed dishwashing is essential; how could the Zapatistas, for example, continue the fight against the Mexican government without dishwashers working hard behind the scenes? But ▶

> " Like Joe Camel and Rosie the Riveter before him, '[Dishwasher] Pete' popularizes the pride in serving capitalist interests! "

instead of indulging in this pastime by being a wage-slave, you should encourage dishwashers to stop dishwashing and do something satisfying to them and useless to the bosses, such as reading, writing, altering billboards, seizing unused land and growing zucchini to feed the hungry. Oh, sorry, I forgot. "Dishwasher Pete"—you don't exist. You're just a tool of the food industry. Your zine is like a television program—allowing dishwashers to relax, laugh, be entertained, and live vicariously so that they may happily wash all the more dishes upon their return to work. So I urge *you*, the secretary who's reading this, to truly serve the American people by sabotaging the Dishwasher Pete myth! Go into kitchens and tell the peons the truth about their false idol! DESTROY *DISHWASHER!!*

On a different note, I really enjoyed the zine itself. It was very funny and informative and I look forward to reading future issues.

> Sincerely,
> Patrick Brennan
> Kennebunk, ME

Dear Pete,
Nothing's changed here. How's the good doctor?

The rent is now up to $100/week. Etc.

This may sound like a dumb question: Are all restaurants filthy? I've never worked in one that could have passed a health inspection without bribery or in one where I was comfortable about eating the food. I come to work, look around, see meat thawing in the pot and pan sink, see the owner walking

66 You should encourage dishwashers to stop dishwashing and do something satisfying to them and useless to the bosses, such as reading, writing, altering billboards, seizing unused land and growing zucchini to feed the hungry. 99

around with a cigarette hanging out of his mouth as he prepares food, see containers of cleaning chemicals on the shelves with food, see containers of food stacked up in the dishroom by cooks too lazy to carry them into the cooler, see containers of food on the floor, food in five-gallon plastic buckets with no label or date, for Christ's sake. ("How old is this soup?" "How the hell do *I* know? Smell it!" "I've got a cold. You smell it." Etc. I'm not kidding.) All I can think is, "Cholera epidemic waiting to happen." Are all of them like this? I may never eat out again.

Anyway—

Anonymous
Chattanooga, TN

Pete,

For a full eleven months, I worked only twelve days. Six washing dishes at Chez What? in Portland and six washing dishes at the B——— in Ohio. The latter is the hip diner/bar in town, as well as the filthiest kitchen I've ever seen. Food rotting in the walk-ins. Giant rats everywhere. I thought of training one of them to do the dishes so that I could slack even more on my ten-hour shifts.

The real entertainment there was Steve, the cook with his mouth wired shut (it had been broken in a fight). Of course, he'd probably be gritting his teeth that hard anyway from all the speed. He told me repeatedly, "Man, you're an outcast! Everyone here does drugs!" Yeah, like the cook who misspelled the word "who" in his query, "how gots the pot?"

I would have liked to have made it an entire year on twelve days, but economic ▶

> **❝** Food rotting in the walk-ins. Giant rats everywhere. I thought of training one of them to do the dishes so that I could slack even more. **❞**

Hearing from Fans and Fellow Suds Busters
(continued)

necessity weighed upon me, and now I'm dishing at a much cleaner place. It's quite slow, and I'm such the pearl-diving prodigy that the boss already wants to move me to cook. That's what I get for efficiency at my chosen profession!

> Love,
> John Gerken
> Ann Arbor, MI

Hi Dish,
Congratulations on your endeavors.

The question here is not how many states you can wash dishes in, but rather, what state your soul, which is your first priority, will be in after you pass on to eternity.

Something to think about in your travels anyhow.

P.S. What famous head of state was a dishwasher/busboy in Durgin Park Restaurant when he was a young man helping out to make ends meet? He is now deceased.

Answer: Ho Chi Minh, former President of North Vietnam.

> Have a nice day,
> Peter Denisi
> Brockton, MA

Hi Pete—
Good to hear you still have a pulse. I guess those assassination rumors were unfounded.

I haven't been spending that much time in San Diego lately. I returned from Montana last week. During previous wanderings through Montana I'd heard the tale of the poached pearl diver, supposedly killed while riding through a conveyor dish machine with the hot water on as part of a dishwasher's initiation ritual. I dismissed the story as an urban legend, knowing full well that no disher would be foolish enough to be baptized with hot water. Turns out there was some truth to the story—with a happier ending. While in the town of Columbia Falls, I was chatting with some long-time residents about some of the odd things that have occurred in their area over the years. Out of the blue, one of them—a former park ranger—brings up the dishwasher story, which he was personally familiar with. Apparently, the disher was one of two brothers employed at Many Glacier Hotel within Glacier National Park sometime in the mid-to-late 1970s. It had long been an initiation tradition at the hotel to ride through the dish machine with the cold water on. Sure enough though—he went through with the hot water on! He had a bucket over his head, which gave him some protection, but received second and third degree burns over the rest of his body. He was hospitalized across the border in Cardston, Alberta, and recovered. The incident was the talk of the town and they're still talking about it more than twenty years later! So somewhere out there is a guy with burn scars all over his body who's trying to explain to people how he got them in a dishwashing accident!

That's all for now. Don't slumber too hard.

Take care,
Tony Slad
San Diego, CA ▶

> 66 During previous wanderings through Montana I'd heard the tale of the poached pearl diver, supposedly killed while riding through a conveyor dish machine . . . 99

Dear Pete:
You guessed it. I got another fucking dishwashing job. So instead of wasting my extra ten bucks a week playing ten-cent pinball, I'm working forty-eight hours a week and passing out after three Old Milwaukees a night. Today I bribed the other dishwasher at J—— B— to work for me, since my carpal tunnel's so bad I keep dropping everything.

God, the owner at J—— B— is insane. For some reason, he thinks his place is so fucking fun that I should just put up with the fact that the job is eighteen hours a week forever—too little to live on, too much to handle together with a decent-sized thirty-hour job. But he'll probably be the only decent job reference I'll ever have, so I don't want to just walk out. Who would he get to replace me? Some lunatic? He won't even let me do something less wrist-destroying like bussing. I know, I know! I FUCKING KNOW! But fuck you, I think I LIKE bussing tables! I hop around like a little invisible creature and if anyone asks me for anything, I act like I'm retarded. They make me do it at my other job (a yuppie lunch oasis—you should hear the conversations THOSE people have!! Today: "My daughter finds it SO hard to go to school with our employees' children …"). The other day some rude woman actually walked into the kitchen to complain because there weren't any clear tables for her to sit her fat stupid ass at.

"There must be SOMEBODY whose job it is to clear off the taaaaaables for us."

> " I think I LIKE bussing tables! I hop around like a little invisible creature and if anyone asks me for anything, I act like I'm retarded. "

YOU OBVIOUSLY DON'T KNOW ANYTHING ABOUT THE FUCKING PIGSLOPPING INDUSTRY, BITCH!!!

Awwwg. My hands hurt. I'm going to try to get some more sleep.

Incoherently,
Ann Sterzinger

Jobs That Never Happened
A Comic Strip

by Pete Jordan and Megan Kelso